DRIVEN BY PAIN
CHANGED BY GRACE
BY PETER LYNDON-JAMES

DRIVEN BY PAIN
CHANGED BY GRACE

I would like to dedicate this book to my wife, Amanda, for staying with me for the last 30 years and to my three children: Tosha-Lena, Peter and Rhyan for standing by me from where I have come from to where I am now.

I hope with all my heart that this book and what I went through changes you and your families like He has mine.

Copyright © Peter Lyndon-James 2020

The right of Peter Lyndon-James to be identified as the author of this work has been asserted by him in accordance with the *Copyright Amendment (Moral Rights) Act 2000*.

Apart from any fair dealing for the purposes of private study, research or criticism or review as permitted under the *Copyright Act 1968*, no part of this book may be reproduced by any process without the written permission of the publisher.

Some names have been changed to protect the privacy of individuals.

Peter Lyndon-James
PO Box 1970 Midland DC WA 6936
www.toughlovebook.com.au

ISBN: 978-0-646-81452-0 (paperback)
ISBN: 978-0-645-3367-0-2 (ePub)

Thanks to the following people:

Jennifer Maly, Head Editor of Paper Lions Australia and her Assistant Editor,
Gemma Hooper for editing the book
Steve Blizard for his assistance with proofreading and editing
Cover Art and Design by Shea Walsh
Artwork on the rear cover by Cherie Mongony

Printed by Scott Print
4 Aberdeen Street, Perth WA 6000
www.scott.com.au

processgreen™

Endorsements

The ultimate geek, I was the polar opposite of Peter Lyndon-James, managing a successful business with a normal family. I have no tatts, was never drunk nor did I ever touch drugs. So when our paths collided nearly ten years ago, little did I know how Pete would turn my whole world upside down. The most unique individual I have ever met, Peter Lyndon-James has incredible compassion for the men of Shalom House. My journey alongside him has brought personal healing to my life and family while totally transforming my outlook towards men who are struggling in life.

Steve Blizard, a Perth-based Financial Adviser

Wow! If ever there was a story about how God changed a man's life, this is it! The awesome thing about this account is that it's 100% true as I know Peter personally. This book candidly recounts the path of a man lost without answers and yearning for change. Its raw detail commands your full attention! Only God, something supernatural, could have made the turnaround in a man who was clearly destined for destruction. I love the transparency of Pete's journey with Christ and the real-life struggles he had to face every day for years to get to where he is now. This book will surely create hope for the hopeless and strengthen the faith of the believer!

Christian Gee | 2010 IFBB Heavyweight Mr Australia
(IFBB - International Federation of BodyBuilding & Fitness)

AUTHOR'S NOTE

I wish to acknowledge that this book is written to the best of my memory and all full names mentioned are done so with the full consent of the individual.

Why was my life stolen from me? It's like these last 49 years, I have been driven by pain. All I ever wanted to be was normal. Even 49 years on as I write this, I cry because I am still sad for what I missed out on and what I went through.

Laying on the floor of my home after waking up after sixteen days of no sleep with a shotgun aimed at my head and "Get down on the floor, get down on the floor" in my ear. A copper's knee in my back with my face plastered to the floor. All I could see was my half-naked wife, Amanda, holding our fourteenth-month-old son. There was a sawn-off shotgun held to her head in the corridor of our house.

I hated me, I hated everything about me. I'd sold a box of dynamite the day before. I was usually selling two and a half kilos of meth a day, guns, steroids and a whole heap more. The Tactical Response Group had just raided the house, I had a helicopter hovering over the roof of my home, making sure no-one could get away.

It was all over red rover.

CONTENTS

Endorsements	1
Author's Note	2
Introduction	5
Part 1 — 1977 to 2002	9
Part 2 Journal 1 — The Initial Challenges Of Changing	99
Part 2 Journal 2 — My Struggle Continues	160
Part 3 — The Dark Night Of The Soul	225
Part 4 — Shalom House: The Strictest Rehabilitation Centre In Australia	230
Testimony — Gavin Lyndon-James	260
Testimony — Christian Gee	269
From Peter to Amanda	277
Family Photos	280
Four Generations of Peters	281

DRIVEN BY PAIN
CHANGED BY GRACE

Introduction

My name is Peter Lyndon-James. I have spent 26 years of my life in and out of jails and institutions starting from the age of seven and HAD a criminal record longer than most. I've broken into houses, stolen cars, mugged many people, I've sold drugs and guns, had genital warts, gonorrhoea, crabs, herpes and more. Have I given it to others? Yes. Intentionally? No.

I've played doctors and nurses as a child, I've fondled another boy's genitals growing up, I've also been sexually molested by an adult male when I was eight years old. I have slept with hundreds of prostitutes behind my wife's back as well as with many other women. For most of my life, I've never paid taxes until I became a Christian.

I, Peter Lyndon-James, have done all of the above and more. Even if it's not written above, I have probably done it.

All I can say is that if you are a victim of my life or my choices, if you are a victim of my selfishness and stupidity — I am sorry, I am so very, very sorry. I have no excuse for what I have done to you or to any other person, what I have done was and is wrong and I am 100 per cent to blame, there is nothing I can say in my defence.

Please, I ask that you would forgive me as I am genuinely sorry for my actions and wish I could change what I have done as well as the life I have lived, but I can't. All I can do is take ownership of my mistakes and I'll always try my best not to do it again.

Today I really care about people. That person is not me anymore, that person is dead, that's the old me. Today I am trying my best to be the best version of me. I care about people, I care about them in the way I need to, not in the way they want me to. I am very determined to make sure my life makes a difference in the lives of as many people that I come across while I can. I don't care if you or any person on the face of this planet like me, not even in the slightest, I am not here to make friends but to change lives. I do care what God thinks of me, though.

I am not a religious man, but I am a proud Christian man, and I welcome any person to look over all of my life including my finances and if there are areas in me or what I do that isn't done with honesty, integrity and transparency, then help me see what I can't see to make the changes that I need to make. I am trying my best, please help me to try better. I started Shalom by accident in 2012, all I want to do is to help people, I only made it to Grade 6 and went to 16 different schools, I have tried my best and will continue to do so until the day I die.

WE NEED CHANGE

Over the past seven years, I have been honoured to play a small part through Shalom House in helping so many families to change their lives. I believe that if you change a man, then you change the entire family.
I would like to be completely honest with you. For the last 10 years, I have been a full-time volunteer who hasn't received an income and Amanda supported me.

It's only recently that I have begun to start to earn an income with my first book as well as through public speaking experiences to create some personal income. My wife and myself, we believe it's not about money, but about people, as we believe people matter, families matter.

WHY I DO WHAT I DO

Why I do what I do is because I genuinely care about families, I care about children growing up with their parents. I care about dads being the dads and husbands they should be, I care about you. I care about what makes a family function, I care about the community and the diversity that we have that makes our community what it is today, this is not a speech, but a fact.

DISCLAIMER

I do not work for Shalom House. Over the last 7 years, I have been exposed to the workings of several local government departments at various levels and I can honestly say that it repulses me what I have seen. I respect the rulers of our day; I obey them and have from the beginning and I have the paper trail to prove it.

I have set Shalom House up to the point where it no longer runs because of me but in spite of me.

As a straight shooter, I don't mess around and I get things done. I uphold honesty, integrity, accountability and transparency with all that I am, even at the expense of all that I own.

Most people think in their brains what I say with my mouth, I don't care what people think of me, you included. I will not tell you what you want to hear, but what you need to hear. I CARE ABOUT YOU, I care about your family, I really do care, that's why I do what I do.

My whole life, all I wanted to be was a geek, a normal person, a productive member of society. Today I am that, I'm a geek, I'm a productive member of society and my heart's greatest wish is to make a difference in the lives of as many people as I can.

We at Shalom have just gone through an internal audit by Ernst & Young, about 8 to 10 people off and on for close to three weeks, they keep us honest as well as the board we have.

We will ALWAYS TELL THE WHOLE TRUTH AND NOTHING BUT THE TRUTH...!!! We have always tried to give it 200 per cent.

peter@lyndonjames.com.au

**DRIVEN BY PAIN
CHANGED BY GRACE**

Part 1

1977 TO 2002

I spent 26 years of my life in and out of children's homes and institutions, starting from the age of seven. I hated who I was and I hated everything that I stood for. The way I smelled, how I felt about me, the people that I hung around as well as what I did on a day-to-day basis. Well, I didn't really hate the people that I hung around because they were like me, I just hated what we did, they were like me and came from where I came from. I hated my parents for dumping me, with my dad running off with another woman when I was a kid and my mum who seemed more concerned about alcohol and men than her own children.

Life has so many twists and turns in it, taking you in many directions, just with one choice, your whole life can change direction. As you read what I have written, I would like to state from the very start that I love both my parents as well as care about their partners. I am not writing this book to have a crack at them, but rather to tell my story. I honestly do not blame them or anyone for the life I have lived, I was the one who made choices which led my life down the wrong path and I do not blame anyone for those choices but me. What I plan to do as you read my story is to explain why I was where I was, what happened as my life unfolded as well as what happened to get me out. I would also like to share my struggles as I started to make the choices to change my life.

From the start, I would also like to state where I stand in regard to religion. I seriously hate religion and I often say if the Church of God was like Hungry Jack's, then it would be chockers, Whopper double beef with cheese, heavy mayonnaise, add ketchup. Me, I have extra pickle DP meaning cut in half. But religion isn't like that, it's made up of all these different mobs and for a person who comes from where I come from (in other words, a faithless background), how do you know which church is the right one? Growing up, I'd never been to church, I've broken into a few but I've never been part of a service in one. I'm not a religious person, I hate religion. I'm a Christian, let me explain.

A RELIGIOUS PERSON

A religious person in my view is someone who goes around swearing, saying Fish, Chips and Salt every second word, where F is F***, C is C*** and S is S***, if you know what I mean, get the drift? They tell everyone to do what they don't do themselves. They lie, gossip, look at women lustfully and go to church once a week. I can't stand religion.

Have you met people like that?

A CHRISTIANESE PERSON

Well, a Christianese person to me is a person who goes around saying Hallelujah, praise the Lord, glory to God. Every second word is God this and God that, glory here and glory there and they set the standard of

Christianity so high that I don't want to be like that and it's too hard for me. When you come from where I come from, it's a standard that for most they feel it's just simply too hard to obtain.

Now I'm not saying there is anything wrong with them, there's a scripture that says, "I would rather you hot or cold not lukewarm or I'll spew you out of my mouth."

GENERAL FLYING FLOPPAS

The third mob I call the general flying floppas who say, "It's okay, I'm a good person, I'm not hurting anyone. If religion works for them, good on them, but not in my circle."

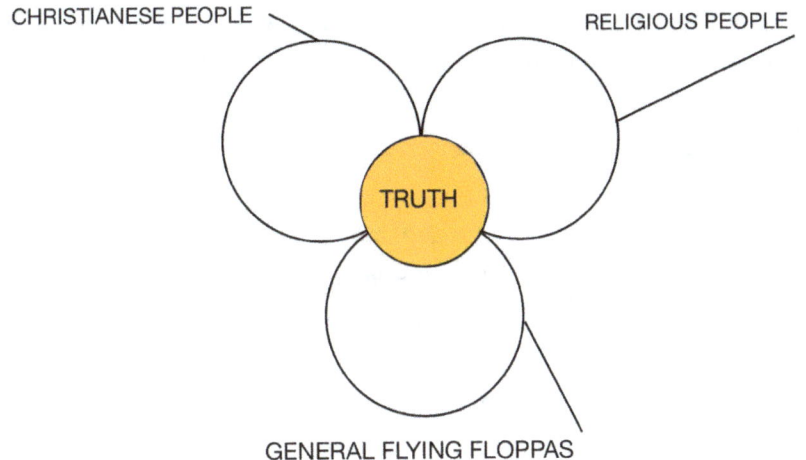

THE CHALLENGE

As you read this book, I promise you it's not all about religion, it's my story: drugs, guns, crime, prison, sexual abuse and more, twenty-six years caught up in a world that I wanted out from but didn't know how to. I personally reckon we're not just a fart in the wind, and I reckon that when we die that there's something up there, well, in fact, I now know there is because of what I have been through and because of what happened to me. How do we communicate what we know to be true without pushing religion or what we believe down people's throats?

I don't believe that it's okay to push what we believe upon people, it's just NOT OKAY. If we truly want to tell people what we believe then I think we should live it. We should lead by example, through the words we speak, and in the thoughts we think, in how we lead our homes and how we are with our finances as well as how we respond when we are mistreated. I honestly believe that our actions should speak louder than our words.

I reckon it all started when my dad took off with Caroline, our babysitter. There were five of us kids all up; Judy the oldest, then me followed by Gavin, Cheree and Graham. We lived at 28 Scanlon Way, Lockridge, and I went to Lockridge Primary School.

I can't remember much, but I remember Caroline was locked out of her house one night after babysitting us so she slept over. Apparently, Mum woke up and found Dad sleeping with Caroline while she was asleep. They had a big fight and Mum kicked him out. He went to stay at the Eden Hill Hotel.

Back then, they used to have accommodation at the back at the hotel. I remember one day clearly, it was Anzac Day and my sister Judy, Gavin and I went to visit Dad at the motel. We all sat down on his motel bed and watched the memorial services on television. That was my last close moment with my dad.

Sometimes I used to pull in at the rear of the hotel to see him on the way to the shops to see if he wanted anything. He would always slip me a dollar or two; as a kid, the money always came in handy. I was smoking at the age of eight and used that money to buy more smokes. Dad wasn't living at home anymore, so I couldn't pinch them out of his carton. Mum was that broke she started to smoke rollies.

Back to Dad and his new-found girl, Caroline.

I think she was about sixteen; she used to live three units up from us. We lived in a two-storey government housing unit, considered the 'bad' part of Perth at the time. All our backyards backed onto a large oval. I remember we used to play tee-ball on there on weekends.

Dad was a mechanic by trade and worked at the back of an industrial shed in Lockridge somewhere; from what I can remember, he was self-employed.

After school one day, Mum asked me to go to the shops for her, so on the way, I decided to pop in to see Dad as I normally would, but there was no answer. I remember going to see someone in the bottle shop and they told me he had moved out. I ran home and asked Mum where Dad had moved to.

All she said was that he had gone away for a while. It turned out later that he had gone up North.

We all missed him massively.

Our family slowly started to fall apart. The repossession people came through just after Dad left, taking the stereo, TV, and nearly everything else. When Dad took off up North on his journey, he left behind a business and a lot of bills. That left us with sweet nothing.

I remember Mum used to have this sugar daddy pull in now and again by the name of Lee, a French fellow she met at the local pub. He worked up in the mines and only pulled in every few months. Mum reckoned that he wanted to take her back to France but didn't want the luggage of five kids. I mean, let's face it – who would?

She was always happy when he pulled up because it meant she could get pissed and feel sorry for herself for free for a few days.

Nearly a year went by with no word from Dad until nearly the next Christmas. It was school holidays. I had just come back from a mate's house up the road and there was Dad, standing on the front lawn talking to Mum. She was throwing pots, pans and everything within reach at him. I tried to talk to him but he was climbing into the car as Mum was yelling. All I could hear him say was that he would see me soon. I remember being angry with my mother because she was driving him away for the second time and I didn't want that!

We got to see Dad a couple of times over the following weeks. He had landed a well-paid job up North in a place called Marble Bar – the hottest place in Australia, they reckon. It was decided by Mum and Dad that a couple of us kids would go with Dad and his girl to their new-found paradise to give her a well-earned break. Adults can be so selfish. Gavin and I went with Dad while Judy, Cheree and Graham went to stay with Mum's mum, Joan, my beautiful grandmother. At the time, Gran, as I called her, lived in Armadale with my Uncle Lloyd who is really my grandfather, we just called him Uncle Lloyd.

Mum went on a holiday with her Frenchman to Mount Newman while we went to Dad's place at Marble Bar in an old Hillman Hunter, fully loaded. I can still remember the time when Dad broke down 300 km south of the town so we grabbed what we could carry and hitched a lift. Dad got a lift back to the car the next day and it was completely burnt out, they had even removed all the tyres.

That always happens up North, they say.

I will always remember the first day up there, 40 degrees plus. Dad enrolled us at the local school; I think we were the only white kids there.

I remember being in the Christmas parade that year, we hid under the stage. We were that scared because we had only just arrived a week before and the whole school was full of wongis (that's what we call full-blood Aborigines).

After a while, it was great. It was around wet season and there were always lots of frogs around. You couldn't even go to the toilet without them jumping up at your backside. On the weekends, we used to go looking for 'tin', a dark black rock about the size of a matchhead. If you collected enough and took them into the local store they would give you money in exchange for them. I reckon Dad did it just to keep us out of his hair. Once he showed us the first time how to find the tin, we started going off by ourselves every chance we could get.

It was sometimes a bit of a problem around home with Dad and his girlfriend. I was around eight or nine at the time. One time, I walked into Dad's room and caught Caroline without her top on. She was pregnant at the time with her first child. Boy, did she go off! I think that's what got us kids an early pass out of Marble Bar.

The following week, we were all booked into the hotel in town. Dad had arranged with Mum to send us back to her; he told her he couldn't handle us.

While we were staying at the pub, I befriended an elderly Aboriginal man named Paddy. I was staring out of the window of the motel when he came out of nowhere with a whopping great big bloody goanna. Paddy had blood running down his chin from having the goanna's head between his jaws, that's how they kill them. Man, that was a spin-out that I can still picture today.

We were in Marble Bar for another three weeks from what I remember because the rain had closed all the roads, being wet season. When it rains in places like Marble Bar, trust me – it rains! You could be sitting in your car one minute and the next minute, BAM, out of the blue, a huge river torrent comes and picks up your car and turns you upside down. Next thing you know, you are floating downstream. It happened to us so I know it's true.

When I moved back with Mum, we never really settled anywhere for long. After the move from Lockridge, Mum put what was left of our belongings into storage. We were never to see that lot again; in it was my only sports medal I had ever been given, along with all my school reports and toys.

Mum was a pretty heavy drinker and had a few boyfriends over the years. One used her as his own little punching bag. His name was Robert. I can remember many, many times running up the street holding my mother's hand as she was bawling her eyes out. At times, her face would be so black, you couldn't tell she was my mother. I also saw her another time, curled up in the corner of the lounge at three o'clock in the morning, crying with two black eyes, her false teeth in her hands. She was trying to glue them back together; she couldn't even see out of the slits that were her eyes, they were that swollen.

During this time, only Judy and me were living with Mum. Gavin, Cheree and Graham had gone to live with Grandma and Uncle Lloyd permanently. Mum needed to sort her life out so Judy and me were then placed in Wanslea Children's Home for six months. We attended Cottesloe Primary School next door; it was probably the best out of all the children's homes that I attended over the years. I have nothing but good memories of my stay there.

When Mum had proven to authorities that she had sorted herself out, we were returned to her. We stayed at the Gosnells Village Caravan Park when Judy and I were reunited with Mum.

Peter and Cheree, 1979

Sometimes, Mum would have a boyfriend pop over. When we stayed there, I befriended a man named John who I met through another boy my age. Over a couple of months, this man gained the trust of my mother and he was allowed to take us places, we were even allowed to stay over at his place occasionally. During a six-month period, this man molested me many times.

Not a day goes by that I don't think of what that man did to me and it will burn in my brain forever. I believe if it were not for my mother having to book herself back into rehab and us having to move away, he would have done worse things to me.

We had to move because of Mum's violent ex-boyfriend Robert bashing her brains in. She would always go back to him, she never seemed to learn. Mum booked herself into Serenity Lodge, but this time, Judy and I were sent to stay with a foster family in Safety Bay. Judy kept running away with her best friend, Louise until eventually, her best friend's parents fostered her.

I remember running into Robert when I was fifteen at Sherwood Heights in Maylands. I nearly died, I didn't know what to do, all I could do was pity him. The whole left side of his face was one big cancerous lump, he was dying very slowly. Robert: nickname – the rat, fitting, don't you think? He died six months later.

I was first placed in Walcott Children's Home when I was ten years old; I stayed at Walcott on three different occasions. The first time I met my best mate, Macka. We were both around the same age and had come from the same type of background. Macka and I ran away from that children's home more times than I care to remember. The sleeping areas of Walcott were up on dormitories A, B, C & D for boys; E & F were for the girls.

We had sawn one of the window locks from the security screen designed to keep us in; every time we wanted to take off, we would go out that way. The staff could never work out how we were getting out. The police would find us then take us back to Walcott, we would get placed in the dorm until an appropriate punishment was considered. By the time it was, we were gone again.

Picture this: two eleven-year-old kids climbing out the window at one o'clock in the morning wearing only their pyjama pants. We walked towards Perth as we were only five kilometres out of the city. Occasionally, we would have to hide in the bush because the police would come past; we were only eleven and had pyjama pants with no tops on, so they'd be sure to want to know what we were up to!

Smith's Crisps vans were always parked near the East Perth Football Club and every time we ran away, we would stop there to break into them. They always provided a good feed, so to speak.

When we arrived in the city, we tried to break into a few places to get a change of clothes. We ended up at the large Wesley Church early on Good Friday, only God can forgive me, I know that now, but we were only kids. We climbed through a window into the main part of the church and started to look around. I found a whole heap of 'God loves you' t-shirts so I put one on and threw one to Macka. At least now we had t-shirts to go with our pyjama pants.

Macka came across a large bunch of keys so we ran to where we had seen a safe earlier and tried the keys.

Out of the blue comes a big bang and a voice yelled out, "Who's in there? I know somebody's in there."

Being frightened, we scattered. I hid under an office desk and Macka hid in the cathedral. I fell asleep and woke up about an hour later with pins and needles in my legs, hearing Macka calling my name, so I tried to stand, only to collapse about a metre from where I started. I still remember my head hitting a cop's boot as I fell to the floor. We were arrested and taken to Perth Central Police Station. I was around eleven and already I knew the cop shop well. We were both sitting on the bench in our pyjama shorts and 'God loves you' t-shirts at 6 am.

The police took us back to the home eventually; we were charged and remanded to a later date. Macka and I were stripped naked and locked in separate dorms with only towels around us. With the help of a couple of other kids, we managed to get hold of two sets of clothes. The ones I had belonged to a guy by the name of Bruce, he weighed about 500 lbs and I reckon ten of me could have squeezed into his pants. They did the job required and we were soon off again.

At about 11 pm, we broke into the petrol station across the road. Once inside, we wedged a storeroom cupboard open and found a massive pile of notes. Our adrenalin was rushing as we had never had this much money before. Macka and I got the hell out of there to count our cash. Ninety-six dollars. We were rich!!!

We wandered around the Supreme Court Gardens. About 2 am, Macka and I decided to go to Rottnest Island. We went to the Barrack Street Jetty to see what time the ferries left. The sign said 9:30 am, so we had seven hours to kill. We were on a roll; how could we lose? We decided to do all the ferries over, we stole lollies and hid them across the road at the park. When we boarded the ferry, we didn't feel too much like lollies as we had gorged ourselves only hours before. It was just as well because we had left them without any refreshments whatsoever.

When we arrived at Rotto, we both took a while to get over the seasickness, but after that, we were fine. We used all our money on the first day. That night, we slept on the beach as we couldn't go to Tentland or anywhere like that due to our age.

Next morning, we woke up dead broke and hungry. We tried to get into a couple of bungalows but were unsuccessful. At the third one, Macka got through the front window. We looked around frantically for any money or goods to convert into cash as well as food. I heard Macka yell out that if I saw any tablets called Serepax or Rohypnol to let him know. Well, what do you know – Serepax 50 mg!

We grabbed some chocolate from the fridge and took off to the beach on the other side of the island. This was my first introduction to drugs of any kind. We had three pills each because Macka had seen his mum take them before and he told me he knew what he was doing.

We waited for a few minutes and felt nothing so we had another one, then waited a few more minutes before having one more, ending up having six each. I can't remember much after that, but apparently, we swam to a boathouse moored about fifty metres out. We had been standing on the side of the boathouse drinking beer when we both fell unconscious.

A passer-by spotted us floating in the water. She swam out to us and dragged us to shore. We were taken by helicopter to Perth Central

Police Station then transferred to Princess Margaret Hospital; we were both on life support, my heart had stopped twice and I had to be brought back to life. Macka and I were out of it for about a week. They discharged us from the hospital because Macka smacked a nurse in the face when she told him I was not going to make it.

When we arrived back at Walcott, we were still doped from the tablets. They stripped Macka naked, put him in the back of a transport vehicle and carted him off to Longmore Juvenile Correctional Centre.

I remember yelling, "I won't be far behind ya."

I grabbed another pair of Bruce's shorts and took off! I was caught three days later and sent to Parkerville Children's Home in the Mundaring Hills east of Perth.

Upon arriving at Parkerville, every kid was supplied with a pushbike, our means of transport everywhere. Every time I ran away, I was always on my pushbike; it was about a thirteen-kilometre drive down the hill to Midland. I forgot that I had no seat on my bike and I went to sit down. You can guess what happened there; it took me an hour of turning ten different colours before I could even stand on my feet.

I stayed at Parkerville for about a year. In that time, I had run away many times. The longest period I was away for was about three months. I was staying at a Good Samaritan in the Midland Gate shopping centre car park the whole time. Dad didn't even know and he ran the car yard at Midland Toyota, only 200 metres up the road.

In the morning, I would wake up at around 4:30 am and do the rounds, pinching anything that was food or could be turned into food. I would pinch the fresh bread left outside of shops or I would break into the key-cutting shop because it was easy.

I came back to my little retreat one day only to find they had changed the lock on the bin. It was no longer my warm home so I caught a train into the city.

I heard of a place called The Cave, a drop-in centre for street kids to pop into after dark. I was on my way there when the police picked me up for a name check. I tried to give a false name but I stuffed it up. I ended up giving them my real name and they rang Dad. I didn't understand why they rang him anyway; I had hardly seen him for a couple of years. Dad came down to the cop shop with Caroline and their daughter, Carla, to pick me up.

Dad took me straight back to the children's home and we sat down with the manager. It was decided that I would grab my gear and stay the night with Dad and Caroline to work out what I was to do the next day.

I felt Dad didn't want me in the first place. I sulked and told him I didn't want to stay with him either. It made it easy for him to decide what he did. They packed my gear and put me in the car.

Destination: Longmore Juvenile Correctional Centre.

It was one o'clock in the morning and I remember Dad getting out of the car to push the button on the gate.

I had never been more scared in all my life; I was only eleven, turning twelve, and all I wanted was my mum and my dad. I didn't want to be put away like some out-of-control animal. The main reason I was placed here was that they couldn't keep me in any home, I would keep taking off, not for stealing, I hadn't done much of that since I left Walcott.

Well, Macka, here I am, I thought to myself.

Macka, however, was gone a long time ago.

I remember going through the front gate, I was as scared as anything. They made me strip naked and wrap a towel around myself. Paul was the name of the male nurse with a moustache and dark black balding hair who walked up to me with a big jar of white cream in one hand and a popsicle stick in the other.

He dipped the stick in the jar: "Drop the towel."

I did so, then he wiped the white cream all over my genital area and then marched me down the corridor. I was to find out later that the cream was for crabs, a form of body lice. They gave me a hairbrush, toothbrush, toothpaste and some pyjamas, along with six comic books.

There were forty-two cells in one wing, twenty-one rooms either side of the corridor. Each room was double-locked from the outside. They locked me in my room; the door had a little security hatch that only they could open from the outside to see in.

That first night laying on the bed in my room will stay with me forever. I remember promising myself if Dad or Mum would come and take me home, I would never be naughty again. I curled up into a ball and cried, rocking from side to side. I did that nearly every night of my life from that night on just to get to sleep, or if I was extremely worried or stressed out.

I stayed in Longmore for nearly three months and when I was released, they sent me to Longmore Hostel just outside the main complex. I tried to stick it out but I wasn't doing too well. I was sent to the local school, Clontarf Boarding School, not far from there. It was also a children's home and I ended up living there, going okay, but they closed it down so I moved on. I stayed at Warminda Hostel in Victoria Park for a little while, but I couldn't stand it. I took off and started hanging out in the city.

I was often busted and every time, they would send me to a different home. When you're twelve years old, without a supportive parent or guardian, you become a bit rebellious and lose all respect for authority.

I got used to the freedom of making my own decisions and was always told I was too demanding. I lived in different squats around the city and under places like the Causeway Bridge or the freeway. If you walked underneath them, along the sidewall, you could dig and crawl into a huge big cave with a concrete floor and lighting.

You couldn't ask for more.

We had mattresses and sometimes the police would do a romp through, so we'd often have to restock it. At the Supreme Court Gardens one day, I ran into a bloke I had met in Longmore named Wade, as fat as you would get for a bloke his age. Wade was two years older than me and had been in trouble a lot more than I had.

We started hanging out together and he showed me the ropes, so to speak. One night around 11 pm, we went to this rust-proof joint in West Perth. I was the smallest so I was the one who went through the window, I climbed in and looked for a way for Wade to get in. I found a way at the rear service bay.

We went through and searched all the offices, collecting what we could. Wade and I ended up with two business chequebooks and about seventy dollars' cash. We went out to the workshop, looked through the cars and found a Mazda coupe with the keys in it so we took it. I rolled open the roller door while Wade drove the car out.

The fewer people who knew the offices had been done over, the better. Being a Saturday, we could have the hottie for the weekend without it being reported. That night, we drove along the coast towards Scarborough. I remember turning onto Main Street in Osborne Park and cop lights coming out of nowhere. My heart skipped a beat and Wade went a bit on the pink side.

Nonetheless, we didn't stop.

We had about five cop cars after us. Wade ran four sets of lights; had it been a peak hour, we would have been busted at the first set. We got up to around 180 km/hr when we reached Wanneroo Road and in front of us came a fully loaded semi. We couldn't stop in time so we both just ducked. I heard the roof get ripped off. During what seemed an hour later, but was only a few seconds, we were both sitting in the car looking at each other, trying to comprehend what just happened.

The police were all over us.

To this day, I am amazed that nobody was even scratched, let alone dead. We were both charged and I was remanded in custody to Longmore Remand Centre. That's about the time in my life when my parents told me I was on my own. I was 12 years old.

I was now on what you would call the chain gang, that's where you're in police custody and are held in these huge holding cells in the back of the courts where nobody can see you. When your name is called, the police make you place your hands up on the wall so that they can do a quick body search before escorting you into the court with their fingers in the back of your pants. If they didn't like you, they would pull your pants up so far you would swear there were two of you.

It was my turn and I was marched into the courtroom. I realised it was not the usual room, but a different one off to the side. I had no idea what was about to happen. When I got inside the room, Mum was on the left of the courtroom with Dad and Caroline on the right, and the judge where he was meant to be.

I was still in shock when I was marched back into the holding cells. In a matter of minutes, both of my parents had declared that they no longer wanted the responsibility of bringing me up, so they made me a Ward of the State. That meant that from that day forward until I turned eighteen, the government was responsible for my upkeep, clothes, food, education and for putting a roof over my head.

I was on my own. If that wasn't bad enough, I got sentenced to six months' strict custody, the longest sentence I had been given so far. The only person to ever visit me on a regular basis was my dear gran.

LONGMORE 1984

Longmore 1985

Longmore is made up of three sections:
- Remand: where you go when you are awaiting bail or are remanded in custody until you are sentenced
- Training Centre: where you go after you have been sentenced to a term of imprisonment
- Hostel: you could go there after your release from the training centre if you had no other place to stay

In the training section, your day was pretty well rostered. You had to abide by the rules and regulations of the place otherwise, they would stick you in choggie, more commonly known as isolation.

Your daily routine would start at 7 am. For half an hour, we had to clean our toilet and sink and mop the floor, then stand by our doors and have our cells inspected. The rooms were marked according to their neatness and cleanliness. Each morning, the rooms would be given a score between one and three and over the course of the prison day, your score would add up. There were eight separate time slots which meant the top score was 24; in dollar terms, that was $2.40.

Over the week, it could add up to a good dollar, depending on what rate you were on because $2.40 was just the basic pay. It went up to $3.50 a day if you were on Level 2, the top level. If you had that, you were doing good and it meant you moved into the nice cell on the girls' side with carpets on the floors and concrete seats instead of having to sit on your bed like we did in the boys' section. The rooms were much bigger and being in there kind of made you feel special.

The only problem with moving over to the girls' side was that it never lasted. The second you got done for fighting or getting a low score over a two-week period, they demoted you, made you pack up all your belongings and move back over to the boys' side which was dirty and cold. It took a couple of months after moving into a new slot to feel at home. You have to be able to relax in your 2-metre by 2-metre square room, it's the only place you can feel safe.

Until you're locked up of a night-time around 6:30 pm, you're not safe and you're always open to attack in one form or another. There were all types of kids in there with a range of problems their parents and the community couldn't handle. This is where the problem child gets sent because nobody could fix their problem.

There was this kid I will always remember, Rowan Hayes, may he rest in peace. Ever since he was three, he was in and out of foster families, his step-mother used to beat him senseless and lock him in the cupboard for days. Rowan was one mean bastard and he was only fourteen years old. He would stand over anybody and wouldn't care who he hurt or how he got hurt, no emotion whatsoever. Over the years, I would run into Rowan on many occasions.

You see when you're in and out of there as much as I was, you always saw the familiar faces and you started to build up a sort of mateship. Every time we'd catch up, we swapped stories of how we got busted and what we were doing when we got caught. You would hear some good ones. Some kids boasted about what they got up to. I'd hear them bragging about breaking into someone's house, spraying the homeowners' bird with oven cleaner and leaving it to die slowly, or defecating on people's lounges; they had no respect for anybody or anyone.

Young and wild, some would say.

I know that I carried out acts over the years that only God can forgive me for and I am not proud of what I got up to. I wish I could make up for the past. As kids, deep down inside, we all wanted the impossible, and for us, that was Mum, Dad and a normal life.

Back to the daily routine. After cell inspection at 7.45 am, we went to breakfast. Each table had ten kids and one staff member. Breakfast finished at 8.15 am and we stayed in the quad until 9 am.

The institution was shaped in a large square with bars all the way around you, you could always hear the sounds of keys jangling or a lock turning somewhere. The centre of the compound had a grassed area where we played most of our sport, if you played, that is.

From 9 am until 3 pm, we would go off to our different workgroups depending on what that was. If you couldn't handle school, you would be on the cleaning party. Every time I was locked up, I would work in the kitchen.

That was the only job in the whole prison that offered the perks, such as not getting locked down 'til late, you're always the first one unlocked in the morning and it paid the most. The worst part was that blokes were always standing over you for one thing or another.

I remember one bloke was always standing over me and one day he went too far. He told me to take his plate up. I refused, he said it again and I lost it. I saw red and lunged at him with a knife across the kitchen table. He was an Aboriginal fellow, but I swear he turned white. Have you ever been that frightened and scared that you pissed your pants? No human being should have to feel this way.

All the staff pounced on me and dragged me down to the secure section where you're stripped and given basics like tracksuit pants and a jumper until they work out who's responsible for what and who should get punished. I got two days down the back.

That's where you have to spend 48 hours cooling off, you get no reading material, just a pad and a pen and you're locked in your cell the whole time. Blankets and bedding are removed in the morning and given back to you when it's time to go to bed, it drives you crazy especially when you're like me and like to keep busy. The meals are basic and served up the day before. You never get enough of anything and are always hungry; especially when you do up to ten days at a time down there.

They only let you out for half an hour a day to exercise in a yard about as big as your slot. From 3 pm to 5 pm, we did different recreational activities, anything from making moccasins to watching TV, lifting weights, playing canasta, even. From 5 pm to 5:45 pm, we had to shower, and by 6:30 pm, dinner was over. If you wanted to stay up past 6.30 pm, you had to pay a $2.00 activity fee allowing you to stay up until 8 pm; you could do weights or make models. Either way, it was better than being locked in our slots.

Once a week, they had a Christian group come in and do different activities or watch videos and talk about God. They were called Broken Chain Ministries and were run by Pastors Alan and Maureen Shepherd. That was my first introduction to Christ.

That was our weekday routine. The weekends were the best, we could receive visits from the outside. On the very rare occasion that Mum or Dad visited me, all I wanted was to go home but I always put up the rebellious front and came across as Mr Independent. Another part of me wanted to get the hell away from them because I blamed them for my being there. I mean, they made love, they had five kids, where's the responsibility lie, in the child? I don't think so!

When I was released, my father lined up some work for me and a place to stay with one of his mates in Midland. I started work at thirteen at a place called Murphy's Tyre Power in Midland. I made ninety-six dollars a week with the tax on that being about nine dollars.

Card For my brother, Graham, 1983

I was a tyre fitter and I tried to hold down that job as long as possible, but it wasn't long before I ran into my old mate, Macka. Macka and I used to go out during the day breaking into houses and shops to survive. I remember we went to the movies once and watched a movie called *The BMX Bandits*. Straight after watching it, we went and pinched two BMXs. We thought we were just it.

We used to grab food out of the rubbish bins around Perth and eat it when we were really hungry. One night, we were broke and a gay guy came up to us in the mall and offered us money to do stuff to him. Macka and I played along and headed down to the Supreme Court Gardens toilet. We were going to mug him for his money, but we argued who was going to hit him first; it ended up being me.

As we got close to the toilet, I walked alongside him and out of nowhere, I swung my right first as hard as I could at his jaw. It sent him straight to the floor, so I followed it up with a few more for good measure while Macka grabbed his wallet out of his back pocket. We then ran as fast as we could; twenty-six dollars was all we got. It was enough to get something to eat, all that mattered to us.

In the city, there were a couple of drop-in centres for homeless kids which opened their doors at midnight and kicked you out at six in the morning.

It was good at times because you could get pies and pasties for only 50 cents each, the only problem was that pasties were vegetarian and had these little seeds all over them which turned me off a bit. There was a bloke named Mark and his girlfriend, Joanne who used to be at the YMCA drop-in centre a fair bit, they were around fifteen and she was seven months pregnant.

I remember one day when I was driving a stolen car with Macka, Mark and Stewart. We drove around looking for a house to break into to get some money, our daily thing. We'd drive up and down the streets looking for an easy target when we spotted one. I pulled in the driveway, turned the car off and knocked on the door; if someone did answer, I would just ask directions or ask if John, or some other made-up name, was home. As it turned out, nobody was.

We piled out of the car into the backyard. Most of the time, we would use a shovel to wedge the back door open, most places had a shovel in their backyard, or we would have a Freddie up our shirts. A Freddie is what we called our best mate — a strong, long-handled, fat-headed screwdriver. We ransacked the house collecting whatever we could that had value: TV, video, stereo, jewellery, etc. It took less than five minutes to go through a house, especially when your adrenalin was going through the roof.

We squeezed into the Holden Kingswood station wagon and drove off. Little did we know, a nosy neighbour had spotted us and called the police. At the end of the street, there were two cop cars blocking the road.

That was it.

The blokes in the car were yelling, "Floor it, floor it, ya not stopping," so I floored it, over the kerb and around the cop.

It must have looked funny — a carload of kids behind the wheel of a Kingswood.

I gunned it down Warwick Road and was coming up to a bloody big T-junction. The lights were red and I wasn't stopping so I tried to make a right-hand turn, but my tyre blew out on the concrete median strip that sent us catapulting towards the nearest power pole, one of those huge steel ones. It got flattened. When we came to a stop and the power pole was on the roof, we all tried scrambling out through the windows.

Because I was the driver, the cops went straight for me, they didn't like smart little kids who have no regard for public property and I don't blame them. They grabbed me by the hair and dragged me out of the front seat. My feet didn't even touch the ground but I felt my head slam into the side of the car. I woke up in the back of a paddy wagon.

You could smell something off in the air. As it turned out, Mark had shat his pants when we went through the lights. When we got to the police station, the policemen made Mark sit in the middle of the floor with everything still in his jocks.

Three months later, we were in the YMCA drop-in centre in the city and heard screams coming from upstairs. We all ran up to see what was happening — Mark was hanging from the ceiling, dead as. He hanged himself because his girlfriend had left him.

Many stories come to my mind when thinking about this time. Once, Macka and I were driving around again looking for a house to do over. We knocked on one door and there was no answer. We walked around the back, this bloody great big dog came out of nowhere, and we thought we might give that one a miss. That used to happen a fair bit.

On the front veranda, there was a little Yamaha 100 motorcycle, we thought *Why not*? and tried to get it started for about half an hour. When we did, we both admitted that we didn't know how to ride one, but we soon learned. There were a couple of helmets accompanying the Yamaha, so we donned them and I was the rider with Macka being the pillion passenger.

It didn't take long to work out. In a couple of hours, I was riding like a pro. We kept the bike for a couple of weeks; Macka never got the hang of riding it himself. He rode down Riverside Drive in Perth City going about 80 km/h in peak hour, it locked up on him and we both went sideways over the kerb, we thought we were goners. We used the bike to carry out a lot of break-ins and all the money we made, we spent on drugs and prostitutes.

We were sixteen, at our sexual peak and on a mission. It was our goal to try every prostitute parlour in Perth and we did just that. One I remember was Happy Haven on Guildford Rd in Maylands which was a shocker.

We walked in and there were only two ladies who both looked well past their used-by date. I didn't care, I was in. When we finished what we were doing, I went back to the lobby and it was Macka's turn. He took one look at the lady's face, all the make-up running down it, he figured she was in her sixties and wanted to leave. She asked him how old he was, he told her his real age and she knocked him back.

We ended up getting busted in Forrest Chase and sent back to Longmore Hostel, put into 48 hours of isolation. As soon as we could, we walked right out. A few days later, we walked through Victoria Park, not having had any sleep in three days because of drugs and we were flat broke. It was around eleven at night and freezing cold. We decided to curl up in a car park and get some sleep.

I woke up four hours later, walking across the Freeway on the other side of Perth. I must have sleep-walked, I was that cold I thought I was going to die. I didn't mean to leave Macka behind, but I couldn't find him anywhere.

A few months later, I got a flat in Maylands with Macka, cheap enough at $80 per week. The amount of meth that we would use, and the energy that it gave us was tremendous, you just couldn't stop. I would do anything to keep busy, from scrubbing the floor to washing the ceiling, it didn't matter.

The worst part was when I was awake for 48 hours and coming down, it felt like hell. After a while, the first thing we ever did as soon as we woke up was work out a way to make money to buy more meth. When we broke into houses, we would look for anything of value including bank books and credit cards. Bank books were great; with a good calligraphy set, you could make a lot of money.

We would change all the particulars and backdate a lot of the transactions, making it look like it had a lot more money in the account. On the weekends, we would go to the bank agencies and take up to $400 out at a time, easy money. They couldn't check with the bank because back then, they had no computer link-up. All the money was spent on meth. Eventually, we were caught for a whole heap of charges and got another six months in custody.

When I was fifteen, Macka and I went to Dad's house at about one in the morning and pushed his car out on the road. A few weeks before,

I had pinched his spare key when I went over to borrow some money. I used it to start the car.

We stole the old man's car, which was pretty low, but I didn't care. *What has he ever done for me?* I thought.

That night, we used his car to do a ram raid on a petrol station near the airport. I rammed the rear of the car straight through the front window while Macka grabbed what he could. I remember driving through a back street in Victoria Park, leaning over the back seat to get a Mars Bar because Macka wouldn't give me one.

I mean, we had ten boxes full, it wasn't like we were going to run out or anything. I was going about 60 km per hour and wasn't watching the road when I wiped out the whole passenger side of another vehicle. By the time we had finished, the old man's car was a total write-off.

Screw him, I thought.

We dumped the car in Como.

About a week later, I got picked up walking through the Perth City for a name check. As it turned out, Dad found out that I had pinched his car and dobbed me in to the cops, I got three months for stealing his car. While I was in there, I wrote him a big 'sorry' letter because I felt bad.

Back to Longmore.

By the age of sixteen, I had been to Longmore over twenty-six times. I was what you would call institutionalised. I had become that used to the system that sometimes after getting released, I would be back in custody within twenty-four hours.

1986 LONGMORE

After being released just after my sixteenth birthday, I pulled into the drop-in centre and ran into an old mate, Chris. I hadn't seen him since Clontarf Boarding School. He used to attend the daytime school classes.

We would hang around a fair bit. I was homeless so he let me move into his place with his parents for a while. Chris and I mostly stole cars. We'd take the stolen vehicles to an elderly couple who stripped them down and sold the parts to various wreckers around Perth.

One Sunday, Chris and I were walking around West Perth trying to make some money when we came across a hire car joint called Econo Car Rentals. We broke in through the roof and went looked for money. Chris spotted a board with all the car keys on it, so we decided to take one of the latest cars for ourselves, a Ford Telstar.

That morning, we did a few break-ins to get some money. We then went to the drop-in centre, rounded up as many street kids as we could and snuck back into the car joint. There were thirteen of us all up and we took nine cars, picking the ones we wanted.

We celebrated by stopping at a pub, having some beers and getting on. We planned one big demolition derby. The Rocky Pools is a big mountain of rock all around you and a large waterhole in the centre. The road up to the Rocky Pools was a hard one, normally only 4WD would attempt to drive up the road, we all made it with only one car getting bogged, but we got him out. When I think about all the damage and destruction that I have done to the property of so many people, it makes me sick.

We put two of the best cars to one side and trashed the rest, we kept ramming each other 'til one of the cars broke down. When it did, we would stop and then jump all over that car.

Then we would turn all the lights and indicators on, push the car over the edge into the waterhole, just to watch it sink to the bottom. We put eight cars in the waterhole that day. At the end of the day, we all piled into the two cars that we had put aside and headed down the hill. The two cars headed their separate ways.

Chris and I were in a late-model Ford Telstar. Because of all the damage that we had done to the other cars, we decided it was best to dump this car the proper way — sink or burn it. In the end, we decided to sink it. We drove to a boat ramp where we would let it go, placing a brick on the accelerator and steering the wheel with ropes. It was about two o'clock in the morning, we didn't think anyone would see us.

We couldn't believe it when the car, instead of sinking, continued to float around the Swan River. It suddenly banged into the side of a boathouse, someone stuck their head out yelling and we started to run. It only seemed like minutes and the police were all over the joint. I had never been in cold water before, but I swam that river from one side to the other three times that night.

We also stole a couple of cars from the Perth Entertainment Centre car park earlier that day to use in a ram raid through the retail store, Archie Martins. We were stopped at the lights and my mate, Brockie was driving; he was one mad driver, that's how he got his nickname.

He was well-known for pulling up at traffic lights and giving police the finger only to have them chase him. He got off on the adrenalin.

Over the next few months, Chris and I stole over a hundred cars from the Cannington area, most of which were stripped and sold. All the money we made went into our veins, and I am talking thousands of dollars' worth.

We once broke into a house in Kelmscott and I found three and a half thousand in cash under the mattress, we were stoked. We bought motorcycles, mine was a Honda CB250 and Chris had a Yamaha Virago. On the way back to Chris's house, he rode erratically, all over the road, in the middle between cars and it wasn't long before the police put the lights on him.

We were going down Welshpool Road coming up to the William Street Bridge. Chris didn't flinch, he went up on the side of the embankment and straight over the side of the bridge, thinking he was some super Evel Knievel or something. The bike was a write-off, I went straight back to his old lady's house which was only 1 km away. The police pulled in the driveway two minutes after me. They were looking for Chris, as they had already traced the bike registration to Chris and we hadn't even had the bikes for an hour. They grabbed Chris at the industrial area and he was charged with heaps, his old lady bailed him out.

Not long after that, Chris and I were asleep at the house of the couple who used to strip all the cars.

It was about 6 am and we woke up to the police coming through the window, yelling: "Nobody move or we'll shoot!"

They carried the police standard .38 revolver and a few of them brandished pistol-grip shotguns.

We were busted again and this time they got us big time. We were charged with stealing over one hundred cars, no MDL (driving without a licence), UUMV (unlawful use of a motor vehicle), UDMV (unlawful driving of a motor vehicle), reckless driving, failing to stop when required by an Officer of the Law, breaking and entering and many other charges. I received nine months' strict custody and was sent to Riverbank Detention Centre. Riverbank was for boys 16-18 and was a hell of a lot harder than Longmore, that was for sure. The complex was shaped the same as Longmore except it had higher walls and it was much harder to get out of.

Riverbank's routine was the same as Longmore's except that you were up at 5:30 am every morning because you had to do ten laps around the oval as part of your fitness regime. The pay was slightly higher, you made $44 per week, but out of that, you had to pay $28 per week rent. You could also get fined for misbehaviour or swearing, smoking, etc. Fighting was a $50 fine, and a week down the back, that was hard.

Over the years, I had learned to use the trampoline pretty well and spent most of my time on it, it helped kill time.

Night-time activities were the same as Longmore. The Broken Chain group used to come and I attended as much as I could. I was learning about God and what he had done for me, but at the same time, I was also just going along for a free feed and to perve on the sheilas who came in.

I had seen Alan Shepherd many times before and always believed in God. I mean, I ain't no preacher and have always been far from a perfect person, but God made me feel loved and I needed to feel loved. I was alone, I still rocked myself to sleep and often cried despite being sixteen years old. It's hard being a kid laying down in a cell, knowing you are always alone.

One night, I attended one of the night-time sessions, I can even remember the date: 18th May 1986. This particular night, they played a video called *"The Cross and the Switchblade"* based on an autobiographical book by David Wilkerson who plays himself in the movie. I remember the second that Alan pressed the PLAY button, I was captivated and locked in on what was taking place. It was like they were telling my story.

The movie's main character was a fella by the name of Nicky Cruz (played by Erik Estrada) who grew up in the Bronx. He was a leader of one of the worst gangs around at that time. It told the story of this skinny-looking preacher, David Wilkerson who was from a country town. He felt that he was called by God to go to the Bronx, gather all the gangs together in one room and tell them that God loved them and explain how He had a plan and a purpose for their lives. Now, when you see all the different gangs, the fights and the muggings, it would have been a pretty brave thing for the scrawny preacher David to do.

In the movie, it showed Nicky's struggles within himself that no-one else could see. He hated himself, he hated what he did, who he hung around with, the lifestyle he was stuck in. He knew no other way, he had grown up that way. All he wanted to be was normal, you know, a geek, a productive member of society free from the influence of drugs and substances. A bloke who did normal things, like have a mum and a dad, go to one school instead of lots of schools, someone who went on family holidays, and all that sort of stuff.

During the movie, I began crying because this was my story he was telling. It was me; it was how I felt about myself, I hated who I was, I hated what I did, I hated everyone and blamed everyone else for why I was like I was. My whole life had been stolen from me. As the movie went on, there were many times where David approached Nicky and told him that God loved him and that He had a plan and a purpose for his life. It was like David had been told by God to specifically continue to tell Nicky that God loved him. But every time David told Nicky about God, it just made Nicky angrier and angrier to the point where he held a knife to the preacher's throat.

"If you come near me again, I'm gonna kill you."

You can see in the movie that Nicky wanted so badly to be normal, to be a geek, but he was trapped in a world he didn't want to be in.

Like me, he didn't know how to get out, there was a battle going on inside of him. David felt called by God to gather the main gangs together in a big hall and tell them all that God loved them and that he wanted to help them change.

The thought of getting all the gangs together in one place seemed impossible: they had African-Americans, Mexicans, Hispanics, Negroes, Italians, to name just a few. People from different races who hated each other who were fighting over their own little patch of turf.

Seriously, to get them all into one place would've been a miracle, even the local coppers told David that he was nuts and that it wouldn't happen, but the preacher managed to do it. One night in a nearby hall, he managed to get all the gangs under one roof to hear his talk.

The police themselves could not believe what was taking place, they had full security around the building and they were scared. When they were in the hall, all the gang members were just throwing rubbish at each other, stirring everybody up, and it looked like they were about to have a big gang fight in the middle of the hall. The preacher got up on stage and started the service, it took a while for the crowd to calm down and to listen but they ended up doing so the preacher began to talk.

He started the service by taking up a collection, an offering to cover the costs of hiring the building. While the preacher was speaking, he was being heckled a great deal by all of the gang members, they were taking the piss out of him and you could tell he was a little nervous. Anyway, David asked for two volunteers to hand out the buckets, picking Nicky Cruz and one of the Negro fellas who happened to be Nicky's number one rival. All the gang members stopped their heckling to see if Nicky and the Negro would hand out the buckets or fight.

They looked at each other and with a bit of egging on, the two off them took up a collection while everyone else was making fun of them.

Most people threw in some notes and some change. When the collection was done, together they walked behind the stage curtain.

Nicky said to his sworn enemy, "Should we split it now? I reckon this preacher thinks we're going to rip him off. Instead, how about we just give this preacher his money?"

"Yeah, let's just give him his money, we'll prove him wrong."

By this time, I was glued to the screen. They walked up on stage and Nicky looked the preacher in the eye. David locked his eyes on Nicky.

"Here's your money, Preacher."

David held out his hand to grab the bucket.

"God really loves you, Nicky."

Nicky dropped to his knees on the floor in front of all the other gangs and started to cry, and I mean cry. David started to preach about how much God loved all them fellas, even if them fellas did not love God or even know God. He loved them. The preacher talked about sin and how it separates us from God and how God sent His Son to die for us and our sins.

Mate, I'm telling you, half the hall broke out in tears. Grown men were crying when David gave an altar call and many came forward and asked Jesus Christ to come into their lives.

I couldn't believe what I was seeing.

For the rest of the movie, it showed how Nicky's life started to change. He started helping the preacher in his work and he started to dress normally. Nicky stopped swearing, smoking, drinking, using drugs and even changed the way he talked to others, changing into everything I ever wanted to be. He quit the gang, he was becoming normal, a productive member of the community.

Honestly, I sat crying watching this movie. I wanted so badly to be a good person and to be normal. I wanted what he had or was getting, I didn't think it was possible to change. I didn't want to live the rest of my life in a prison, doing crime and drugs, but I could see that it was the path I was on and had been on for many, many years, since I was seven years old, in fact.

I remember going back to my prison cell that night, getting on my knees and I prayed for the first time in my life.

"God, if you're real and you can change Nicky's life, I know that you can change mine. Please forgive me for all my sins, I believe Jesus is real and I want Him in my life".

I tell you what, an overwhelming sense of unconditional love washed over me. I couldn't stop crying, wave after wave after wave of emotion crashing over me. I wept uncontrollable tears of joy as I felt the love of Jesus Christ fill my heart. I honestly felt love like I had never experienced before.

It was like the whole world became new and I heard an inner voice that said to me, "John 8:32," a Bible verse that says: "You shall know the Truth and the Truth shall set you free, or make you free."

I felt like God had revealed to me the truth of the gospel of Jesus Christ and that I, like Nicky Cruz, had now broken free of my old life and I was going to start living a new life like Nicky.

People cannot fathom that there is a higher power they call God, that He created Heaven and Earth and all things in it. It's a bit unreal, hey, but when you feel Him in your life, you know that He is real. I used to carry a pocket-size Bible in my pocket and read it every day. I used to cop all that the other kids would dish out at me for it. They would tease me, but it didn't matter because my mate was there, I felt Him, that's all that mattered to me.

Close to the end of my sentence, I held Bible study groups in my cell with a few of the other prisoners, we had gained special permission from the guard in charge to do this on a regular basis. I remember one time when one of the strongest, scariest and worst kids in there came to me and asked me to pray for him.

I had three weeks left of a nine-month sentence and still had to appear at court for one break and enter with intent. I had pleaded not guilty for the past eight months because I did not do it. Stupid me, then I pleaded guilty just to get it out of the way and the judge gave me another four months accumulative which meant on top of the sentence I was already serving.

I was completely shattered.

That meant I had to serve another two and a half months. In total, I would serve slightly less than twelve months. When I returned to my cell that night, I cried and ask God why. I was a changed person, I felt that I had been given a new chance at life and now it was put on hold.

Everything happens for a reason, I thought.

Six weeks before my release, I was asked if I wanted to go on a Challenge For Youth camp for young offenders. That was probably what showed me there could be another side to life. I stayed an extra week in custody just to go to that camp.

They picked twelve boys along with four staff members and we went on a three-week journey up North. First, we went to Kalbarri and walked from one end of the gorge to the other. It took us three days and we had a ball. We were supplied with an army issue ration pack which made your number twos come out a bit bigger than the norm; sometimes you just wanted to yell for help, you thought you were giving birth, and for a bloke, that's pretty scary, I tell ya.

After the gorge, we went to Mount Augusta, and we camped at the bottom of the mountain for the night. The plan was to walk up the mountain on one side and come down on the other the next morning. Colin and I got lost and it took them an extra six hours to find us.

We then headed towards Yallalong Station where we spent six days with no food or water, walking from one side of the station to the other. We were taught basic survival skills, how to light a fire with sticks and how to extract water from a tree. In the last four days, we were paired up, given a map and told we were to navigate our way using nothing but a compass and the stars. There were certain checkpoints along the way and if we did not leave a sign that we had been there by a certain time, they would come and get us. After a few days of eating nothing at all, you tend to lose some weight.

I had to use a shoelace tied around my waist to hold my pants up. There were a lot of goats on the station, and someone came up with the idea to catch and eat one. We chased the goats and I grabbed a really big one by the horns. It took me about fifteen minutes to get it down, only to learn that the older they are, the tougher the meat. I had to let it go as it was too old. One of the other blokes had caught a baby goat that was supposed to be good eating. We held it down, cut its throat, hung it up and skinned it.

We made a spit from a bit of fencing. The meat was the best I'd ever tasted, probably because we hadn't eaten anything except Quandong nuts. We also drank from mud puddles, so that would have made the meat taste so good. We left Yallalong Station and headed north towards Exmouth. There we walked across the tough ranges in Exmouth right up to the point.

Survival Camp 1987

Three weeks later, we arrived back at Walcott Centre in Mount Lawley to a 'Welcome Home' meal. Then we were released back into society.

Before my release, I had organised with the pastor, Alan Shepherd to stay with him in Clayton Street in Midland, so he picked me up from the function. I had very little time to read the Bible in the three weeks that I was away, so my Christian faith had worn a bit thin. You see, you have to feed your soul in order for your faith to grow. It's the same as the need your body has for food; in order to grow, so does your soul. If you do not feed your body, it dies; the same goes with your faith. Mine had slowly dwindled and I started to feel uncomfortable.

I was working back at the tyre store where I first started out when I was thirteen and it wasn't going the best. I was broke and unhappy.

I decided to go out one Saturday night and ended up running into Chris at Pinocchio's nightclub in the city. One thing led to another and I had too many beers, someone mentioned wiz — nothing better than a shot to sober you up. I didn't even go back to Alan's place.

I started using very heavily again and would do any crime I could to get money. At the time, I was still hanging around the streets and I met a girl named Nicolette. She was different because she was more upper-class than a typical girl hanging around the streets. We sort of hit it off even though our personalities were totally the opposite. We had a flat in Wembley for a while and my income was still crime. We argued a lot.

Chris and I had about a grand between us when we decided to go to Adelaide in South Australia to have a look around. Neither of us had ever been out of Western Australia before. We caught the bus to Adelaide. I remember arriving in the city at about 10:30 pm and not knowing where we were going so we just checked into the nearest hotel.

It makes you wonder when adults see two sixteen-year-old kids paying for the bus tickets and booking into hotels, but don't bother to do anything about it or even question what they're up to. After a couple of days, our money started to run low and we were scratching for a feed.

It was a Sunday morning; all the shops were closed and we were in the city. We tried wedging a few different doors open when one gave way. We didn't know what business it was, we walked inside and up a flight of stairs, it turned out to be a nightclub. Chris ran for the till and I found the office — I couldn't stop yelling that there was a pile of cash sitting on the bench. Chris ran over, we found a couple of bags and started to push the money into them. We didn't bother about the change, there was too much and we weren't greedy. We left the club the same way we had come in, down the stairs and out the door.

We hired a motel room, sat down and counted our cash, there was a little over $10,000 — we were stoked! We went out, got on and decided to go to the casino. We had to get some decent clothes, but all the shops were closed, so we walked up to total strangers and offered them $100 cash for their shoes, $300 for their pants. We did this to many strangers until we had enough clothes to pass the casino dress code.

Three grams of bad meth and $10,000 later, we were broke at the casino. All I had to show for my share was some ugly sheila hanging off me like a bad smell. Once the deed was done, Chris and I decided to go back for the change at the nightclub we left behind earlier.

It was about 5 am on a Monday morning and the day was about to start. We were hoping the cleaners hadn't been there yet, otherwise it would be too late. We were in luck and this time we came prepared with bags.

Chris opened the safe and had another look inside the safe, there was a big bundle of notes that we had left behind only twelve hours before. The sun started to come up and judging by the amount of traffic outside, we had cut it pretty fine. When we got back to the room, we counted our last pile of cash, there was just over $6,000. We decided there and then, no more casino, we were going to have a holiday. We went car hunting and hired a taxi to drive us around for the day until we found the car that we wanted. It was an old Holden HQ Kingswood and it cost us just under $2,000.

We decided to head to Kings Cross in Sydney, New South Wales, so we drove non-stop for two days until we got there.

We hung around the Cross until our money was all used up on drugs and sold our car to pay for our tickets back to Perth.

Not long after my Adelaide trip, I stole a two-door LH Torana with two friends, Steve and Gary. Steve was driving and Gary and I were in the back and we were heading past the casino when the police spotted us. Gary was massive, his body seemed to be larger than the car. Steve planted his foot and had no intention of stopping. He took us through a few back streets, but he didn't have a chance of getting rid of them in a four-cylinder Torana, so he booted the car around the corner.

The rule was that if we ever got chased by the police, the passengers would always remain in the rear of the vehicle. It was just as well because, with Gary's size, it would have been impossible to get him out of the two-door car. Steve had run away already when the cops ran up to the car and the two of us were still sitting in the back.

"Don't move!"

"We were just hitching!"

The police had to let us go because they had no proof and we were given the benefit of the doubt because we didn't try to run from the scene. Steve was lucky and we caught up with him at home later.

I was driving with Steve through the city centre in a Ford Laser hatch I had stolen from West Perth only hours before. Someone happened to leave the keys in it and I noticed as I was walking by. Steve was staying at the Kings Ambassador Hotel in the city, an upmarket hotel.

We were approaching a traffic light which seemed to go red a bit quicker than normal and I had stopped past the line by about half a metre. Without looking, I put the car in reverse and smashed into the car behind me.

I couldn't believe my luck — it was a Porsche!

I didn't realise what I had done straight away, I panicked and floored the Laser through the red light, but the car behind followed me.

I turned another hard right and ran another red light. The next thing I knew, the Porsche had pulled up alongside me. I could see the anger on the driver's face and there was no way I was stopping, so I rammed him. Steve didn't look like he was doing too well in the passenger seat.

There we were on a Wednesday in the middle of the day, having a smash-up derby on a busy street. The Porsche driver rammed me back and I rammed back even harder. We came up to a sharp bend and I clipped him. He lost control and flipped his car. I was too busy watching him roll over to notice my car start to spin sideways. We went straight through the Jesus people front window. Our car was on its side, we climbed out the door and started to jump fences to get away, and then we headed straight to Steve's hotel.

At this time, I had been back in Perth for a couple of months and started to get a discharge from the end of my old fella, it was starting to get a bit sore down there. I had a funny feeling that I had picked up some sort of VD (venereal disease) from that chick in Adelaide.

I knew it didn't feel right when we were doing it, I thought.

I had to go into the VD clinic in the city, but I was a little scared to go by myself so I yelled out to Macka while he was in the shower and said that a chick named Tracey was on the phone and she wanted to speak with him. Macka told me to tell her to ring back and I said she couldn't. I lied, saying Tracey asked me to tell him that she had just gone to the VD clinic to get herself checked and as it turned out, she had syphilis and that he should go and get himself looked at as well.

I couldn't think of any other VD except gentile warts and I'd already had them, so I knew you didn't need a doctor to tell you that you had them. Syphilis was the only disease I could think of and the worst type you could get, so Macka freaked out.

As soon as he got out of the shower, we went into the city to get checked out. It was painful, to say the least, with all of these cotton buds shoved in all the wrong places. I couldn't even imagine what Macka was going through. He was getting checked out for the worst of them.

Being checked out for syphilis involves this big steel rod stuck right down deep into the eye of your old fella.

I was lucky this time, it was only gonorrhoea for which they gave me tablets. Poor Macka came out of there, leaning forward and cradling his privates in the palm of his hands before he sat down gingerly, he was so bloody sore!

I couldn't help but laugh.

"How'd you go?"

He said he wouldn't know for about six weeks when the test results came back. I couldn't let him wait that long and explained that he didn't have anything, it was me who had gonorrhoea and I had told him that he had syphilis because I didn't want to go in there by myself.

Macka got up and went berserk, started smashing the walls with his fists and he stormed out of the hospital.

The doctor asked what the hell was happening, so I told him the story and he couldn't stop laughing. As it turned out, I would get mine. I was drinking and taking drugs that made the antibiotic not work and my left testicle grew to the size of an emu egg, no exaggeration.

I had no wheels and had no other choice but to hitch to the hospital. When I got in there, I had to strip naked, put on a back-to-front gown and get on the bed. In came the doctor and a whole heap of trainee doctors, about fifteen of them. Each one of them wanted to play with my left testy. Problem was that it was so sore and if you even blew at it, I was in tears. They twisted and they squeezed my poor testicle until I'd had enough.

I told them where to go, put my clothes on and, against their advice, hobbled out of there. The next day, I couldn't move, they had to call an ambulance as I couldn't even stand. I had the biggest swollen testicle man had ever seen on this planet to date, I tell you. I had to endure all the pain of the day before all over again and more, there was nothing I could do. I spent over a week in the hospital and had three needles a day in my backside.

By the time I turned eighteen, I had spent seven birthdays in a row at either Longmore Juvenile Correctional Centre or Riverbank Detention Centre for boys (not to be confused with the Riverview Church mentioned later in my story). Every time I was released, I would get back into the drugs and go again.

I finally started to grow up a bit at the age of 18. Nicolette was pregnant with our first child; we had a three-bedroom house in Midland and I decided to start my own lawn-mowing business. I used to knock on doors asking people if wanted their lawns or any gardening done. I would generally pick up a lot of work and had a lot of regular customers. As a kid, I used to go to old people's homes and ask them if they wanted their windows cleaned or any odd jobs done. I have and will always admire old people because they carry with them grace and knowledge, only to be respected.

Our beautiful daughter, Tosha-Lena was born in October 1988. It's different when you have the responsibility of bringing up a child, it's not an easy task and Nicolette and I didn't last long. We split up three months after Tosha-Lena was born.

Just before I broke up with Nicolette, my mate Todd and I decided to go to the Avon Descent, a canoe event that lasted two days and went from Northam to Perth. We packed five cartons of beer into a small Ford Cortina wagon and headed to the overnight camping spot where every year, about 20,000 people rock up for a big party. We were full of piss and decided to go sheep chasing. We put on our backpack full of supplies (beer) and headed towards the hills. We chased several sheep until Todd tackled one. Full of piss, I cut off its head, skinned it, gutted it and then slung it over my shoulder. We had to swap the dead sheep over quite often as it got heavy.

I can't remember much, but apparently, we walked back into the campsite and grabbed a tent pole to make a spit. A large party began at our fire. The police found me at four in the morning in the back of my wagon, it was minus sixteen degrees.

I had the worst hangover you could imagine and to top it off, I had a raw meat taste so strong in my mouth, it wasn't funny. I was that drunk, I had eaten raw meat and the police denied me a drink of water, I was to find out why later. I was taken to the Toodyay Police Station and charged with the unlawful killing of an animal. I got fined $236 and as it turned out, the owner of the sheep was the Sergeant of the local police station.

Back to Nicolette.

Our personalities and her expectations of me were totally different. She wanted somebody who would go to work and do all the normal stuff, but I found it hard over the years to straighten up. When you grow up the way I did, it was hard. I have cried many times because all I wanted was to be normal.

What I called 'normal' was Mum, Dad, family holidays, school, BBQs, weekends, holidays, etc. I can't remember ever sitting down at the table having a family meal.

I was eighteen and was slowly waking up to myself, I would get into trouble a lot less, thanks to my daughter and Nicolette. Even though we weren't living together, I have had constant contact with my daughter over the years.

I was at the stage of my life where I hated and blamed my parents for everything that I had done in my life. I hated them for ripping off my childhood memories.

Where had my Christmases, my birthdays and Easters gone?

I was locked up constantly for the previous ten years and I had no real memories to hold onto. All the stuff I write about in this book, I am in no way proud of. When you grow up the way I did, you tend to let the wrongs you do justify themselves because of the situation at the time.

Throughout my whole life, my grandma and Uncle Lloyd have always been there for me. I knew I could always go to my gran when I was in trouble, but it wasn't the same as Mum and Dad.

I was staying with my grandmother when I met my wife Amanda, I was working as a tyre fitter.

I used to hang out at the Kelmscott Hotel a fair bit. I was still heavily using drugs, mostly speed (amphetamines). My pay would never be enough to sustain my addiction and I always did a bit of crime here and there.

The fifth of March 1990 was when we met. Amanda walked into the bar at the Kelmscott Pub after moving down to Perth from Wongan Hills to study Horticulture at TAFE.[1]

I was the local drug dealer at the pub. She never went to pubs before but one of her friends from TAFE talked her into it. When she walked through the door of the pub and saw me from like twenty-five metres away, she fell in a puddle on the floor, melted she did, just from gazing upon my good looks and glory (I had that effect on women back then).

Her friend scraped her up off the floor, helped her to her feet and Amanda said, "Who is that man?"

"You DON'T want to go near him, he's BAAAAAADDDDD," advised her friend.

And the rest is history.

I was flat broke one Sunday and I had a service truck supplied to me as part of my job so I decided to pull up to the truck sales yard on the Great Eastern Highway. I brought with me a whole heap of jarrah logs. There was a couple of twenty-two-wheeler semis parked in the yard. I jacked them up and took all the trucks' tyres off them, leaving the truck and trailer sitting on the logs. I could picture their faces when they arrived for work the next day.

---

[1] Courtesy of Peter's Facebook page

Over the next ten years, I was in and out of court but was never given a prison sentence. I had started several small businesses, each one failing because of my meth addiction. It was hard giving up crime, but as you get older, the types of crime you commit changes. As a youth, I was continually breaking into shops and stealing cars. My whole life has been like a train going flat out 100 miles an hour without doors, no stops and no conductor to let you off when you want to. You simply can't get off! You just keep going around and around. You want to get off, you want to stop doing all these things you are doing, but it's hard.

As I got older, the crimes were mostly driving-related, maybe the occasional stealing charge here and there. We used to see our escapades a lot in the papers. When you grow up like I grew up, to have no contact with the law was a miracle which I wasn't to be blessed with for a few more years to come.

Like I said before, everything happens for a reason, whether it be God's path or life's path, we all have a destiny to look forward to. It's how you find it or what you experience in order to find it that can change your life forever. Some of us have to experience different situations in life, whether they be good or bad.

I got my first adult jail number in Hakea in 1991.

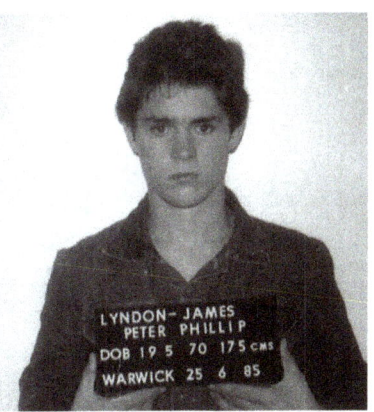
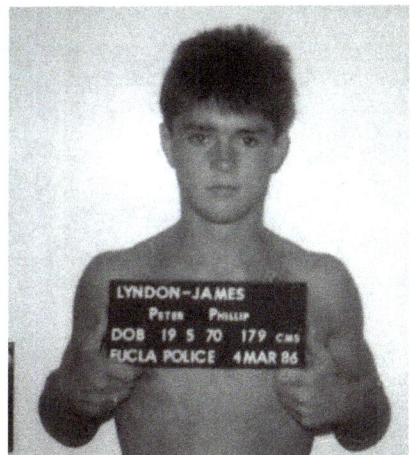

2

Mugshots from my time as a juvenile offender

---

[2] False name and date of birth given which was accepted by police officers.

Adult mugshots

Peter and Amanda, 1992

By 1993, Amanda and I were living in Bassendean, still on the drugs and doing the same old stuff, trying to break free from crime and all the people involved in committing crimes. I was working at a place in Bayswater and ended up quitting because amphetamines and other drugs had got a hold of me again. I decided to start a second-hand shop and got myself a $2k credit card. My plan was to go to the auctions, spend the money on stuff and then have a garage sale to make some cash. On my first weekend, I turned my $2k into close to $5k. Every week for about six weeks, I did the same thing while still hitting the gear pretty hard. I did think about opening a shop. I looked around and found one in Midland; *'Pete's Garage Sale Shop'* opened for business. I ran it the same way you would a garage sale, everything's open to offers.

My drug use was off the charts and to tell you the truth, I don't know how I managed to grow the business and support my habit. One night, I was at home off my face on magic mushies and the security firm rang to say the back door to the shop was open. I had forgotten to lock the blooming thing. I told them I would be there in five, it felt like a year.

I jumped in my Toyota Celica hatchback and started to drive from Bassendean to Midland. If you have ever been smashed off your nut on magic mushies and try to drive, I can tell you it's like life goes in slow motion; what should have been a ten-minute drive turned out to be two hours.

Luckily there were no coppers around because I was driving at 5 kms an hour, but it felt like 200 kms an hour to me. I remember it as if it were yesterday. I made it to the shop, locked it up and went through another spaceship drive home. Seriously, I don't know how I made it, but I must be honest and say that I enjoyed the buzz.

At the time, I was not just using drugs, running a shop but also selling drugs. One of my closest mates, Macka who I will always love as a brother, was locked up in Wooroloo Prison Farm. It was his birthday so I thought that I would give him a visit.

In those days, you didn't have the big fences and all that stuff around you in prison. You were allowed to bring in cakes and cold drinks so I made a Kudda chocolate mull (marijuana) cake to take in. Kudda, by the way, means *filthy,* which also means in your words: extremely good and potent.

So we had the kids carry the cake into the prison so it looked less suss and we all sat on the lawn and pigged out on the cake. My God, if I thought the drive home from the shops on the mushies was bad, I was so stoned I could hardly walk. It felt like I was about to pass out and someone told me I went ghostly white. We stayed for two hours and when I was leaving, it was a mission to look straight. I know it ruined Macka, I don't know how he could have stood up for muster. I tried to drive, but then I had to let someone else drive even though they were in no better shape than me.

Anyway, back to the shop. I was staying up for days on end on the gear and one day, I got pulled over by the coppers and ended up getting charged for driving without a licence. I knew it was going to be another trip to jail as it was my third or fourth time in a year.

I decided to do what I always did: run.

I thought: *If I stick around for court, then I'm screwed.*

I came up with a brainwave and talked Amanda into travelling around Australia with me. I looked around for a mobile home and I ended up buying a 1952 Mercedes-Benz camper bus, old but it would do. I had the house packed up in two weeks and sold my shop to my sister, only to skip the state to avoid jail.

Karratha 1993

We travelled from Perth all the way up the coast to Exmouth for some fishing, stayed there for a few days and continued on our way to Broome. I still had a heap of meth and pot on me that didn't run out until I hit Broome. I was in a little bit of a hurry to get out of the state as the police were looking for me. The drive to Broome was the slowest, most painful and expensive drive I'd ever done. The bus itself was getting 200 kms to the tank because of the diff and the Holden motor. It was just one big juice guzzler. I had to carry six jerry cans of petrol as we ran out of fuel many times.

When I got to Broome, I wanted to get rid of the juice guzzler as soon as possible. I put up a post on a local buy and sell board and within two days, this young fella wanted to swap a WB Holden ute for it.

Mate, I didn't hesitate, I gave him the bus and a whole lot more.

Amanda in Darwin, 1993

The next day, we were in the ute heading for the border. I can't explain the relief that I felt crossing into the Northern Territory, having lost the coppers and not going to jail.

When we hit Darwin, we rented a long-term caravan. It didn't take long before we were back on the pot, then the gear and the cycle continued again. We did some work up there for a while, but it was hot and sweaty, I hated it. You were drenched in sweat from the minute you woke up until you went to bed. Being repulsively smelly and sweaty was not for me. I came up with another brainwave, to swap the ute for a motorbike and then we could travel from Darwin to Townsville. My brother Gavin was in the army at the time and my old man was also heading to QLD. We could meet them there. I swapped my vehicle, this time the ute, for a Suzuki GSX-R750. The buyer also ended up with a lot of camping gear as we couldn't take it on the bike, even as it was, you should have seen how much crap I put on the back of that bike.

So we loaded the bike and headed for Brisbane. We changed our mind about our destination by the time we got to Mount Isa because our butts were that sore from being on that bike for 12 hours straight, Townsville looked closer. Three days non-stop on that bike from Darwin to Townsville. My butt was so sore. After I got off the bike, I was walking bow-legged for about a month. I had been hit in the face by a wasp and nearly killed by a cow coming through Mount Isa. Amanda slept most of the way on the back of the bike.

All these stories may sound like fun, but I was running from me, my old life, from who I was and who I did not want to be. I just wanted to be normal. No matter where we went, I attracted people like me. I could go into any town in Australia and score gear. If it wasn't amphetamines, it would be trips, ecstasy, meth, heroin, mushies, alcohol. You name it, I used it. Why couldn't I be happy without any drug or substance? Why did I always feel uncomfortable around geeks, normal people? I felt I was a weed and that they were judging me, so I stayed away from them.

Except the problem was that everyone who I felt comfortable around was doing what I didn't want to do, but I ended up doing it anyway, I had to in order to fit in.

Between 1993 and 1996, I kept running away from myself, going from town to town, job to job. We stayed in Townsville for a while and that didn't work as the drugs, alcohol and the people that come with that lifestyle started to overtake my life. I wanted so badly to be a normal person, I just didn't know how. The running took us right across the eastern states, Cairns, Maryborough then to Sydney, Melbourne and Adelaide. We kept moving every three months until one day, we finally ended up heading back to Perth.

I say it often: "You can take the prisoner out of prison but then you have to get the prison out of the prisoner."

Even though I was not in prison, I was still in prison. I hated who I was and what I kept doing, it's not easy to say stop.

Perth did not last too long as I got right back into the gear and I knew I was going to hit the wall with the coppers still looking for me, so I had to get away. Amanda rang her parents because we needed a place to stay and it just so happened that they had an old farmhouse on the other side of their farm. We moved up to a place called Konnongorring, about 35 kms south of Wongan Hills.

Same stuff happened there, I was making trips to Perth often to score gear as well as stealing truck tyres and getting myself into big pickles. The coppers raided the farm and I was caught with a whole heap of stolen truck tyres and other stuff.

I got married to Amanda in 1994 after being together for about four and a half years. We got married at the Wongan Hills Pub. The getting married bit was great, although having both of my parents under the same roof was always toxic. My old man and my mum were always at each other and on our wedding day, something was said that caused my dad to leave. It sucked as we were always put in awkward positions if we did have a get-together, having to choose which parent to invite because my parents always stuffed it up.

After getting married, we thought we would go to Exmouth for a honeymoon and then we headed up to Karratha. I decided to stay there and get a job so Amanda headed back to the farm to pack the house up then she drove back up to join me.

We were running again.

The same stuff happened, I got work but was full-on into the gear. Amanda became pregnant with our first son, Pete, not that I remember it too much, his birth just another excuse to get wasted.

The coppers in Karratha had it in for me, we had been there for over a year with Amanda working for the Shire and me working for an engineering company as a boilermaker. There was this one cop who had it in for me, every time I pulled out of my street, he would pull me over trying to charge me with something.

I knew I was going to get done soon as I was flying to Perth every couple of weeks, picking up ounces of amphetamines, selling a fair bit, plus my habit was through the roof. Me and Amanda decided to pack up all our gear and do the midnight run and leave town, the last thing I wanted was to go to jail. At midnight, we packed the trailer and off we went, driving south to Perth.

By 1996, Amanda and I were living in Parkerville with young Peter. I was self-employed with a business called Total Professional Services. I did everything from boilermaking and welding to mowing lawns, the business was doing quite well, but as always, I had my drug addiction to deal with. I was still using large amounts and tried to hide it in any way I could. Even Amanda didn't know at times how much I was using. It was hard trying to lay there at night, pretending I was asleep.

I was starting to feel closed in.

CLOSED IN.

When you start using drugs, you feel on top of the world until you start coming down. You don't want to sleep because you achieve so much while you're awake, while you're on the go. After a while, when you do sleep, the first thing you do is get on or if you haven't got the money, you try to pull some scam or try to steal what you can to pay for your next shot.

The amount of times I would justify buying meth to complete a task or to do one big bender or a mission is endless.

I would see a car on the road for sale, for say $2,000, and think to myself, *one gram of speed (amphetamines) and a good 24-hour sting and I could fix that up quick, restart and would easy get $5,000.*

To start with, I always made a profit but when drugs really get you, you start to lie to yourself or block out the truth from your brain.

I know that subconsciously what I was doing was wrong, but I would justify it by one means or another. How do you get off meth?

I have been on meth and I have tried many times to give up meth. I wrote that last sentence and realised I just lied to myself.

I have tried many times to give up meth and every time I was about to put the needle in my arm, I subconsciously thought of the repercussions of my actions. I knew that by putting that needle in my arm I would be destroying my life. What made me do it was the rush, the feeling, the energy, everything was exciting and never-ending, no matter who I rang at any time, 1 am, 3 am, 1 pm, they were always awake and if they weren't, there was always someone to answer the phone. It was never long before the person you wanted originally got your message because when you're a meth freak, you don't sleep long unless you have just completed a bender. My biggest bender would have been sixteen days and I reckon during that time, I would have had five hours sleep in total, mostly at traffic lights or in petrol station driveways.

I remember one time sitting at a traffic light next to Midland's Hungry Jack's and when I woke up, the light was green and there were all these people banging on my window.

"Are you, alright mate, anything wrong?"

I just looked at them, looked at the light, it was green, I floored it not thinking about the poor man hanging off the car.

I felt like an idiot, but I had done that many times before. I would push it to the back of my mind as if it doesn't matter, being a looper.

What is a looper, you would probably ask? It is someone who is awake 24 hours a day, lives and breathes whippa whether they wish to admit it or not. Me, I was different, I would always tell people when I met them that I was a meth freak. I mean I didn't know many people that didn't know about meth and never really spent the time trying.

When you use meth, you tend to block out the people who you love the most, including family and friends. I distanced myself from my parents. I know that I blamed my parents for my past; when you're that age, you blame who you can, you're frightened.

Stop and look at an elderly person when you walk past them next. Try to put yourself inside their body and imagine having seen what they have seen and experiencing what they have experienced.

You would be blown away. They deserve to be respected. You picture something really deep like life; sooner or later, we are faced with the choice of what you are going to do with it, or what you want out of it. You could be like a large number of people that I grew up around who decided to avoid answering that question.

I have always, up until now, put it in the 'too hard' basket and never imagined living another 50 years. I mean 50 years still left!

What would I like to achieve? Go to work, come home, go to bed, get up to go to work, get pissed, go to bed.

Sooner or later, you will be a faced with the question "Why I am I doing it, do I want to be married, do I want to raise kids, do I want a family, do I want to travel or do I want a life where because of my actions, at any second, the police can come and take me away from my wife, my family and my kids?"

They are who you love the most.

Getting back to feeling closed in, my bills around my addiction were growing and I tried to hide my use from my wife to reduce her use.

I decided that I had to get away from the people I was associating with because I was going downhill fast. I got a job as a boilermaker in Kalgoorlie to start the next day. Amanda stayed behind in Perth with our only child at the time, Peter. For the first two weeks, I slept in the back of my Toyota Land Cruiser because I was flat broke.

It's hard when you try to stop using meth after using it constantly. All you want to do is sleep, where even lifting your head is a task only the strong can endure. It feels like you've been hit by a truck. I found it hard going from using meth constantly, then straight to work, away from my wife but I felt I had to do it, I had to break away.

I eventually moved Amanda and young Peter to Kalgoorlie after I had made enough money to support us. I kept my business going and it was growing rapidly.

In fact, too rapidly. I was that busy, trying to do too much myself and again, I turned to meth in order to cope.

I started using heaps at first, convincing myself that all the money I was spending on meth was justified because I could look at my assets and see how fast my business was growing.

At first, it's always good. Yep! At first!

Soon everything always comes tumbling in on you bit by bit and you don't know what to do, where to hide or who you can talk to. My business suffered badly due to a couple of large contracts I had going at the time and because of my meth addiction.

We felt closed in, so we decided to run again, selling what we could and giving away the rest. We headed east. We had enough meth to get us to Eucla; Amanda, Peter and myself in an old Dodge truck I had done up. It was worth at least seven thousand. I sold it at the petrol station because I could not be bothered fixing the radiator that had blown. All I wanted to do was sleep.

I got $900 for the truck and we booked into the motel for the next three days just to catch up on sleep and even that was hard, every muscle in my body was as hard as a rock.

We caught a Greyhound bus to Adelaide and decided to settle there. Why Adelaide I don't know, but anywhere was better than where we were. We rented a two-bedroom unit in Kilkenny, about fifteen kilometres from the city. I sat there and watched Peter sleeping; I used to cry a lot, all I wanted was to be off the whippa, it made me feel disgusting to stick that needle in my arm. I will have those scars forever, not to mention the scars on my arms. It's what I decide that they represent and do about it that matters.

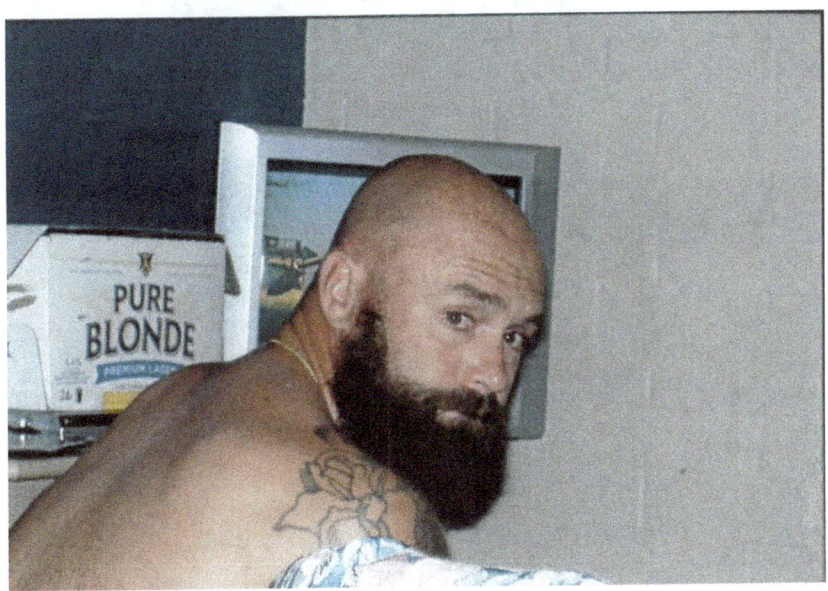

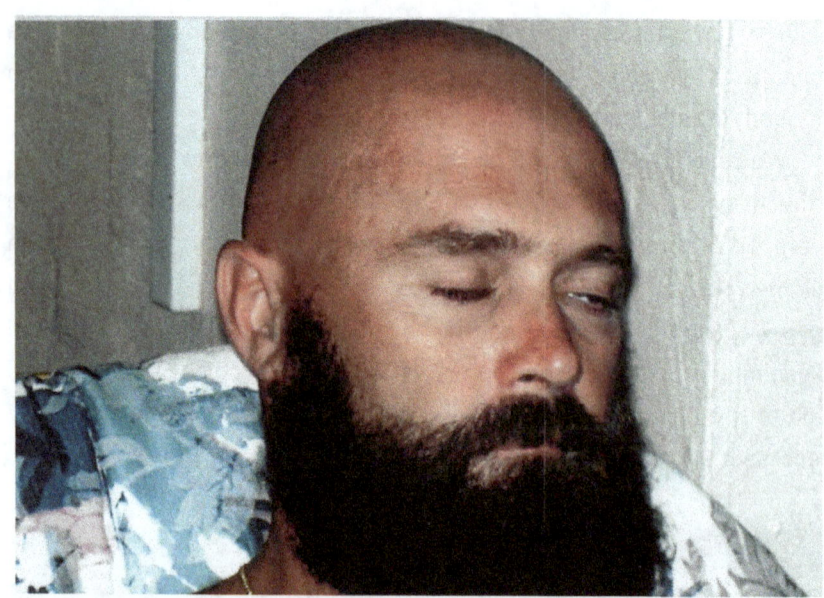
Karratha 1996

Midland, 1998

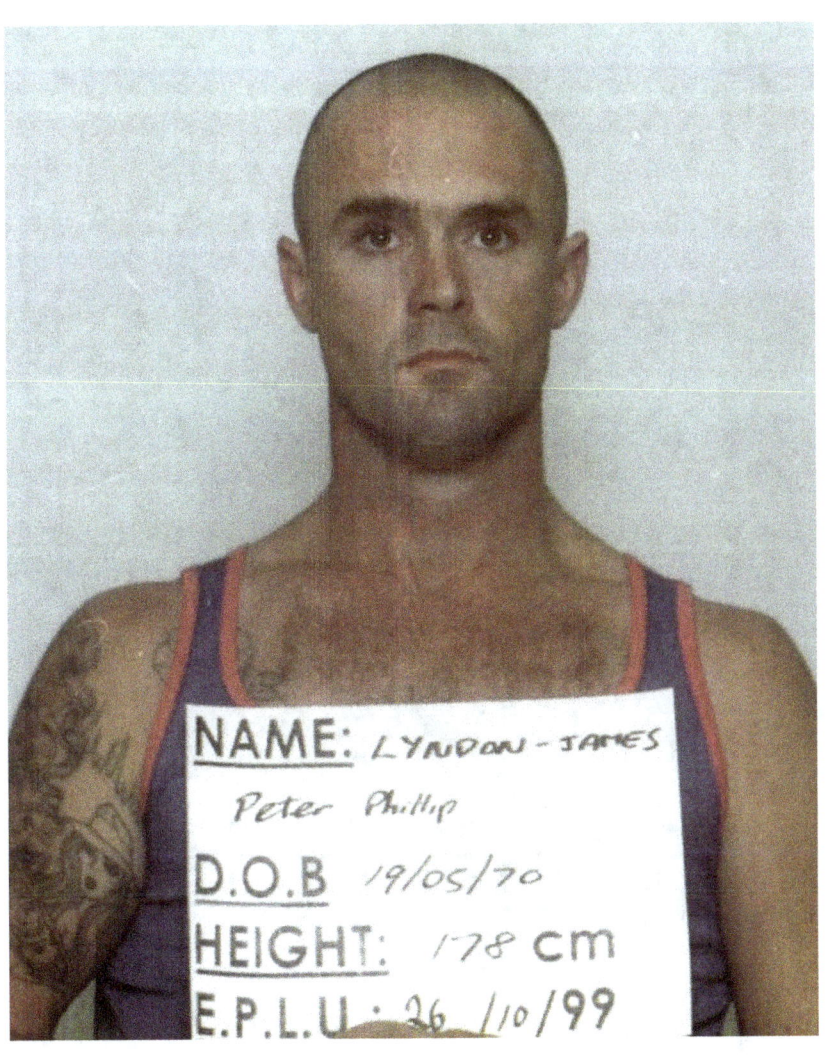

Peter and Macka, Canningvale, 1999

I had just got out of prison. It was November 25, 2001, having served twelve months of a three-year sentence for fraud, break and enter with intent, burglary and driving without a licence, reckless driving, causing an accident and a few other charges. I was driving down Sevenoaks Street in Queens Park in my Ford F-250.

I hadn't slept in about eight days, I fell asleep at the wheel and went straight through a stop sign and wiped out a Mitsubishi van and I mean wiped out, there was nothing left of the vehicle. I was shocked but not amazed that it happened. I was in a bad way with my drug use and had no conscience whatsoever. That was one of the charges that led to me being jailed.

When I was arrested and sent to prison, my wife and I were half in transit so our stuff was everywhere. One month before I was sent away, our second son, Rhyan was born so you can imagine the hardships my wife was facing. She is a very tough and courageous woman for whom I thank God every day. For the twelve months that I was in custody, Amanda stayed with Gavin and his wife, Tammy. Eight kids and three adults in the one house, pretty squashed.

My time in prison was hard. For the first two weeks, I could hardly feel my head coming down off the drugs, then reality began to set in. In a way, I was glad because I was cleaning up, I was starting to feel me again, I could taste food and started to develop a sleeping pattern.

For all the charges that I faced (58 in total), I sat in front of the magistrate for around two hours pleading guilty after he read each charge. I received three years on each charge, to be served concurrently and five years on each aggravated burglary charge. I spent two months on remand waiting to be sentenced. After the sentencing, I was transferred to Canningvale next door for more long-term prisoners.

While I was there, I received a visit from my wife and kids. After my family left, I went back to where they strip-search us. While I was being checked, an officer claimed to have seen me swallow something. I was handcuffed and taken to Unit One, the punishment block. I was stripped naked and placed in a padded cell with a surveillance camera inside.

I spent 24 hours in that cell and was refused a shower. I was there under suspicion of bringing drugs into the prison. The way in which the prison officers treated me was degrading. How can any man sit back and watch another man in pain and laugh? Prison is a place where bullies breed, there is always someone standing over someone for something.

Pot in jail is worth a fortune, so if you had pot, you were IT as soon as word gets around, which doesn't take long, trust me. The only way to do your jail time is to be a dark horse and throw off whenever you can. Prison is full of bullies who take kindness as a weakness.

During this jail term, I was moved around for one reason or another. I went to Wooroloo Prison Farm, to Casuarina Prison, to Bunbury Regional Prison and I was released from there. It was in Casuarina Prison that I began to write my journal which is Part Two of this book. This brings us to the main part of my story and the main reason for writing this book.

After my release from prison, I was staying with my brother Gavin and his family in High Wycombe, but it was a little bit cramped. Across the road were a bunch of teenagers who were always up doing something or other, no matter what time of the night, so I decided to walk over to them one day and ask them if they knew where I could get on; of course, I was right on the mark.

I started getting drugs from them on a regular basis and it was costing me money, so one day I said to Amanda that I might as well sell meth for a living. I mean, I know enough people who use it. Up until that time in my life, I had never dealt drugs before, not in a big way. I started off getting eight balls on credit — three and a half grams. It cost me $1,300 and after a few months, I was getting up to four ounces a time on tick (credit) and was selling in excess of $40,000 a day of meth (methamphetamine or crystal meth).

I was using at least two grams a day myself. Most of my shots would be a half a gram at a time, an amount that could send me looping for days. I was renowned for giving people shots that would drop them. I would get off on their reaction, I didn't care how much it cost me. I used to tell them to try the next level, it was different than anything that they had experienced before and it was.

Everybody's reaction was different; I was soon to suffer the consequences.

Across the road from us in Bayswater was a park, then a large area of bush, followed by a transfer station. After a period of time, I started to see things and hear things that nobody else was aware of. It was sending me crazy.

I was in the shower and this 'thing' poked me in the foot, I looked down. It was a stick that was glowing, I swear it was a high-tech camera, it had come up out of the drain at me.

Another time, I was in the park at three o'clock in the morning, looking up trees with a flashlight. I was looking for what I called 'little people'; they were the people who followed me, they drive cars, they climb trees, they blend in everywhere, no matter what you do, you can't find them or prove they are there.

Some nights, I would jump up in the air next to my neighbour's fence at 1 am with my digital camera in hand and would take surprise pictures, the flash would scare the living daylights out of whoever was there.

Nobody was there, of course, it was just me looping. I would accuse the neighbours of looking over my fence at all hours of the night. One time, I spent 17 hours looking through a hole I had drilled in the roller door. I was looking for the police, it was a strong paranoia that they were coming, they always come sooner or later, they always come...

Because of the type of upbringing I had, I was a person who could get hold of anything from cars, bobcats and trucks, all the way to drugs, guns and explosives. There wasn't anything that I couldn't get hold of, including chemicals to make meth.

I woke up on a Monday at around 11 am, hearing what I thought was my mate, Crash, banging on the roller door. I was sliding my pants on when I heard voices coming from everywhere. I heard a large bang outside and told Amanda to get on the floor. At the time, she was holding my young bloke, Rhyan.

I knew it was the cops, I had been through this many times before. We were already on the ground in the kids' room before they came through the door, there were about fifteen of them, all carrying guns or rifles and some wearing vests. The warrant was for suspicion of selling explosives and detonators. Like I said, I could get hold of anything.

We were arrested and charged with a large number of charges, from the possession of two firearms, pistols that they had retrieved in my roof to possession of amphetamines, possession of cannabis with intent to sell and supply and possession of an illegal weapon, a stun gun. Amanda spent time in the watchhouse while she waited for her sister to bail her out early that morning. We received two separate bails of $10,000 surety and I was remanded to appear at a later date. The police seized a large quantity of cash and goods.

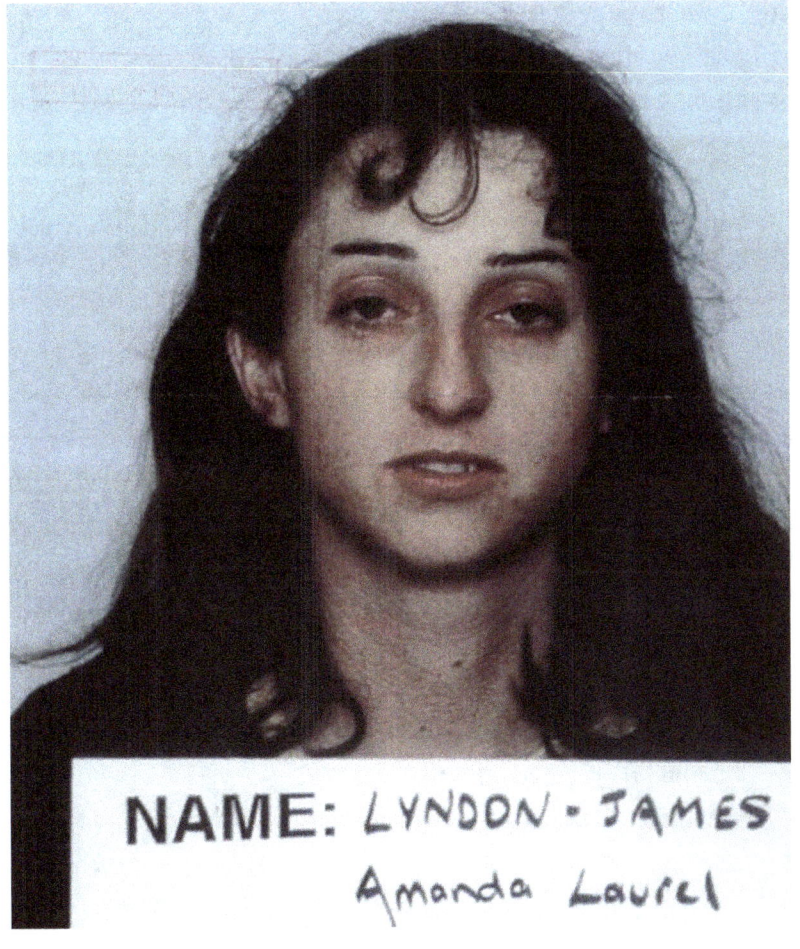

Amanda's Mugshot, May 2001

After the day that the light had come up out of the drain at me, I was convinced that somebody was trying to show or tell me something.

Meth was getting the best of me. I spent two days driving all over Perth following the flashes of light coming from brake lights on cars, they had me going from place to place following the flashes. It was like a car would be two steps ahead of me and the driver would tap on the brakes a few times and I would hear a voice in my head saying, "Peter, Peter, I want you to follow me," so I did.

I followed the car in front of me. The car went left then right, then left and then it pulled over in a carpark near a children's playground. I pulled over and the car drove off.

I remember looking around and I saw a husband and his wife with their children, the dad playing with his children and I heard a voice in my head saying, "Peter, I'm offering you this."

I couldn't help myself, I just broke down and cried.

The voice in my head was offering me everything I ever wanted, I just wanted a family. I wanted my mum and my dad, I wanted to go out like other kids. My whole life, I just wanted to be normal, to go on family holidays, go to one school, to run up the corridor in the mornings and jump into bed with mum and dad for a cuddle. My parents never attended any school events that I can remember, I've never even sat at the kitchen table with my parents or family and had a meal. I wanted to change so badly but I didn't know how. I remember sitting in the car for about 20 minutes, bawling my eyes out, I wanted this so badly. After I got my act back together, I cleaned the snot out of my beard, tidied myself up and then drove off.

Now I don't know what was happening, but something weird was going down, I was hearing voices in my head. I know it wasn't the meth, but this voice was leading me all over Perth, offering me everything I ever wanted, to be normal. A geek, a productive member of society, a mum and a dad, one school, friends, a person free from the influence of drugs or substances.

A normal person. After about 15 minutes of driving, the same thing happened again, a car's brake lights flashing, so I followed this next car and it did the same thing. It went left then right, then went left and left again and then it pulled up in front of a brand-new home. The house was at lock-up stage and it had no landscaping done, so I pulled up and the other car just drove away.

As I looked at the house, there was no-one around but I heard that voice in my head again and it said, "Peter, I'm offering you this."

I just bawled my eyes out, crying for about 10 minutes in the car.

This voice in my head was offering me a home. I've never really had a home, I've moved every three months my whole life. Running from place to place to place, running from myself, but wherever I went, I went.

I was the problem.

All I ever wanted was to be normal, to have a place to call home, where I wouldn't have to move all the time. I sat in the car for 15 minutes: crying, confused, exhausted and lost. I didn't know what the heck was happening. Something weird was going down. All of this happened over a period of two days, being led all over Perth and being offered everything I ever wanted. A house, family time with my children, stability.

Man, I was tired.

I went home to the missus.

"Something weird is going down, Amanda, this has been happening for two days."

My wife just thought that I had lost the plot on methamphetamines, that I was going through a period of drug-induced psychosis, but I knew that I wasn't.

At the time, I was on bail for a pound of pot, two handguns, intent to sell and supply drugs and a whole range of other charges. I knew I was under intense police surveillance, that I was being followed and that my phones and my house were bugged.

I got up the next day and I decided that I would lose the police. I got on my motorbike, a Kawasaki VN1500 Cruiser, brand-new. So I rolled up the roller door and booted it out of the carport. I rode it across 20 metres of beach sand to get through a very narrow path for pedestrians and across the Tonkin Highway onto the other side of the island.

I lost the coppers as I drove down the Tonkin Highway, I had no idea what was happening, I was mentally exhausted.

Half an hour later, I found myself out on the coast, riding my bike when I heard that voice and it said, "Peter I want you to follow me."

As soon as I heard the voice, I pulled over to the side of the road and I took my helmet off and pulled it apart, I wanted to find out where that speaker was in my helmet. I couldn't find anything, so I put my helmet back together and rode off.

The same thing kept happening for most of the day. I would hear the voice in my head telling me to follow the signals, so I would follow the vehicle a couple of cars in front. It would lead me to a place, then that car would drive off. I would look around and again, the voice always offered me something I always wanted but had never had.

Every time, I cried.

At about 2 pm, I was 15 kms past the Neerabup Roadhouse. The vibration through the bike had been the best I've ever felt and the tune that was coming out of the pipes was off the charts. Now, if you like bikes, I'm telling you, it was like the whole universe came together for me, it was the most perfect 'in sync' moment of my life. I remember it clearly like it was yesterday.

I was sitting on about 110 km/h when my bike started making funny noises. The handlebars started to shake and all of a sudden, my bike spluttered and I made it to the side of the road. I had no idea why it broke down because it was a new bike and had a full tank of fuel. I pulled my bike apart trying to work out the problem. New bikes don't make those noises and nor do they vibrate like that unless you do modifications to them, which I hadn't.

I even thought that the police had wired my bike to do what it did when I couldn't find anything wrong with it. I was stuck in the middle of nowhere so I decided to hitch a ride. I left my bike parked on the side of the road and I crossed to the other side of the road to hitch a lift back to the roadhouse to call my wife.

So I stuck out my thumb. After a couple of minutes, a young couple stopped and picked me up and I got into the back of their car. We started driving up the road and they had music playing and it felt like the words in the song were speaking to me.

After about five minutes, the young fella in the front seat turned around to me and said, "I feel like God is trying to tell me to tell you something."

"Yeah, what's that?"

He felt that God was telling him to tell me that God loved me and that He had a plan and a purpose for my life.

As soon as the young fella said that, I broke down crying big-time. I told the girl to pull over to let me get out of the car. So they pulled over to the side of the road and let me out, then they drove off. I took my leather jacket off and hung it on a post on the side of the road and went into the bush to cry.

I was at breaking point after three days of this weird stuff happening and then some complete stranger picks me up and tells me that God loves me and that He has a plan and a purpose for my life. Like I said, I am not a religious person. I have always believed that something was up there, but have never been to church or anything like that. Sorry, that's a lie as I have actually broken into a few churches over the years (not okay, I know).

After half an hour of crying in the bush, I cleaned the snot out of my beard, wiped my face and got back out onto the side of the road and started to hitch. A car pulled up, a matte black Ford F-250. The driver had really long, black hair and tattoos covering half of his face.

"Is that your motorbike back there on the side of the road?"

I told him it was, so he offered to go back and pick it up as he had a set of ramps in the back.

"No, I just want to get to a phone box to ring my wife, something weird is going down."

We got about 5 km up the road and then out of the blue, he turned to me and said, "Mate, I feel I've gotta tell you something."

"Oh yeah, what's that?"

"I'm sure God is telling me to tell you that He loves you and that He has a plan and a purpose for your life, that your life is not a mistake."

I sat in his car and I cried for the next 10 minutes until we got to the nearby roadhouse. Mate, I was so confused.

I used to wear a whole heap of bling (gold jewellery and diamond rings). I remember getting out of his car and taking all my gold jewellery off my fingers as well as the gold chains from around my neck and I threw them in the bin at the petrol station. I went to the public phone box out the front to ring my wife's number.

"Something weird is going down, my bike's broken down and lots of weird stuff is happening. I need you to come and pick me up."

My wife said she couldn't pick me up as she had to pick the kids up from school. So I was forced to hitch again.

I had walked about one hundred and fifty metres on the highway when an old granny stopped to give me a lift in her old Datsun 200B.

I remember her leaning out of the car window saying to me, "I don't normally pick hitchhikers up, son, but you look different."

The elderly granny must've been about eighty years old with curly platinum hair and false teeth. I got in the car and thanked her for the ride. The reason I could tell she had false teeth is that when she talked, they flip-flopped inside her mouth. She had to use her thumb to push them into place when she spoke. We got about five kms up the road near Joondalup when she turned to me and said, "Honey, I feel I've got to tell you something."

"Yeah, and what is that?"

She told me that God was telling her to tell me that He loved me and that my life was not a mistake, but He had a plan and a purpose for my life. I instantly, uncontrollably, burst into tears, I was a mess. She drove me all the way home from Neerabup to Bayswater.

That was three Christian people in the space of not even 20 km over a one-hour period who told me that God loved me and that He had a plan and a purpose for my life. Each one of these people did not know me or each other.

Despite all the evidence that it was God talking to me through these people, I still didn't comprehend or understand the truth, that God was reaching out to me. A couple of days later, things escalated.

That was around the time I was on the way to see my old lady at Australind. I don't know what made me go because I hadn't seen my mum in almost a year. I started to notice signals from other cars, double tap on the brake or a flash from the headlights a long way off. I don't know where they were taking me or where they wanted me to go but I knew I had to follow. I ended up at some recreation centre. I told the kids (Tosha, one of her friends and Pete) to wait in the car and I started to follow the light in the sky. It was not a continuous flash but when I started to go the wrong way, it would flash again.

I followed the light into the bush and I ended up standing for three hours in the same spot. I didn't know it at the time but I was only one hundred and fifty metres from the car. It started getting dark.

I must admit that I am hesitant to share this bit, but I know what I saw and I know it's true. When I got to a certain spot in the bush, a light began to shine in the sky, from heaven; very small at first, then it began to grow bigger. I could not move, my feet were frozen and all I could do was cry. The light became so bright and the ground around me began to move and I mean move, shifting in waves like an ocean in front of my eyes. You might think I'm nuts but I would pass any polygraph test you give me because what I saw and heard was real.

As I was staring at the light, I heard a voice coming from the light say, "BE STILL AND KNOW THAT I AM GOD," clear as day.

I had my hands behind my back as if I were standing in front of a judge, continuously crying. I couldn't move, the ground was moving, the light was bright and I know what I heard, felt and saw.

After what seemed like fifteen minutes to me, I crawled out of the bush because the ground was still moving. I finally stood up and walked toward my car when the moving sensation stopped. When I got near my car, I saw that the coppers, Amanda and Nicolette were there. I was wondering what the heck was happening.

It turned out that I had been gone so long that Tosha had gone inside the recreation centre after waiting a long time and she told people there her dad had gone missing. Like I said, I thought I was gone for only fifteen minutes but it turned out to be over three hours. Amanda and Nicolette had driven from Perth, more than a two-hour drive.

I was a bit stunned to tell you the truth, I was on private property so I told the coppers where to go as well as everyone else. Amanda got Nicolette to take all the kids including Peter back to Perth as I refused to leave the property. I wanted to see the ground in broad daylight, I mean the ground don't do that sort of stuff normally. My thoughts were that someone had put scaffolding in place to make the ground do what it did and I wanted to see the marks where the boards were placed to stop the scaffolding fall over.

I had an argument with Amanda, she slept in her car and I stayed in mine. At first light, I was searching through the bush looking for cracks in the ground as well as the marks for the scaffolding that held the light in the sky, nothing there. Everything was normal, I was so confused. I know what I saw was real and I will stand by it until the day I die.

When I walked back out of the bush, I tried to explain to Amanda what had happened over the last couple of days: the lights, the ground moving, the light in the sky, me feeling like someone was wanting me to follow them, but then they wouldn't show themselves. I was peeved off. We decided to meet each other at home and Amanda went her way and I went mine, then it started happening again.

A car would tap on its brake lights and I would hear a voice saying follow me, so I did. I have done this on many occasions and sometimes I found myself as far as Lancelin, right in the middle of the bush. Walking God knows where, looking for only God knows what. Whoever it was, they were offering me everything I ever wanted, and that was to be a normal person.

When I was driving back to Perth alone, I saw a car stop on the opposite side of the road. I stopped too and by the time I did, the other driver drove off, so I parked on the verge where that car had been stopped and began searching for some message left for me. I found an address on an old piece of paper and looked around for some sort of confirmation that the information was correct, but there was none. I returned to my car and headed to the address in South Perth.

I headed towards Hungry Jack's in South Perth and decided to wait on the corner of Canning Highway and Berwick Street. I was standing there for a few minutes when several people started signalling for me to get into their car, or were they? They looked angry. I didn't know. I couldn't tell what was real and what was not. I was meeting somebody, but I didn't know who or for what.

Why was I here?

I didn't know, all I knew was that I was tired and I wanted whatever it was they were offering me, which was to be a normal person.

When you sell $40,000 worth of meth a day, you tend to stress out and mix with some heavy people. Along with selling that amount of drugs, not to mention the amount I was using each day, I was also selling handguns, ammunition, explosives as well as dealing with stolen goods. I had good reasons to stress out. I was at a stage in my life where I wanted out of the destructive life I was living, but I didn't know how to do that.

As I was standing on the corner, I started to panic, I started thinking that people around me wanted to kill me. An Asian lady was walking towards me from Hungry Jack's with a handbag over her shoulder and her hand in her handbag. As she was walking towards me, she was looking really suspicious to me, looking to her left and right. It felt like she was going to shoot me.

I started to freak out, yelling, "She's got a gun, she's got a gun."

I was petrified.

At the time, I was selling brand new .22 calibre pistols in the box with silencers fitted to them, that's what I thought she had.

Why would she want to shoot me? Well, because I knew too much and now was the perfect time. I mean, everybody already thought I was crazy. My wife, my brothers and sisters, my friends. They all said I'd lost it but to me, this was all real. I got scared and I didn't know how to get out of what I was doing or who I could talk to, someone to take me seriously.

Cars started to rev their motors as they drove past me. I thought that they were also trying to kill me. I started running down the road, cutting in front of cars, yelling and screaming.

There was a car rental yard on the corner. I jumped on the bonnets of the cars, trying to bring as much attention to myself as I could.

I was yelling things like, "Help! Police! Somebody's been shot!" and "She's got a gun, she's trying to shoot me," and "He just shot her!"

The people in McDonald's, across from Hungry Jacks, must have thought I'd lost it as I was banging on the windows while I was yelling.

The more people who knew I was there, the more chance I would have of surviving the night. I thought I was going to die and all I could think of was wanting to spend time with my wife and kids before I did.

It took ages before the first cop car rocked up. It was a traffic car, we called them Mickey Mouse cars back in the day because they were sedans with the lights on the roof.

Anyway, out hopped two female officers.

I looked straight away at the car's registration plate, thinking it looked dodgy as the vehicle was on an angle and the plate had no surrounds on it.

I ran away, yelling: "They're not coppers, they're not coppers!"

I was thinking that they worked for the people I got the gear from.

Not only did the number plate look dodgy, but why weren't there any other police cars around? I mean, I had just spent the last hour jumping up and down on cars, yelling and screaming.

I was hysterical.

The Mickey Mouse car disappeared and a paddy wagon pulled up, the officers trying to coax me into the car, but I bolted.

I thought that one cop was trying to put me in the back of the paddy wagon and take me somewhere to shoot me. I mean, why not? It's the perfect way, put me in the back and take me out to the Gnangara Road bush and put a hole in my head. Everyone thinks I've lost it on the drugs, what better way than this?

I was terrified.

I ran flat out trying to get away, down the middle of Canning Highway, again yelling that these were not police officers and they were trying to kill me. The cops grabbed me, trying to put handcuffs on me.

I was laying in the middle of a two-lane highway on top of the median strip, my head pushed down hard into the bitumen with a knee in the back of my head on the road and my body on the verge. I swear they were trying to break my neck, or at least I thought they were. While the copper's knee was in the back of my head, his hand was on my jaw with the other hand on the back of my head. I seriously thought I was going to die.

There were about five officers and they still couldn't get the handcuffs on me. They sprayed my face with a large amount of mace, but it had no effect on me.

I was screaming, "Please don't kill me, I'll do it myself, I'll give myself a hot shot. Please let me see my children one last time."

I was fighting for my life as I didn't really want to die. They used two sets of handcuffs to partially restrain me.

When they tried to push me into the back of the paddy wagon, I was fighting it with everything I had. I had a foot on either side of the paddy wagon doors, screaming at the top of my lungs, exhausted.

I remember feeling like I was about to pass out when all I could think of was to cry out to God for help. I started saying the Lord's Prayer out loud, I mean I hadn't read a bible or prayed in 20 years at that time.

"Our Father who is in Heaven, hallowed be thy name, thy kingdom come, thy will be done, on earth as it is in Heaven," then I passed out.

I awoke the next day in Royal Perth Hospital, tubes down my throat, in my arms and even one in my penis. Amanda was beside me. I was so dazed and confused and I didn't know what the heck was happening. I needed to go somewhere and think. I ripped all the tubes out including the one in my penis.

Man, did that hurt!

I had no idea the blooming thing had a balloon on the end of it. I still recall the pain now twenty years later as I write this.

I said to Amanda, "I can't go home, we need to go somewhere and think, something weird is going down."

The staff tried to stop me from leaving but I told them to bugger off, that they couldn't keep me there and I left the hospital.

I drove around with Amanda for a while looking for a motel to book into so I could rest and think, I was so confused. I didn't understand what was happening or why, I was scared and broken, I was at the end of myself, I wanted out but didn't know how to. I had decided I would gladly give that life up for my wife and three kids: Tosha-Lena, young Peter and Rhyan. What makes you want to change from being the person you are after 18 years?

I booked into a room at the Wanneroo Tavern. When I got in the room, I covered all the windows with towels as well as the mirrors, it was a paranoid thing I used to do in case THEY had cameras behind the glass. I laid down and I slept.

Three o'clock in the morning, I woke up. I had had a dream, probably the most realistic dream that I had ever experienced in my life and it wasn't just any dream. I believe the dream that I had was from God.

God had told me, "Peter, Peter, you are going to travel the world with a group of Christian people and you are going to tell them how I changed your life."

I woke up, sat bolt upright in bed, crying my eyes out with His presence all over me, the same presence I remember feeling when I was in the prison cell when I was in Riverbank as a child.

To describe His presence is impossible with words, but I will try. Love, acceptance, forgiveness, grace, truth, mercy, all in its purest form. An overwhelming sense that I belonged as a part of who He is, there are no words I can find that can or would describe who He is or what I felt, ten trillion times better than any drug on the planet and more.

It was a Sunday morning and we had the two boys with us in the motel. I told Amanda about the dream and told her that I had a really strong feeling that I was supposed to go to church.

"Church?" she said sceptically.

"Yep, church."

At that point in time, I had never been in a church in all my life. Like I said before, I've broken into a couple but never attended a service.

Now I don't want to blow wind up your back end and I also don't want to push religion down your throat and I am trying to tell my story the way it is without all the religious mumbo jumbo, so please forgive me if some of what I'm about to say offends you or makes you angry. I reckon religion has a lot to answer for, I know many people who have been hurt by people who call themselves Christians and I really don't want to come across as one of those to you.

I told the missus that we were going to church. Pete was six, Rhyan had just turned two. We got all churchified and I mean churchified.

I honestly thought I had to dress up, so I went and got myself all dressed up, the missus got dressed up and so did the kids. Trust me, if you came from where I came from and did what I used to do, you don't get dressed up, I had me a three-piece suit that I went and bought from the shops and felt like a real knob. The family jumped in the car and started looking for a church.

Honestly, we drove around most of the day trying to find THE church, but with each one that I saw, I had a really strong feeling in my heart that it was not the right one. I must have checked out at least sixteen churches until about 3 pm on the Sunday, I pulled into the car park of the New Life Church in Morley.

I read the sign; service starts at 5 pm. I knew in my heart that it was the right one. So we went up the road for a feed and came back at 5 pm. When we came back, there were cars all over the joint, we got out of the car and started to walk toward the building when I started to shake and began to cry for no reason at all. These people took our kids from us and told us they would take them to kids' church. Amanda and I walked into the church and people were singing while I was just crying and shaking uncontrollably.

The preacher started to preach his message and when he said, "How dare these uncircumcised Philistines defy the armies of the living God," all I could do was cry.

At the end of the preacher's message, asking if there was anyone there wanting to change their life, if anyone had had enough of who they were and were serious, not half-hearted, about wanting to change.

My heart was pounding as I got to my feet and I was called to the front. Amanda also stood up and came to the front, not because she particularly felt the need to, but because she didn't want to be left in the seat on her own.

Me, I was a blubbering mess as the preacher led me in a prayer where I asked God to forgive me for all that I had done, and I prayed, asking Him to come and live in me and help me to change from the inside out. My God, there He was again. I felt Him, He was with me and now, well now, I could feel Him in me. All I could do was cry.

As I fell to my knees, I heard Him say, "Peter, I want you to give up everything you own and follow me."

From that day on, my life began to change.

For me, the hardest thing I ever did with my life was to become a Christian. Seriously, everything that was acceptable to me wasn't acceptable to Him. I mean, if I wanted something, I just took it, I used to use every drug there was to get high: meth, trips, pot, ecstasy, you name it, I took it. Everything that I owned was bought with drug money, everyone I felt comfortable around was doing things that I was not allowed to do and more.

For the rest of this book, I want to share with you the struggles that I went through to change my life, the things I had to confess, the people I approached to ask for their forgiveness and the things that I had to change, not just IN me but ABOUT me, who I was as a person, how I spoke, how I responded to people when they spoke to me and how I responded when I was mistreated. I also had to learn to start telling the truth, as over the years, I had told myself so many lies that I believed them and those lies became my truths.

Anyway, what happened from there is that we left the church and went back to the motel, but I knew I couldn't go back home. Monday morning, I was as crook as a dog coming down from the meth and all the other stuff in my system, still very scattered in the brain and all over the shop mentally.

So we spent the day driving around trying to find a place and we ended up right out the back end of nowhere; Gingin to be exact, about an hours' drive north of Midland where we booked into a caravan park and I just slept and slept.

At the time, Amanda and I were on bail for a pound of pot, a couple of handguns, intent to sell and supply and a whole heap of other stuff. I had a dodgy lawyer at the time and felt strongly that I was supposed to swap him for a legit one, which I ended up doing.

You're gonna hear me say many times I get to do this or I feel like God was telling me this so I might just explain it to ya. When I got nuked (I call becoming a Christian getting nuked), I felt God come into me, and I felt Him alive. When He comes into you, He starts to change you and to give you the strength you never used to have. Anyway, He was in me and His voice was getting louder.

How I explain hearing his voice is, picture going to Coles Supermarket and buying a whole heap of shopping. You load your trolley up and push it out of the store, you unload the trolley into the car and push the trolley to the side and go to jump in the car.

You hear this voice saying, "Take the trolley back," then you hear another voice sayin', "Na, stuff 'em, they pay people to do that."
Those two voices, one Right and one Wrong. One is part of the solution and the other is part of the problem. Me, I always followed the problem voice, the one that made me feel good for the here and now, the one that always gave me the easy way out.

God was starting to teach me how to hear Him and not only hear Him, but he gave me the strength to obey what it was He was asking from me.

I was on the way into court and I felt in my heart that I had to swap lawyers, I had to get me an honest one. So I told my new lawyer the truth about my charges, confessed it all straight up. I was remanded for four weeks so my lawyer could get prepared and over that short time, I was led to clean up my life.

I remember the first two weeks at the caravan park, all I did was sleep and eat, sleep and eat. I woke up one morning, and God actually prompted me to write my story down

He said, "Peter, sit down and write out your life."

I did and that's this book.

I wrote that many years ago and forgot that I had it until recently when I was going through some old files and found it. Back then, I would sleep, wake up, eat, sit by the computer and start to write, then go to bed again when I was tired. When I awoke, I did the same thing again, God told me to write what I've written above, I remember the day I got up to the point where I was laying in the hospital bed with all these tubes hanging out of me.

I heard Him say, "Right, now shut it up and stop writing, we have written the first half now let's write the second."

Over the years between then and now, He has been writing the second part and now I'm about to put it all into words.

Over the next couple of weeks leading up to court, I started to give everything I owned away, it was all bought with drug money or was stolen. I went around and paid all the bills I had as well as the one that I had to the man I was getting my gear from. I gave away all of my cars and jet ski, I got a trailer and loaded all my power tools into it and donated it all to a church. I honestly gave nearly everything I owned away, by the time it was my court date, I'd caught up on my sleep, all the stuff was given away, I had a legit lawyer and I had cut off all ties with my past. I was still smoking pot and I had an ounce or two, well, maybe five or six aside. I went to court thinking that it was going to be a remand, but I ended up getting four months prison, four months wasn't much, a drunk's lagging (prison term) basically, I was sent to Casuarina Prison.

I must admit that it was the best prison term that I had ever done, I was put in the best part of the prison with all the fellas doing life so it was nice and quiet, no misbehaving or standover stuff. I got the best job in the place and was put on the quad bikes delivering all the food to the blocks, I was even given top pay.

All within the first week.

Mate, that's never happened in my life, I had complete and total favour, God was letting me know that I wasn't alone.

It's a pretty surreal feeling knowing He is real and that He's there, kinda creepy, but at the time so comforting. I seriously can't express to you how much I love Him for what He has done, not just for me, but through me and also through my children and those who I love. I spent four weeks in Casuarina Prison where I was going to chapel and reading the Bible. To tell you the truth, I needed to go to prison, this stint helped me to focus, to draw closer to Him and to learn how to hear His voice and seek His face. It also helped me to put a bit of discipline in place within my life.

You might remember earlier in this book, I talked about getting nuked after going back to my cell and praying.

"God, if you're real, I want to know you."

His presence came into my cell.

Well, back then, He gave me a scripture verse and it was, *John 8:32* and it said, "You will know the Truth and the Truth will set you free." I looked that scripture up again fifteen years later and just before *John 8:32*, in Verse 31, "If you abide in me and my Word, then you will know the Truth and the Truth will set you free."

Man, did I cry, it was like God had spoken to me loud and clear, and He said, "Peter, just like your body needs food, your spirit needs food and my word is the food that you need."

I remembered back in 1987 when I was released from Riverbank, I used to get prompted to read my Bible, read my Bible, but I just pushed those thoughts aside until they shut up, I didn't realise that it was God trying to instruct me, I thought it was just me.

Slowly, my heart started to harden against the things of God to the point the last thing I wanted to do was to read the Bible and that's how I fell away from Him last time.

God was telling me this time, "Peter, if you don't want to fall away from me again, YOU MUST read your Bible daily, as just like your body needs food, so does your spirit, my words are life to you."

I really hate religion, seriously. I often say that and you will hear me say it often: If the Church of God was like Hungry Jack's, then it would be chockers; full, that is. At least when you go to Hungry Jack's, you know what you are getting, but with churches, you might not have a clue, there are so many of them, so how do you know which one is the right one?

Often, people have been hurt by one particular mob and they put 'church' in the 'don't go near' box because of their experience, or many people have been hurt by people who profess to have faith but don't live what they believe, where their actions don't line up with their words. As Christians, I reckon the best way to communicate what we believe is through the way we live our life, our actions should speak louder than our words. People should see our faith in us, not just in the words we speak, we have no right jamming it down people's throats. If we want to tell people about what we believe, then we need to live it, not just say it.

After four weeks at Casuarina, I was sent to Karnet Prison Farm. As far as prison farms in Perth, this one's the best. Again, I was favoured, I was in the cushiest block with the least trouble, scored the best job up in the abattoirs, killing the cows, making top dollar too.

It was while I was in prison that I started to get prompted to go to Bible College, yeh, I know Bible College.

Me, who had been to sixteen different schools and only made Grade Six, who can't even read running writing. Every time I listened to the radio, all I heard were ads for it, picked up the paper and there it was again, I talked with people and they just kept mentioning it. I asked a prison officer for a Yellow Pages and sent a letter to all the Bible Colleges in Perth.

Amanda was left to clean up our old house and look after the kids. Luckily, she ended up getting a farm rental in Gingin, a two-bedroom joint. She was driving up to see me every weekend, bloody long drive, it was about an hour and a half each way. In a prison farm, you have a lot more freedom than in a maximum-security prison, also it was a lot easier to get stuff in. On one of her visits, I asked Amanda to bring me some pot next time and she did.

When I got nuked and became a Christian, I didn't change overnight, it's taken a long, long time and I'm still changing. You try getting one of those huge container ships and turning it around in one spot, it's impossible. Over ten or fifteen kilometres, a ship can do a complete turn as long as its path is clear.

Well, with me, it was taking me a bloody long time.

I knew in my heart I was not going to let her bring some gear in but I ignored the prompting. I thought to myself that it would be alright, that I wasn't hurting anyone.

I remember that night, I was sitting out underneath the stars after a couple of cones (pot), stoned off my face and really loving life when all of a sudden, I felt this massive hand come down from heaven, point at me and yell, "STOP SMOKING POT."

"Woohhh," I said.

First thing I did was get all the choof I had and throw it away; I know it was God telling me not to smoke any more. I had so much to learn as a Christian, it wasn't funny.

Speaking of funny, well, I find it funny, some of you may not, but it's a good testimony about how I stopped masturbating. As a bloke who used to masturbate a bit, especially away from my wife and in jail, I had a high sex drive and still do. I remember waking up one morning with a full-on boner and did what most blokes would do, relieve the pressure if you know what I mean, but the problem was it was right on muster time, so I did what I did and did it fast. The call came for us to come out of our cells and stand by the door for inspection. In prison, you have tracksuit pants on and I tell you, everything shows.

As I stood by the door, it was like the whole prison was looking directly at me and it was like they all knew what I had just done, I had never felt so embarrassed in all my life. From that day on, I have never taken my Jack Russell for a walk again (masturbated).

Now I honestly don't believe they were looking at me but God had told me: "Peter, it's not okay to do that," and I know it was Him speaking to me because of the conviction I felt in my heart.

There were so many things about me that needed to change and the job ahead was a big one. While in prison, I continued every day to read my Bible and learn about God. Out of all the letters I sent out to various Bible Colleges, only one got back to me. On 98five Sonshine FM, I used to hear about this particular Bible College at Riverview Church, a fairly big church located just out of Perth City.

We tossed a few letters back and forth and I arranged for an appointment after my release date. Six weeks later, I got out and moved in with my wife at the Gingin farmhouse. I know this may sound funny but I used to hear God speak to me through music. I was on the farm doing some work and thought to myself that I might have a few cones as I still had a few ounces of pot leftover from before I went to prison, so I did. I got stoned off my brain and jumped on the ride-on lawnmower with the radio blaring and I was actually feeling really good when as clear as day, I heard God speak to me. This overwhelming conviction came upon me and I turned the mower off, ran inside and asked the missus where all the pot was, so I took it from her and scattered it out in the paddock.

Amanda asked me what was going on and I just said that God had spoken to me and she said, "What did He say?"

It wasn't until she asked that question that the full impact of what had happened and I broke down on the floor and I wept.

God had spoken to me very loud and clear, He said to me, "Peter, Peter, I love you, STOP SMOKING POT."

Now I would like to say to you that was the last time I smoked pot, but it wasn't.

You're going to read a great deal about all my faults and flaws in this book, you're going to read about the mistakes that I made, the things that I put my hand to. You're going to read how I slept with prostitutes after ten years of being a Christian man. The hardest thing I have ever done with my life was to become a Christian, everything that I enjoy that used to give me pleasure, one by one, I had to lay them all down and it was not easy, I can say that for sure. And with everything that I had to lay down, there was a lesson that I had to learn in the process. When you become a Christian, you don't wake up the next day and be completely new; nooooooo, the battle begins.

I went to my Bible College interview and was accepted so the next thing was to decide where we were going to live. My wife's parents owned a unit just up the road from the Bible College and it just so happened that the unit had become available. They offered to rent it to us for $80 per week; mate, that was cheap. Unless it happened to you, then you would not believe it but everything was lining up and I mean everything, the timing how it all unfolded was like clockwork. I have never held a driver's licence and always used to drive under suspension or I had what they call an extraordinary driver's licence that allowed me to drive during certain hours but at that time, I was not allowed to drive. We moved into the unit and basically, we owned nothing at all. Most of the furniture we had we got from the side of the road, we only had a mattress on the floor and most places we went to, we walked because either the car was broken down or we couldn't put fuel in it because we had no money.

I went on Austudy, Amanda was on a parenting pension and I was to start Bible College a week later, but first I had to go on a Bible College two-day camp where I was to get to know those people I was about to study with. Man, was I a fish out of water! The camp was held from Friday night to Sunday afternoon. I have never felt so out of place and uncomfortable in all my life, all these people were so far from who I was, they were all off-the-charts kind, happy and doing stuff that there was no way I was going to do. They were playing getting-to-know-you games like dodgeball and other stuff, I refused to take part as I was feeling really awkward.

That night after dinner, I hit the sack and I woke up at 3 am after a dream. This was not just any dream. I had dreamed that Satan was telling me that I was a weed in God's garden, that I did not belong among these people, that I would be better off dead and I had an overwhelming, almost overpowering feeling to go and kill myself. I was bawling my eyes out, I didn't want to die, I wanted to live, but yet the desire to kill myself was extremely strong.

I got out of bed and walked out of my room across the lawn when one of the leaders saw me, ran up to me and asked me what was wrong and if I was okay. I couldn't control myself and just kept crying. He grabbed an elderly lady nearby and they both took me into a room where they prayed for me.

They asked God if He would reveal to me what was wrong, I got a picture of my mum. I really hated my mum and other people for what they did to me, but my mum especially. I felt unforgiveness towards her for putting me through what she did and for her choosing men and alcohol over me. I blamed her for what I went through in life and was angry at her for stealing my childhood and I shared this with those who prayed for me.

They both prayed again and asked God to show me what He wanted me to do; when they did, I wailed again, crying out loud. God told me to forgive my mum, but I cried out that I couldn't, and He told me He would help me if I did. I prayed that day out loud to those who prayed with me, I prayed and asked God to forgive me for hating my mother and I also chose to forgive her for what she had done to me. When I prayed that prayer, I'm telling you, something really big, heavy and dark lifted off me, it was like a weight that I had been carrying for years lifted off my life.

After about five minutes of me crying, they prayed for me again and asked God what else He wanted to show me, then a picture of the man who molested me as a child came into my mind and again, all I could do was weep. God said I had to forgive that man from my heart for what he did to me and that I had to release him into the hands of God.

I prayed, I forgave and boy, did I weep.

By the time the prayer session had finished, I was exhausted but I felt clean, I felt alive and I felt free. I remember this time as if it was just yesterday.

Who would have imagined the effect that unforgiveness could have on your life?

I came back from that camp a changed man, strengthened and empowered for the next season of my life, Bible College.

**DRIVEN BY PAIN
CHANGED BY GRACE**

Part 2 Journal 1

THE INITIAL CHALLENGES OF CHANGING

The following sections of the book are made up of snippets from my two personal journals I kept from January 2002 starting in Casuarina Prison until early July 2010. These experiences have positively altered the way that I live my life to this day. I am not saying that any of the things that happened to me will happen to you, even if you make the necessary changes to your lifestyle, particularly when facing struggles with addiction. I wish any addict could simply improve their life by saying they are committing to God, but it isn't always that simple. There will be lots of hard work ahead on a long and difficult road. We all take different paths and my new life was made possible by my perseverance to changing myself inside, something that needs to happen before any addiction is conquered.

I consider that these memories are true accounts of the events as I witnessed or felt them. I tried to write these recollections down as accurately as I could afterwards. Some of these recollections overlap events I have already mentioned in Part 1 of this book, so I am sorry if they are repeated.

8 January 2002

Well, this is going to be the start of my journal. I'm going to write in it every day. Never in my life have I woken up at 4 am on a regular basis without an alarm clock.

God is changing my life and it feels great. At 4 am on Channel 10 was a show, *Enjoying Everyday Life,* based on the book *Life In The Word* by Joyce Meyer.

God wakes me up. It started last week. As soon as I would wake up, I would go have a shower, then sit down to watch the show but I would miss the first half. Now, out of the blue, He wakes me up at 3.30 am, giving me time for a shower.

I know it would be hard to face the day without this show. For two hours, it's good Bible Study time.

My stars are out tonight, there seems to be a lot more and they are sitting a lot lower than normal. It's good to see them, they reassure me that I'm not going crazy.

The last few nights, I have been having the same dreams I had years ago. They're pretty bad ones, last night's one was a bit frightening.

I know God is changing me day by day and I wake up knowing something else has changed.

I still get headaches quite often and I pray to God for answers.

If you had seen what I have seen, you'd think you're nuts too.

I wonder what God has got planned for me.

9 January 2002

The dream was that I would meet a professor in a wheelchair who has no use of his limbs and talks with the use of a headset by touching a keyboard by using his chin. There is more to this dream but I feel I cannot talk about it because, in my dream, I was told not to...

10 January 2002

Last night, I had a dream where I was flying over the prison and the Holy Spirit was in me. The prisoners were outside looking up but not at me. As I flew over them, I could pass on the feeling that the Holy Spirit gave me to the others.

Today, God has changed my thoughts. You know, how your brain can think bad thoughts, particularly about women. One of the Christian fellowship prisoners says that he feels that I will become an Evangelist. He imagined me talking to thousands of people at a time, winning souls for God in the name of our Lord Jesus Christ (God's Warrior).

11 January 2002

I went to a Catholic church service today. I go to worship God, but I find the way that Catholic churches preach is too routine. I can't wait for Monday; I know God is going to do something special. I have made up reminder pamphlets for the prisoners I have already talked to.

12 January 2002

Up at 4 am. A good start to the day except for another bad dream. Next time I have a bad dream, I am going to rebuke the Jezebel spirit in the name of Jesus. I made an oath to God today that if He provides a secure financial future for me and my family, whatever I own will always belong to God.

I will serve Him with my mind, body, spirit and soul.

I went for a walk when I gave my oath. I know He heard me because it's broad daylight and I saw a star shine brightly and then disappear. I know He is watching me because it's happened on other occasions.

13 January 2002

Sometimes I think I'm going crazy when I tell people that I can see a star flash at me in broad daylight and what I see at night. They think I'm nuts — so do I. Maybe it's an after-effect of the drugs I was using, but that's six months ago. I know I see what I see. I wish I had someone to talk to who understands and who could help me understand.

It's hard all by myself. I've made up my mind from now on, I will not tell anybody what I am experiencing unless they approach me and know what they're on about without me having to say anything. As if. I feel so alone and frustrated.

I'm not crazy.

14 January 2002

My wife Amanda told me yesterday about one of my mates who just got out of prison. He has only been out one week and already he is doing credit card fraud. What an idiot!

Prison fellowship in one hour. I saw a star flash at me today and it was good to see as I thought God was angry with me because I had told somebody what I saw.

Prison fellowship was great, only 16 people but that's okay, and there was one new face. I feel a strong frustration with the pace of things that are happening. I wish things would pick up but I'm still in prison.

Well, it's pitch black outside, but my stars are there to reassure me. Without them, I would have no hope at all. I pray to God that they stay there.

Patience, Pete, patience.

15 January 2002

I think I have worked it out. In order for me to be a part of what is happening, I must **never** tell anybody about what I see or do, not even my wife. The quicker I put this into practice, the quicker the ball will start rolling. I can't wait.

I know that everything I do is being watched, everything I say is being heard — I will **never** tell another person. Persistence leads to perfection. Nothing is impossible.

Nothing.

Things can only get better.

I know God is trying to show me something but I don't understand.

16 January 2002

Last night, I saw the stars join up in a straight line like a laser and they formed different shapes, it was clear as. I can't help but think that there is somebody else involved, maybe they work for God, who knows?

Like the following people:
- The doctor at the Midland Health Centre
- The old fella at the Gingin Caravan Park
- Fernando and Yolanda
- The people I saw in Army greens
- The security guard at Joondalup Health Centre

It was like each time I met these people, I was being interviewed, but for what, and why me? I ain't nobody special — I'm just me — why do I see stars flash during the day? What is the purpose — is it to reassure me — I know I could have my lights switched out in a second — that scares me a bit.

WHAT IS HAPPENING!!

Why do I wake up in hospital with 13 stitches in my head, a tube in my penis, an IV drip in my arm, wearing a name tag on my wrist saying *name unknown* — D.O.B. 1/7/1969? They knew who I was at the hospital, I had told them there was nobody to talk to except this journal, and it doesn't give me any answers.

17 January 2002

Yesterday, I was going through a bit of an attitude problem. I was worrying about what I was going to do when I got out, like if I was going to Riverview Bible College and how would I get there every day from Gingin without a driver's licence, because I want to give it everything I have. God has told me to relax and leave it up to Him. He knows what He is doing and has a plan for me.

18 January 2002

3.15 am — what a day. I wonder what I will learn today. I keep seeing the stars do weird stuff, they move from one spot to another. I can't wait for it to explain itself.

I reckon my wife knows what's happening.

19 January 2002

I had a disturbing dream about a young lady who was seducing me. I was going to have sex with her but turned her down because God was telling me it was a sin. How strange was that? It feels good that I turned her down. Something has changed inside of me, I don't know what, but I feel weird.

The four months prior to coming to jail and the two months I have been here so far have been the best days of my life. This time in prison has brought me so much closer to God.

Thank you, Jesus.

20 January 2002

Today I was up at 3.30 am and watched the church service. With what I see at night and during the day, something big is happening on Earth. Everything points to the second coming of Christ our Lord.

I can look at the night sky and stars move. I watch shooting stars come to a stop and light up like a Christmas tree. It can be broad daylight and no matter where I look, stars will pierce the day sky and I see their light.

21 January 2002

Another perfect day. Two more days until I go home. Just finished another Monday at prison fellowship. I am getting a strong calling from God, I know it.

I can't explain the taste of vinegar in my mouth all the time. I have a coffee and I taste vinegar — I have a Coke and I taste vinegar very strongly.

Over the past week, the book of Daniel keeps coming up — it refers to the second coming of Christ. I feel God is calling me to do something big. I know that God would not call on me to do anything that I could not handle. I pray that when the time comes, He gives me the strength — wisdom — and courage to do whatever he wants.

I must give up smoking.

22 January 2002

Well, it's the day before I am to be released and I reckon it's Summary Day, a day to look back over the past two months and twenty days.

I want to write not only what I have learned, but what I should put into practice when I am released.

1. Everything in this world belongs to God, we are just caretakers.
2. Try to know God through His Word and follow the example that Jesus left us.
3. Don't be negative, make firm decisions to act and be positive.
4. Always ask God for guidance in regard to the paths I must follow.
5. Live by God's Word and trust Him in all matters. He will make the path clear for me to follow. Stop trying to figure out what's happening — Trust my Lord.
6. Don't be jealous of what other people have.
7. If you are not faithful over little things, how can God put you in charge of bigger things?
8. Always wait for God's direction in the tasks that I undertake.
9. Whenever fear and trepidation grip me, turn to God, He will never leave me.
10. Without God in my life, I can do nothing. God is love.
11. Control my mind. Through prayer and thanksgiving, I can control my thoughts.
12. I can do anything through Christ who lives in me, He is the hope and glory.
13. The mind of the flesh is death.
14. Hold onto my peace in times of trouble. The first thing I should do when trouble comes is to calm down. Refuse to get upset and don't talk about my problems. When I start to feel pressured or sad, I will praise God.
15. Do everything in my power to keep my peace. Don't let events upset me — go with the flow. Peace is God's purpose for His people.
16. I cannot be defeated — nothing is impossible — nothing is too much for me to handle because Christ my Lord lives in me.
17. The joy of the Lord is our strength.
18. It is God's Will to be happy even when I have problems.

19. Listen to my inner self. Keep my opinions to myself — a fool reveals all of his opinions.
20. I need to mind my own business.

23 January 2002

Get out today — I had an amazing dream last night. I dreamt I was going to run a camp for displaced youths and teach them new skills and the way of God. I did my ankle today, I twisted it coming down the stairs at my parole meeting. Sometimes I upset myself so much — it wasn't funny.

I swore at my wife and accused her of being in on what is happening to me. I thought that my phones were tapped and holes were drilled all around my workshop. I still can't explain it.

I smoked some pot today and boy, did I feel bad. It made me sick and I chucked a whitie.

The farm property I have moved to is unreal. I plan to spend the day cleaning up the yard, it needs it. I tell you, my wife is the best ever.

Thank you, Lord.

24 January 2002

I'm going to Riverview Bible College on Tuesday morning for an interview. I'm going to see if I can do full-time study. It's been that long since I went to school. I don't know what I will be studying.

25 January 2002

Well, it's 6 pm and I've decided to stop smoking pot because my conscience is driving me mad and I can't think properly.

26 January 2002

Today and tomorrow, I am going to spend time with my wife and my kids and my God. I'm looking forward to going to church tomorrow. I've been praying to God to show me which church to attend and what he wants me to do with my future. Maybe it's Riverview Church, I'll have to wait and see.

    Not being rude to God — but He's slow.

    I wish there was somebody who would say 'Peter, do this' or 'Peter, don't do this'. All this guesswork is making me nuts.

27 January 2002

God told me today through music that I was to stop smoking pot. Cigarettes are still troubling me — I need to give them up. I'm going to head towards Midland or Morley to check out the churches there.

    It is taking a lot of effort to build up my courage to walk into a church. I need to be a part of God, I want to do everything I can to praise and worship my God.

    I am going on a camping trip with my son on the 8th and 9th of February with the other dads from the church. It should be great. I never did anything like that when I was a kid. My dad was never there. I love my kids and want to give them the sort of life I never had.

    A normal one — whatever that is.

28 January 2002

Well, it's Monday morning and I've got my beautiful daughter and my sister's daughter staying for the next few days. The next church activity is on Saturday, a business networking lunch. It's for people who want to start a business for God in His kingdom. No matter what positions I will have over the rest of my life, I will always remember that everything belongs to God. I am the caretaker only — when you die, you can't take it with you.

29 January 2002

Yesterday was a funny day — one minute I was up and the next minute I was down. My wife's mother rang yesterday and told us that her boarder from her unit in Como was moving out. We asked her if we could stay there and she didn't have a problem with that.

I had an interview this morning at Riverview Bible College where I enrolled for the Bible Study course. My hunger to build a relationship with my God is being fulfilled. I am thankful for His Love — Affection — Forgiveness — Patience — Guidance and for his Word. I stare up at the sky and tears of joy flow from my eyes. I feel his love and it's overwhelming.

30 January 2002

I've spent the whole day looking after four kids. Pretty cool day, it's nice and quiet here in Gingin.

I can't wait to start Bible College. It's going to be hard at first because I am changing my whole life. I'm going to have to learn to hang around 'geeks' — I categorise geeks to be normal people. I have always wanted to be normal.

I can't even remember sitting at a dinner table with any member of my family. I've never been on family holidays. Enough about the past, it doesn't matter anyway. I thank God for my whole past, as it has made me who I am today. Praise God.

31 January 2002

As recently as September 2001, I was selling up to $40,000 a day of drugs (methamphetamine) as well as other drugs, guns and explosives, not to mention stolen goods. In the past six months, my life has been one big rollercoaster ride, up and down. A lot of things have happened that nobody would ever think was real. But I know that everything I have seen is and was real.

We are moving to the unit in Como near the city, 5 kms to Riverview Bible College. We will save money on rent. God has a plan for me and the wheels are turning. When I start College, I am going to give it everything I can. I know I may trip up a few times, but my God is a God of love and he will be there to pick me up.

Recently, I had a dream where I met Professor Stephen Hawking, the famous physicist who is an expert on stars. In my dream, he was going to ask me to start up a secret organisation. I know my dreams will come true.

3 February 2002

This morning me and my son, Peter rode our pushbikes from Como to Riverview Church in Burswood. After church, we rode into Perth for an ice-cream and from there, caught the ferry across the river and rode home. Never in my life, did I spend time with my parents like I spent with my son today. Thanks be to God.

My church is unreal, I feel at home there even though it was only my first day. I felt like yelling and screaming, my God lives in me. I am addicted to the Word of God. I rode there again tonight for the 6 pm service. I intend going to church as much as possible because when I'm there, I feel close to God.

I only smoked about 5 smokes today.

I can't wait to be baptised in the Holy Spirit.

5 February 2002

Last night as I lay in bed listening to Joyce Meyer tapes, I had the light off and the door shut. I could see a spirit hovering above me, so I raised my hands towards heaven and the spirit rested in my hands, the palms of my hands glowing white. Poor Peter had his first day at another new school and he was pretty upset and I don't blame him. Me, I went to about 30 different schools and only made it to Grade 6. The rest of my 'schooling' was in Longmore or Riverbank.

6 February 2002

Last night I went to Riverview Church for Bible Study, or Discovery as they call it. They laid their hands on me for me to receive the Holy Spirit, but I suppose it wasn't God's Will. Sometimes, it gets frustrating trying to please God and it pisses me off not knowing what to do.

God doesn't give you straight answers, it's a bit like a game, you have to look for the signs. That's what I think.

9 February 2002

Today was a good day, I've been having these days when one minute you're up, and next minute you're down. My wife and I took the boys and rode our bikes to the zoo. Tonight, Pete and I rode down to the river and Pete caught two fish. I've always dreamed of spending times like this with my kids.

10 February 2002

God never ceases to amaze me; I have been thinking a lot about what led me into the arms of Christ my Saviour. I also keep thinking there must be a human force there somewhere, I know there is. God with His love is unconditional.

18 February 2002

Over the past few days, I have been through a tough war between the Devil and God. I am very weak and gave into sin. I felt myself slipping away. I smoked cannabis for the past two days and lost control of my thoughts. I felt the Holy Spirit leave me.

I have never been so petrified and alone. God told me I am too ambitious and selfish, and I worry too much. I must live one day at a time.

I am going away to Bible College camp for four days. Every minute of every day, I must think of my God to keep me strong.

Everything happens for a reason. The main thing is what you do with what happens. Just take one day at a time. Every day will make me stronger. There is life in the Word.

I'm starting to understand.

20 February 2002

I've had the best three days of my life. I went away on Riverview's Bible Study camp, attacked spiritually in a dream by Satan who told me I was a weed in the House of God. I was petrified because the dream left me spiritually empty. I spoke to my leader about my dream. I was overwhelmed to finally have somebody to talk to about the events of the past six months. It has been me and God, but I know Satan has been attacking me through the parts of my life that I haven't really repented of or forgiven myself for. My leader and a senior member of our group prayed for me together, we cast Satan back to the pit where he belongs.

21 February 2002

In my dream, God was telling me the future where I would lay my hands on people and the love, peace and joy from the Holy Spirit would go into them. They would break down crying. God has told me this morning not to be afraid of what I see. He says he has an army of love over the land and the sea. Revival.

4 March 2002

This is my second week at Bible College and I'm having a ball.

I gave my journal to somebody to read in the hope that they could help me explain what I am going through. This person has had my journal for the past two weeks but did not read it. I know that this must be God's Will so I won't show another person until he tells me.

10 March 2002

Over the past few weeks, I've been blown away. I feel God's Holy Spirit, it's sensational. The other day, I was given some tapes by the principal of Bible College, Dwayne's Mum, about moving in the Holy Spirit, achieving the Spirit Realm within — wow.

I laid my hands on Amanda spiritually for the first time. I felt the Holy Spirit touch her heart and the feeling was so overwhelming, I had to stop — I couldn't stop bawling. I mean, I wasn't too sure at first, but if you love somebody in your heart, you MUST have faith in God and that is a MUST. It's like my dream coming true.

I dribble...

My dream about Stephen Hawking bothers me — I'm pretty sure it was from God.

I still see all kinds of weird stuff in the sky with the stars and the clouds. I saw the stars join up like one big grid.

I don't know what this is exactly, but it's the best representation of what I think I see. This sounds silly, but this is what my brain tells me that our earth is like, one big hydroponic chamber surrounded by a grid of stars — I see things moving along the grid — during the day, I see sections of it light up. I feel kind of stupid writing this, but it's what I see. I still see spirits. Maybe Professor Hawking has something to do with it — maybe God wants me to tell Him something after all because He does star stuff.

God is awesome.

11 March 2002

Today was a sad day. I rang a member of the prison fellowship who used to come to Karnet called Len. He told me that our friend Noelene from the fellowship had been in a car accident and was in intensive care. I was extremely saddened, so I got Amanda to give me a lift in to see her. I felt I had to pray for her and when I was praying, I couldn't stop crying. A nice lady like her should not be in hospital. God will heal her. I also typed up my testimony and posted it to Len. I have a strong desire to share my testimony with whoever I can.

17 March 2002

Today was great — my mum, grandmother and grandfather came to church for the first time in 20 years. They all enjoyed it immensely.

I think I have a bit of a big mouth and talk too much, it's just that I get excited about what I am going through and can't wait to tell somebody. But, at the same time, I feel that some experiences are best kept to myself.

Today I did my practicum which was at the 'Get Connected' booth, meeting people and telling them how to volunteer at the church. I prayed for someone and I'm not sure if I should have.

I'm all confused, is there something I should be doing or shouldn't be doing? I don't know. I don't want to upset God, learning to walk with God is not easy.

I'm trying to give up smoking again because I can smell the smokes on me and I know I have to give up. I'm using patches, they seem to take away the craving. It's only when someone comes over that I have one. I'm getting there.

I start an evangelism course on Tuesday which will be great.

24 March 2002

Today was cool. My sisters Judy and Cheree and their kids came to church today.

The other day, I sent an email to Cambridge University trying to get hold of Professor Stephen Hawking. Today, I got a reply so I sent him an email about some of the things I see. He probably thinks I'm nuts and I'll never hear from him again.

28 March 2002

Because of the pain in my back, I had to spend the whole day lying down. I spent a lot of the time laying on the trampoline and while I was lying there, I saw a star that was bright as. Instead of flashing, it shone for about 15 minutes then another one lit up next to it and zipped through the sky. This happened at about one in the afternoon. I'm not too sure why God is showing me this.

When He is ready, He will show me.

31 March 2002

I have just come back from church. I can't stand it when I don't feel close to God. When I do feel close to God, I feel joy, happiness and His love. His presence is humbling.

2 April 2002

Tonight when I looked at the sky, it's like there is a mist across the bottom half of my vision like a varnish; you can still see through it and then it moves to cover my whole vision. I'm pretty sure God is showing me something new, I hope so.

4 April 2002

It's one in the morning and I have just woken up from another dream where I was spiritually attacked. I felt that a spirit had just been inside of me that did not belong. It tried to make me think that I did not belong in God's kingdom and that I was a weed. I could actually feel it inside me and I felt an intense fear within me, I felt it in my throat. I went out to the loungeroom and left Amanda in bed. I laid my hands on my throat and I rebuked the spirit in the name of our Lord Jesus Christ and told it to come out of me.

All of a sudden, I felt this thing come out of my mouth and then I saw a massive swirl of what looked like steam that swirled in front of my face and then it took off. Scared the crap out of me. It says in the Bible that when a spirit is cast out of a man that it runs to and fro across the face of the earth looking for a place to rest. When it can't find anywhere, it goes back to the home it was kicked out of and finds it swept, clean and empty, then that person is seven times worse than the first. This is what it felt like for me. What had come out of me when I was saved tried to get back in.

11 April 2002

The other night, Amanda and I went to bed and I woke up many times. I laid my hands on Amanda while she was sleeping. I saw spirits moving over her. When I asked her if she could see anything, she said she couldn't. I could feel the Holy Spirit within me. I knew that **she** couldn't see anything but **I** could because God has given me new eyes, hard to explain.

Amanda knew that I had been seeing something for some time, but she thought I was nuts. To prove to her that I wasn't, I asked her to hold her hand up with her palm flat and relax. Amanda relaxed and I saw the spirit rest on her hand. I told her it was there and asked her what she could feel — pins and needles and a tingling feeling was her response. I was stoked. It's the same feeling I get as well. At least she finally believes me now.

I did it again to Amanda last night to make sure she felt it and she did — awesome, eh?

I see and feel the spirit in many different ways. I'm sitting in the kitchen at 4 am writing this and I see it now. I have rebuked this presence several times in the mighty name of Jesus Christ and it has not gone anywhere, so it must be good. I will not take any chances though. Each time I see it, I will rebuke it just in case Satan or one of his mates is trying to pull a fast one.

In my dream, I was levitating. At certain times, I thought it was the power of God. I had also been chosen to present a very important document of seven pages, each page representing a day of the week. Each page was very special but I can't remember what was written on them. I was supposed to give the pages to people in the government. There was a lot more to this dream because when I awoke, I was excited, but I left it too long to write it down. I'm not saying this dream was from God because I know when I have a God dream.

Yesterday, I laid my hands on Amanda and the Holy Spirit went through me to her. I thank God for what He did.

Last night when I was praying, I made my best mate, Macka, the focus of my prayer. He's like a brother to me. I asked God to bring him back home into His care. You see, if you have a past like we have, he needs healing too.

Macka needs to feel loved and God loves us all, we all belong to God and with God. I thank God for his deliverance and after I had finished my prayers, the phone rang within a minute.

Yep, it was Macka. God had got him to ring. He had not rung me in a long time, so thank you, God!

I'm meeting Macka today and we're going to spend the day together. God is amazing.

14 April 2002

Today was another awesome day, it seems every day, I can feel God's presence within me. He is more than a father to me. I have written down what God has done for me and how He has changed me.

He has stopped me:
- Using drugs, smoking and drinking
- Swearing, a symptom of my anger, depression and hyperness

He has:
- Taught me to be a good husband
- Looked after my finances
- Healed all my past
- Filled my soul with love
- Given me Bible College
- Taken away **ALL** my pain
- Made me feel comfortable around normal people
- Taught me the importance of spending quality time with my kids

Every day, He is teaching me about His character.

HE HAS AND HE IS.

Last week, I asked him for a push-bike so I could get around. On Friday, we received a refund cheque for $50, but we didn't know what for. When I was on my way back from church, I saw a racer for $50 at the bike shop. I don't care what anybody says because I know it was from God, He is looking after me in every way possible.

Tonight when I was down at the park, I saw clouds in the sky all around me. I saw millions, yes millions, of stars flying through the sky. Imagine laying on your back and looking up. Picture clouds making a ring around the stars zipping past at different speeds. This is not the first time I have seen this, and I know it won't be the last.

If I told anybody about this, they would say I have lost the plot. Some people already do.

Sad! Very, very sad.

What have I sacrificed for God to deserve all this love He has shown me, what have I done to deserve all these blessings? I can think of nothing that would make me a worthy recipient of all this goodness. I have given up nothing of value, but God continues to love me.

19 April 2002

It's been a weird couple of days. Up until the 17th of the month, I could feel God's presence all day and night. I was filled with joy and happiness. Over the past few days, I haven't felt close to Him at all.

This feeling comes and goes and I was wondering today if I had done something wrong.

I typed up my résumé tonight because I need a couple of days' work to catch up on the bills, the car is playing up and we keep on getting a lot of dirty mail which we don't bother opening. It makes me feel bad.

I had to re-sit my New Testament exam today because I failed my first one on Wednesday. It was the first exam I had ever taken and that's why I failed. I was the first one to leave out of the whole class.

Here are two diagrams showing the difference between Religion and Christianity, highlighting the importance of Christ dying for our sins and Man's separation from God.

24 April 2002

I am seeing into the spirit realm heaps now, I know there is a lot more yet to see. Every day, no matter where I am, I can see spirits in the room at night-time. What will I be building 'kingdom-wise' for God? I don't know. If it is something using my hands or energy, I can do it, but if it's words, that will be God.

These prayers God has answered and things He made happen:
- Touched Amanda and Macka spiritually
- Money for a push-bike and the bike itself
- House/College/Life
- Healed Rhyan when he was sick
- Peter and Rhyan
- Answered all my prayers so far

I often think about the dreams I had about Stephen Hawking, it will come true.

2 May 2002

Amanda has gone home to the farm for a couple of days and I'm by myself. I just came back from the bottle shop.

Six months ago, I smoked a joint and got in big trouble with God and I haven't touched the stuff since.

7 May 2002

Today was my second day back at College for Term 2. God has used me to touch others spiritually twice today. The first person I interacted with during Spiritual Formation was Jody when we broke into pairs to pray. I was so happy that he felt the Holy Spirit, I could have yelled.

The second time was during Theology. I felt the Holy Spirit within me and I started to cry. A name came to me: Kim, another student. Something told me I had to see if he was alright.

I had a really strong urge to check if he was okay. Before I left my seat, I asked another student, Maria, what I should do.

She told me to speak to Kim.

He said nothing was wrong when I asked him. But I could see something wasn't quite right but I went back to my studies. The Holy Spirit told me to pray for him so I did. I could feel Kim's pain.

I think it must have had something to do with his wife because when we had a break, he went home.

What blows me away was being privileged enough for God to use me to give His Word to another. I can't wait until it becomes a regular occurrence.

Thank you, God!

8 May 2002

Today at Pete's footy practice, I joined in to help train the kids and as I looked at my boy training, I felt like crying. If it wasn't for God, I would never have had the privilege to spend time with my boy in such a way. I would have been in jail, I'm sure of it.

My life belongs to God, I pray He uses me to the full.

19 May 2002

My birthday today, the big 32, getting old.

I have always told Amanda something big is going down, but who knows? With what is going on in the world at the moment, I don't understand how God can stand by and let people do what they are doing.

I feel useless just sitting here day by day. I sent emails off to Cambridge University and Stephen Hawking yesterday about what I see. I think I might have upset God by doing that, the last thing I want to do. By me telling people what I see, am I holding back more that God wants to show me?

I wish I was more mature: it's coming.

23 May 2002

Today at Bible College, we had a prophet come and people were screaming and yelling and dropping like you wouldn't believe. I had fasted from food for 24 hours hoping God would tell me what I see. What do I do with what I see, and is it from God? I didn't get an answer, but it was good to see God touch so many people.

How can anybody not love God? He is everything that is good and He is love.

Amanda received the gift of tongues and she is getting baptised on Sunday. How God has blessed this family is very special.

I owe God my life. He has saved me from a lot of pain.

30 May 2002

All I do is study two days a week and then wait for the next week to come. Yep! I'm growing fat and lazy. I cling to my dreams and know that every day is a step closer.

4 June 2002

Today I learned an important lesson. Over the past six months with everything going on in my life, I have been wallowing in self-pity. I thought God wanted to use me here and now. I haven't wanted to do anything but serve God and I still don't.

I am in a lifetime walk with God.

It just blows me away how loving, patient and forgiving He is. I have been acting like a two-year-old child, wanting everything to happen **NOW**. But I realise I must stop, grow and wait for God. I must serve God and wait on HIS timing. He will know when.

Sometimes to understand what I have written, you have to be me.

12 June 2002

Amanda told me about someone who says he has been going through what I have been going through. She met him today at Riverview's Discovery. I can't wait to speak to this guy face-to-face. Now I have met Dion, I feel disappointed that I have to wait to see him again. I've started work at Riverview one day a week. It will help me cover my school costs.

13 June 2002

I can't stop thinking about my big mouth. I mean, I have seen some weird stuff and I feel God would have shown me a lot more if I had kept it to myself. If I stay quiet, He might show me more.

16 June 2002

Dion told me he sees the End Time, the Coming of Angels. I know that something big is going down.

23 June 2002

Tonight, I took the dog for a walk down at the park. There were a lot of clouds, but I still saw stars flash in the sky.

27 June 2002

One week to go before mid-year exams. I think I should go pretty good this time. On Tuesday, we had prayer group and I prayed over a couple of people and God touched them, that was a blessing to me.

I went and had tea over at my brother Gavin's place last night. I planted a seed, now it's up to God to water it at His Will.

4 July 2002

I have finished the second term of my first year at Riverview Bible College.

7 July 2002

I think often about the dreams I have had, especially the one where I meet Professor Stephen Hawking. That dream was so real, I felt the power of the Holy Spirit in me big time.

We are on three weeks' study break. I have started to study the Old Testament books to get ahead on next terms' study. People comment on how my life has changed and I just can't thank the Lord Jesus and my God enough.

9 July 2002

Today I went to a newsagency to buy a ream of A4 paper and it had $14.65 marked on it. I didn't have much money, but I grabbed the ream and went to the till to pay. Without me saying anything, the sales assistant dropped the price to $10 — nearly $5 off — and that does not normally happen to me. My brothers were with me and I told them it was God looking after me. Another day, I went to photocopy some pamphlets at church and it cost $10. At the time, I didn't have any money on me but the receptionist said I could pay it the next day. Five minutes later, a member of the church, Neil came up to me out of the blue.

"Here is $10, don't complain, just take it."

I was stoked that God had paid for my photocopying. On another occasion, I was on the Midland to Perth train and I only had a $50 note in my wallet which I didn't want to break buying a ticket. The ticket inspectors came and they gave me a fine of $50. I didn't complain, just took the fine. When I got off the train in the city, the inspector came up to me and asked me for the fine back and told me not to worry about it.

God is awesome.

10 July 2002

Today is my sister Cheree's birthday. I'm sitting here at the computer with the door shut and 98five Sonshine FM on, just thinking about what's happened over the last eight months plus. I think about all the events that have unfolded — reality is setting in.

My life is just starting.

11 July 2002

Tonight, I saw every star in heaven move.

12 July 2002

I was thinking about when I moved into the Como unit, how I had a cone of pot and God told me off big time. He stripped me spiritually and I curled up in a corner. I was petrified, all I could do was cry, I was so scared and confused. It gives me reassurance that one, it was God and two, He has a plan for me.

15 July 2002

Yesterday was a good day, my little brother Graham came to church of his own free will to the 11 am service where Penny Webb was speaking. After the service, Graham was shaking and he told me he was close to tears.

I thank the Lord my God for the work He is doing in my family's lives.

8 August 2002

Today I had a visit from the Organised Crime Department. They asked me questions about guns and other things and I gave them some information. What makes me write this in here was a dream where I was climbing through a window. A shot rang out, I'd been hit. That was it — lights out. This dream was about six months ago, but now, I'm not too sure if it was God telling me how I was going to die or not. This also could be part of my dream to do with Professor Stephen Hawking.

24 August 2002

I'm a bit depressed at the moment; one minute I could be going so well and the next, I feel so guilty. Over the past two weeks, I have not had more than six or seven smokes, today I only had a puff. Apart from the occasional beer and my bad temper raising its ugly head now and again, everything is going so good.

I'm doing well in my studies, but sometimes I don't understand the questions.

The pamphlets I have been sending out over the last six weeks have been generating a lot of work. I know God has a hand in it somewhere.

Sometimes I feel that I let God down, like today when I had five cans of beer, and boy, do I feel guilty. You would think that the least I could do in appreciation is that I could stop smoking and drinking full stop.

29 August 2002

I have given up smoking but I still have one drag a day, but it's hard to just forget it.

I have tied a reminder string on my wrist to:
- Think before I say things
- Act more mature
- Be more positive
- Apply wisdom to my life

If I want to be a leader, I must be more positive and ask God for help. He has helped me so much so far, I owe Him big time.

3 September 2002

Today at Bible College, we had a speaker called Phil Baker, the Head Pastor of the Riverview Church. Phil talked about hearing from God, how opportunities will arise in our lives that will lead us in God's direction, but only if we stop and look at the signs.

This brought to mind two experiences that I have had from God:
- I took a book out from the Baptist Theological Library on Spiritual Warfare
- I was outside Riverview Church and someone told me about another person being spiritually attacked

On both those occasions, I felt the presence of God in a very big way. From what Phil said today, I can take these two experiences as signs from God. If only people could feel what I feel!

8 September 2002

Today was awesome — I worked at the church doing voluntary work for half of the day. God asked me to pray for a young bloke named Andrew Matthews. Andrew agreed for me to pray for him, so I did and God touched him. Amazing. The second episode with God was this afternoon when I was asked to do a quote for an Asian couple who had prayed for someone to do their gardens and we each shared our testimonies of how Christ had changed our lives. It was one huge blessed day.

13 September 2002

Why me? I am not worthy! The grace of Jesus is overwhelming and I never fully comprehend it. I go to court on Monday for fresh charges for crimes dating back two years. I am hoping I don't get any more time added to my parole. By the 25th of January, if I don't get any more time added, I won't have anything to do with government departments, for now anyway!

On the 23rd of September, I will celebrate my first birthday: one year to the day since I gave my life to Christ.

What a year ... if only people turned to Christ, they would feel his awesome love.

16 September 2002

I went to court today, hopefully for the last time. I received 100 hours of community service and another six-month, 150-hour order.

22 September 2002

Today, the things I need to ask God to work on are:
1. My temper
2. How to be a father
3. My willpower
4. My study ability
5. The needs of others

Before I went to church this morning, I asked God to open Graham's heart. My brother came to church and gave his life to Jesus — how awesome is God, hey!

6 October 2002

One more week and we're into the last term of my first year at Bible College. It goes to show you that nothing is impossible for God.

My parole finishes in late January next year, only 3 months left. With any luck, I will have finished my community service and paid my fines by then. Then I will be able to go for my extraordinary driver's licence.

7 October 2002

All of a sudden, a lot of memories and 'what ifs' have come flooding back. The doctors, the questions they asked me, the men in army clothes in Midland, the tape, Gingin, Wanneroo.

"It doesn't pay to be smart."

I was told the stars are moving. I wonder what is behind that grid... All I know is that I must keep it to myself.

"WHAT IF!!"

15 October 2002

Just started back at College today after two weeks' break. Man, it's hard to get back into it. I need direction.

I have so much work on, it's not funny. But I want God's Will for my life, not my own. Which way please, God?

    I bought a packet of smokes yesterday after not smoking for two months. How stupid am I, but I only have one a day.

23 October 2002

It has taken two months, but I now own everything to run my own business.

25 October 2002

Because of all my work, I feel guilty that my studies have had to come second. I honestly don't want to do what **I** want to do, but I want to do what **God** wants me to do. But what it is **exactly**, I don't know. I don't want to get lost again; I don't want anything to do with my old life.

9 November 2002

Well, I am growing. I have not had a beer or a smoke since Amanda's sister's wedding seven days ago.

Here are some important dates in my life:

- 23 September 2001   I became a Christian
- 25 January 2002   Got out of jail
- 23 February 2002   Started Bible College
- 3 November 2002   Stopped smoking and drinking

I tried to think of what to write in this journal, and I am not exactly sure, so all I write are my thoughts.

I also think about the people I met during the time when I was coming to Christ:

- **The family standing on the corner**

I had gone through a lot of crap over the last week or two at this time. Mentally, I was tired and I was just looking for a place where Amanda, the boys and myself could stay for a while. Somewhere where I could cut off ties with everyone I knew and detox myself as well as process all the stuff I had been through. I was driving on the coast north of Perth and took a right turn towards Gingin. Standing on the corner in what seemed like a family photo pose was a family of four, all holding hands just looking straight at us. I turned the corner, headed up the road and they just kept staring at us while still holding hands. I said to Amanda: "That's weird," but inside, I felt I was on a new road from here on in. At the end of that road, about 30 kms away was the Gingin Caravan Park where we booked in and stayed for the next four months.

- **The three lots of people who picked me up when I was hitchhiking** (mentioned in detail previously)

- **My walk through Lancelin bush**

Amanda and me were staying at a motel in Mindarie because I couldn't go home due to all of the stuff that was happening. We had had an argument because she thought I was losing the plot, so I said, "Bugger it, I'm going up north to get sorted out and when I get up there I'll send for you." I left the hotel around 11 pm and started driving, then the flashes of light started again. I was in the middle of nowhere and pulled over in the middle of the road, not a car to be seen and I got out of my car and started to yell, "Why the hell won't you speak to me, who are you, show yourself," but nothing. I even threatened to set my car on fire and still nothing, so I kept driving. I was twenty kilometres out of Lancelin and on my left-hand side, I saw the flash of light again. I thought that this presence would finally speak to me. I pulled the car over and followed the flash of light. I must have walked in the bush towards the ocean for about an hour and I heard a voice asked me if I could do it here. I remember saying that I could, then I laid down and slept. In the morning, it took me a few hours to find my car, I still don't know what that was about, but I feel that one day I will be doing something on that plot of dirt.

- **The people at the doctor's clinic in Lancelin**

I was supposed to go to court but I didn't as I was too busy following the flashes of light. I ended up in Lancelin with Amanda and I thought that I would go to the doctor's surgery to get a note for why I was not at court as Amanda's sister had bailed us out. Anyway, when I came out from seeing the doctor, the coppers were there. At first, I blamed Amanda, but apparently the doctor had thought I'd gone nuts and had called them. They put me in the back of the paddy wagon and took me to Joondalup Mental Health Centre. Yep, they put me in a nut house.

- **The so-called crazy people in the hospital**

The next day, I was transferred to the Midland Mental Health Ward and put in an observation room. A couple of hours later, they allowed me to mix with the other residents. I was thinking to myself, how the heck can I get out of here? I'll pretend I'm a doctor or a counsellor. I started sitting with each patient to make sure they were okay, the so-called 'crazy people' and encouraged each person that everything would be fine. By late that afternoon, they let me go, they must have been doing an assessment on me to see if I was nuts.

- **The old bloke with one leg at Gingin** (mentioned in more detail soon in this journal)
- **The ground moving** (previously mentioned)
- **My other dreams** (mentioned elsewhere)

My kids are going great and I know that God's hand is on them. Little Pete told me after I had finished praying for him that his eyes were watering, that means the Holy Spirit gave him some loving. My beautiful wife, Amanda, works as hard as ever.

Man, I thank God for her every day. Until next time...

20 November 2002

On the way to College, I had a strong feeling that I had to pray for Nathan. During Spiritual Formation at College, I got a picture in my mind of Jesus standing on a mountain. Many people were walking up the mountain, with every second or third person turning around to help someone else. As I explained to Nathan about the vision, I got what the message meant — that we as Christians are to help one another. I found out that the reason I needed to pray for Nathan was that he was seeking direction in his life. What spins me out is that if this is a word and a picture from God, they would be my first.

25 November 2002

Well, this is the last week of my first year at College, with next week being my final exams. The last few days have been great; I have felt joy and know God is with me. I feel at the moment that He is helping me with the way I talk and act. I've got a long way to go before I will be used by God, but it will be well worth it when I am. I haven't put any pamphlets out in the community for two months and I am still receiving calls for quotes all the time. Thank you, Jesus, you have blessed my life.

29 November 2002

Only five days left until exams. Sometimes I feel after a year at Bible College that I haven't learnt anything, but that would be a lie. Man, have I come a long way in a year. I haven't had a smoke in over three and a half weeks, thanks be to God. The business is going great. I haven't put out a pamphlet in two months, big jobs are the best jobs.

2 December 2002

Man, I am stressed out. Gran called me today and told me two police officers had been there looking for me to be a witness, or so they said. I think it's suss, why would the police go to Gran's house looking for me? My address is in every police computer there is, and I haven't used her address in 15 years. I will ring Detective McKenna from the Organised Crime section first thing tomorrow. I haven't felt God in a few days and I'm really stressed. Man, I need him so much.

6 December 2002

The other day, I must have been going through a trial of some sort and man, did I fail. AS you can see from my last journal entry, I let my brain go all over the place. What I should have done, or better still, what I will do next time is rejoice — *James 1*.

12 December 2002

My graduation is over and I have officially finished my first year. Awesome! I feel there is so much more that I could have learned if...

15 December 2002

I have just got back from the Christian Outreach Centre (COC) in Perth City. It wasn't bad, it's been good over the past few weeks to look at other churches. I want so much to be used by God and today, I felt it in my heart, wanting to make a difference in somebody's life. I want to start something that will help others! But what?

I thought maybe a place for people to come down off drugs — who knows? I will spend some time in prayer to God and ask Him to guide me in the right direction. This is very confusing because if I am going back to Bible College next year, this would be impossible. Maybe it's just a phase.

17 December 2002

Today I finished my second lot of community service.

My brother Gavin had his housewarming yesterday. I had a few beers and felt a little bad about it, but at least I didn't have a smoke and I tell you, I was tempted.

I get on so well with my wife and kids now, it's amazing. No more yelling and screaming, no more smacking the kids, no more going off at Amanda. My life has changed so dramatically, it's great.

If Jesus can change me this much in eleven months, just imagine... YOU CAN'T PUT HIM IN A BOX.

27 December 2002

We just got back after four days at Mandurah, catching up with Mum while we were there for a bit of a holiday.

In the past few days, I've felt like crying in my spirit. I want so much to be in his presence. Maybe after I finish my parole in one month, God will use me. I have no financial problems at all, and that's all because of Jesus Christ. I can't wait to get back to College in four days' time.

31 December 2002

It's the last day of the year, so I went to Casuarina Prison to visit Leo just to see how he's going. I'm sitting here feeling rather miserable. Why am I not like other people, why am I such a loner? I've never had any real friends to hang out with, not anyone I would see on a regular basis or do anything with. When I'm around people, I feel like I don't belong and I don't fit in. This feeling isn't just today, it is all the time.

A Christian friend just rang to tell me he was planning to have fellowship and prayer with some friends. I am so jealous when I hear him talk like that, he is so mature and focused — I want to be like that. I suppose I have had to overcome a lot in the past year with more work coming up. I got my extraordinary driver's licence today, thanks to God, how my life has changed. ONE DAY AT A TIME.

5 January 2003

I'm going to stop drinking for a month because I've been having a couple of bottles of beer a day, something I'm not supposed to do. Another area I feel I need to work on is my maturity and the way I act around people.

Some of my goals for the future are:
1. Complete second year at Riverview
2. Stop drinking completely
3. Think carefully before I say things, taking time to consider who I'm talking to
4. Be more of a people person
5. Put God first in all things
6. Serve with a servant's heart
7. Grow in Christ

9 January 2003

This morning, I woke up at 4 am with an erection, finally confirming that God wakes me this way when He wants to show me something. An example of this was when He woke me every day for two months at 3.30 am to watch Joyce Meyer when I was in jail. It's almost like a year ago.

This morning's show with Joyce Meyer was about anger and how to harness it. I feel the love of Christ within me and my cup is running over.

Joy, joy, joy — if you know what I mean.

13 January 2003

It's incredible, the ups and downs you have on your journey. At the moment, I feel that God is focused on helping me keep control when faced with adversity (my anger). I am failing pretty badly, but after I do get angry, I apologise for my stupid outbursts.

16 January 2003

I shocked myself today. I went to a house to do a quote and was offered a beer by the owner of the house. I told him that I don't drink.

What a spin!

I am still seeing flashes in the sky, even in daylight. I walked to the post office to pay some bills, raised my hands in the air and I could see and feel the spirits. I know this is not the result of any drugs.

I have read over some of this journal and laughed at some of the things I have written. Sometimes I have to pinch myself, asking if this is all real — how my life has changed. I look forward to the day when Christ opens the door for me and puts me to good use. Until then, I'm going to learn and give it all I have. I know there will be lows, but I will be a better person for them.

Man, has my life changed!

Matthew 5:13-16

24 January 2003

Last week, I had the DNA taskforce come and charge me with a burglary that I was supposed to have committed in 1999. I couldn't remember if I did it or not, so I went to court and pleaded guilty. Thanks to God, I was placed on a Good Behaviour Bond for a year. If it hadn't been for God and the work He has done, I would have been jailed. It felt good to stand in front of the whole court and testify about all the work God has done in me.

As of yesterday, I am no longer on parole, have any unpaid fines or community service orders.

I am no longer accountable to any government authorities, only to Christ. This is only the start of what God has planned for my life.

Thank you, Lord Jesus.

Psalm 46:10

28 January 2003

I know that I am growing in many ways and constantly think about what I see (such as the stars and lights) and why I see it. I also think a lot about what I have been through over the past 12-18 months. I can't make any sense of it all or even explain it. I just hope that in the future when I share what has happened, that I tell it as it is and give God the glory He deserves.

What does the future hold?

4 February 2003

Peter Elliot rang me today about Emil, a man who has just been released from jail and who was thinking about enrolling in Bible College. Peter asked me if I could give Emil a ring which I did. I was excited at the prospect of telling Emil about the changes that had happened to me because of Christ when I attended Bible College. Emil told me that he had been given several hours of community service when Big Mouth Me started to tell him how I completed my community work thanks to God. Suddenly, the phone went dead.

As the dial tone rang in my ear, I knew I was about to tell Emil the wrong thing. Man, if I was going to tell him what I was gonna say, I would have caused problems for both of us. I knew it was God who cut the phone off because all I could feel at the time was God's presence as I was talking and then nothing. I rang Emil straight back and made a time to see him in person later that day. I learned a very valuable lesson — to think before I yap and slow down. Not only that, I now have another God encounter to put in my treasure box — deep in my heart!

6 February 2003

Over the past three months:
- I have stopped smoking, drinking or using drugs
- I have finished my parole and probation
- I have paid off all my outstanding fines
- I have paid off my College fees for the year in full
- Our credit cards are paid off
- I have $1,500 worth of savings in the bank

This is just a brief list of what God has achieved in my life lately. I still have over $8k of work on the go and should be completely debt-free before I start Bible College in eleven days with money in the bank.

I have to pinch myself to try to come to terms with how my life has changed. Thank you, Lord!

10 February 2003

I am happy and my life is going great except I want to be more about God's business and not my own. I am not ungrateful and thank God for his blessings but man, I want to praise and speak His name.

    I don't want to settle down and be a 'stay in one place' Christian, I want to be a growing one — a person who is active for God.

I sometimes wonder why I have no interest in reading books. I love the Bible, but anything else doesn't appeal to me — should it and if so, why doesn't it?

5 March 2003

It's been three weeks since I wrote in this journal. I just started my second year of Bible College, but I'm not too sure if I'll be continuing. It's frustrating not being able to understand what is required of me when doing the essays. I sit in class, but I don't have a clue what I am learning because I'm having trouble figuring out words and things like that.

I won't give up even though I say to myself I'm gonna quit because of my frustrations. I stress out so much it hurts my head.

I must not give up if I want to know what God wants for me. You ask God for some miracle understanding of the text, but it doesn't come. I know he could give it to me if He wanted to! He probably is giving it to me, but there is bound to be something on my side of the fence holding me back.

I feel so much love for Him — thank you, Lord!

11 March 2003

I'm finding it hard at the moment because I feel that I'm not putting the effort I should into my studies. Even when I do study, I find that I don't notice the hidden meanings that other students see.

I have been feeling God's presence for weeks at a time, but He slowly goes away. Each time I say or do something wrong, I get this tingle in the top of my head and I feel the anointing leave.

My work is pretty busy this week, but I won't let it come before God. If I get a tutor, it would help.

I just don't understand.

13 March 2003

We have prophetic people come to College and man, did I get a Word! I thank my Father for His blessing. I am growing and this week, I feel different. I have noticed that when I get angry, my head tingles and it feels like some of the anointing from God is leaving. I have felt this on three occasions.

22 March 2003

I am experiencing different levels of joy within my spirit. One example would be yesterday when I was rude to a man at the petrol station and I felt the familiar tingles in my head. The joy that I have experienced so strongly depletes over time to nothing and right now, I feel empty.

This has happened more than once over the last few months. The Holy Spirit comes back to fill me with His presence when He sees the cry of my heart. I need Him now and I must learn to walk in the anointing of God. Abba[3], Father!

29 March 2003

Macka rang yesterday, telling me he was arrested and refused bail until Monday. I went to see him today and all I could think was, *Why me, why me?* when I was leaving. I mean, why has MY life been turned around like it has? I mean, I'm not knocking God, but I've done nothing worthy enough to be helped to the extent I have been. Only I know it is God who has overcome my addictions for me. Other people say I must have done something — I know that I didn't, it was all God.

I thank my wonderful God for His Love, His friendship, His Patience, His Compassion, His Plans and His Purposes. Only God knows what the future holds!!

30 March 2003

Just sitting here reading a book on church history and I can't help but think of the old bloke with one leg who hitched into Gingin Caravan Park last year. I met him at the ablution block as I was shaving. He had what seemed like a Scottish accent and he started asking me a whole heap of questions. I asked him where he was staying and he told me he had a tent at the back of the caravan park.

I got Amanda to make him a plate of food and then I took it down to him. The old bloke seemed very grateful.

The next morning, he came to our caravan, bringing with him a Centenary of Federation stamp release 1901 to 2001. He got Amanda and me to sign it.

---

[3] in the New Testament — God as father.

He told me that one day my name would be written in gold. When he passed me the stamp First Day cover, we both broke down crying.

I don't know or understand what happened that day, but I do know it was rather significant, the events that led up to it were ... unexplainable. Man, I went through some things, it was like being interviewed. One day, I will find out why and what it all meant, but by then, it will not be important.

The Bible says that God will have mercy on those who show mercy and He also says that some have entertained angels without even knowing it. Thank you, Lord!

I was unworthy, but you have given me life!

CENTENARY OF FEDERATION
1901–2001

On 1 January 2001, the Commonwealth of Australia marks its centenary. In 1901 the six separate colonies federated to become one nation.

Although the idea of federation had been voiced in the 1840s, serious attempts to introduce it only began in the 1890s with a series of national conventions. Approval for a federated system was finally achieved when all colonies voted by referenda for a new constitution and an Act was passed through the British parliament.

The inauguration of the Commonwealth on 1 January 1901 was celebrated around the new nation. In Sydney a grand procession was watched by an estimated 250,000 people. It culminated in the proclamation of the Commonwealth and the swearing in of the Governor-General and the new ministry in a solemn public ceremony in Centennial Park. The streets were lavishly decorated with flags, bunting, branches of eucalypts and electric lights. Ten triumphal arches, spanning the road at various points, were constructed to represent aspects of Australian life. The inauguration was followed by a state banquet in the Sydney Town Hall and days of celebrations across the nation, including picnics, sporting and musical carnivals and fireworks.

The stamps adopt an historical approach focusing specifically on the events of 1 January 1901. They capture the enthusiasm and sense of hope that pervaded events on that day; the notion that Australia was beginning a great new adventure.

Stamp and minisheet design: Asprey Di Donato Design, Melbourne. Pack design: Australia Post Design Studio
Stamp and pack photographs: Courtesy of the National Archives of Australia, Image Library, State Library of NSW, National Library of Australia

6 April 2003

Every second day or so, I feel God's beautiful presence. My relationship with my boys is getting better, it's so hard trying to be a father when you never had one to show you what to do. I am a bit of a grump. Me and my main man, Little Pete, are getting on great, he even gives me a real good cuddle. You know how it feels when your kid comes up to you and rests their arm on you and it is so comfortable. My business is going good, it's incredible the type of work we are pulling in.

I have some God stories to tell ... one day.

Two weeks until the end of first term.

Man, it's going quick.

8 April 2003

Yesterday, I had a meeting with the principal of Riverview, Duane. We talked about where I was at and what I was going through. I told him about my dreams and about what I see, but I am not sure God is okay with that. Maybe Duane can point me in the right direction?

My three good dreams and the one bad one where I got shot and died, it was so real. Is this a warning about how I will die?

And Amanda was watching this happen in that dream. It's all I can think of for the past day...

15 April 2003

Man, one minute I am up and the next, I am down. I can see what I am doing wrong, yet I continue to do it.

- The way I carry on gets to me.
- The things I say get to me.
- The things I don't do get to me.
- I work myself up over nothing, but at the same time, it is something.

I don't see as much as I used to, I still see spirits and the sky looks different. Out of the corner of my eye, I will see a flash now and again. I feel deep inside that the dreams that God has shown me will come to pass, I know they will. I am just growing, I feel that I can be immature in the way I handle stress as well as the way I act.

Things that need to change:
- I need to be more mature.
- I need to think what I am going to say before I say it.
- I need to keep calm through all situations.

I have committed this to Christ this morning.
I know things will now improve.

16 April 2003

It is now the end of first term with two weeks' break coming up. God is great, I am looking at the jobs on the go for the next ten days and they add up to $8k. I haven't put out a pamphlet for over 3 months.

I know it is God ... it is just not possible otherwise ... IT IS GOD!

25 April 2003

Man, I am sore, the past 4 days of work brought in over five thousand dollars. We already have another $2k of work for next week. God, God, God, I know in my heart that it's not about money, it's about the blessings of God.

I think God is a personal God meaning what works for me might not excite another person. It's hard to believe that the God in the Old Testament is the same one. All I know is that I love Him, His Presence and His Ways ... imagine if I could only walk in the spirit daily!

30 April 2003

I just came back from a walk and I'm positive I saw a shooting start fly and then stop in the sky. Just after noticing it, I felt the Holy Spirit. What I see has something to do with my future.

I read *Romans 8* yesterday for about the tenth time and it finally makes sense. At the moment, I am learning to hold my tongue. My prayer is to seek wisdom and maturity. Back to College in four days for second term. I have a flying start to the term with 90% of my assignments completed.

I prayed over my boys this morning and I asked Little Pete five minutes later what he felt and he told me that he felt the Holy Spirit. Seven years old!! Doesn't that touch your heart!

Thank you, Lord!

4 May 2003

I went to Graham's house today. I am so grateful to him as I know I couldn't have got through this without his help.
- I never wanted to be who I was.
- I hated me and what I stood for.
- I hated what I was doing to my kids.
- What sort of life would my kids have had if had continued on the other path?
- How much more time in jail would I have spent?

It has been six months and 3 days since I last smoke cigarettes. It's been 5 months since I last drank alcohol and more than 14 months since I smoke pot.

I saw my daughter Tosha today. Man, I love her.

It is mind-blowing, the change in me. Every day, it keeps getting better. Over the past week, I feel that God is teaching me wisdom, maturity and the power that is in the name of Jesus Christ. Our tongue is sharper than a two-edged sword. God spoke and it was ...

16 May 2003

The last few days have been great. My prayer life has improved, my time with God is awesome. I am growing, I have gained revelations of the power of Our Lord Jesus Christ and I am learning the authority of His Name.

I have had the opportunity over the last few days to speak into several people's lives and it's been great.

Psalms 51 and 91 are burnt into my mind for altar use. All I can say is teach me, O Lord. I have asked the Lord for direction in my life and I know that slowly, doors will be opened.

Thank you, Lord!

30 May 2003

Two days ago, we bought a new van for $12k, surprisingly paying cash for it. If that isn't a miracle, what is? Our first van cost $250, the second was $2,050. Over the past few months, I prayed to God for a decent van, and now this one is like a limo, exceeding all my expectations.

Next week at a church in Fremantle, I give my testimony. I am not nervous now, but I have placed my faith in God's hands.

Sometimes it's like I'm dreaming ... why me??

3 June 2003

I seem to be having trouble with my attitude. While everyone else is going 'Wow' during our ministry sessions, I just don't get it. We went on camp and the problem then was that I verbalised when I didn't get something. I don't think I fit in well with other people, I can't relate. What is wrong with me?

I am not getting anything from reading books. I am a practical learner, hands-on, doing stuff, I reckon.

6 June 2003

I took the dog for a walk tonight and in the sky, I saw a star disappear. It zipped through the sky then it wasn't there anymore. It was not a plane or a satellite, believe me, it was definitely a star.

8 June 2003

I gave my testimony how God has changed my life at the Fremantle church tonight. It was my first time talking in front of people, it was about tithing. They have asked me back in a couple of weeks to give a full testimony. Thank you, Lord, I hope it glorifies you fully.

Proverbs 3:5-6

14 June 2003

Today I got a call from Mick and Kim, they wanted to let me know that Mick had just been released from rehab. When I went over to their place, I found that they had both been awake for two days, back on meth. They had fallen away, you might say.

I led Mick to accept the Lord and he prayed the prayer of resistance. He began crying. I don't know if it was a cry for help or a cry for the Lord, time will tell. God knows the hearts and minds of all men, all I can do is pray.

Kim has been going to a Bible Study group every Tuesday at a Christadelphian Church. I had heard they were a cult because their doctrines were based on works leads to salvation, not faith. I will have to look into other religions not only for my sake but for those who will ask me about them.

20 June 2003

Tonight I went to the prayer night at the South Perth Church Of Christ. They were looking for direction about starting a youth camp or school for young offenders. That's exactly what has been in my heart. They need money or land to get it happening.

I will commit this to God and be a part of it if it is His Will. Not all things are possible with Man, but with God, all things are possible.

Amen.

I was given *Psalm 28* today by Gayle and David from Waterford.

30 June 2003

Two weeks ago, I had the best two days since becoming a Christian, days full of joy, maturity and wisdom. The Holy Spirit was definitely in me. Since then, I haven't felt that presence, but I know that I am just going through a growing stage and the Holy Spirit is still inside me.

We have exams this week, I will rely on the Lord to get me through.

2 July 2003

Who could believe that I have completed my exams and the first half of my second year of study? Jesus is my rock, I love Him with all my heart. I want to be able to share His Love with others in a tangible way ... one day I will, I know it.

3 July 2003

I took a friend's girlfriend over to Shirley's house for some spiritual deliverance and prayers. My heart went out to her when she told her story to Shirley, I felt so much love and compassion. Heroin, death, prostitution and abuse in many different ways. What I have been through is nothing compared to her.

To see God working in her life as well as in her brother's life was a very rewarding sight.

Man, I love Him.

13 July 2003

Today I gave my full testimony at the Fremantle Church in front of about 30 people. I think it went well.

25 July 2003

Sitting in front of my computer, I consider how incredible it is that I will start the second half of my second year, how did I get this far?

My business is completely set up now: new van, new trailer, complete set of equipment and signwriting. Maybe I will start to see my money grow in the bank.

I went to bail Macka out of jail last night, but I wasn't allowed to because of my own criminal past. Macka made a bit of joke out of it. The next morning, I successfully bailed him out of the Central Law Courts without any problems.

I am going through a bit with my dad at the moment, it's like he doesn't care. Not once has he asked me about how my studies are going.

29 July 2003

This is my second week of Discovery classes and my first time as a leader. I had five people in my group including me. We all had life issues to deal with. God is a loving God. Grow, grow, grow.

Over the past week, I have prophesied three times that I can remember. I am not positive it is what it is, but I will wait on the Lord.

14 August 2003

My business has grown at a phenomenal rate lately, my life has done a complete 180-degree turnaround.

Thank you, Jesus, Praise, Glory and Honour belong to you!

18 August 2003

Amanda and I went for our first home loan last week, we'll be very excited if we get it. There would a bit of travel involved, but that's okay.

My dad rang tonight to say that he has a new job overseas setting up a new company. Good for him. I asked him why he shows no interest in my changed life. It's like he is all for himself. The path to healing is not an easy one, but at least it has started.

I head off to Cambodia on the 25th of next month for ten days, then Singapore for five days after that. I hope that being in Cambodia will help me grow.

31 August 2003

We got knocked back on our loan application due to our bad credit rating. They have asked us to provide valid explanations why we have defaults. If this does not work out, we will rent.

Our business is going off, fully booked for the next month.

As far as me and the Lord go, it is okay. I spend time with Him every day. I don't feel His presence as much as I did when I first started Bible College. It would be good to have a verbal conversation with him.

5 September 2003

I just spoke to my grandmother about Uncle Lloyd who is sick in hospital. I told her he must confess that Jesus is Lord before he passes on, otherwise, he could spend all eternity in Hell.

"Oh, Hell wouldn't be that bad, would it?" was what she said.

How does that make you feel, I mean, how sad is it that they can think like that? All I can do is pray! I am looking forward to going to Cambodia and Singapore, three weeks to go — I hope I will grow.

10 September 2003

I had a brief talk today with Duane about going it alone. I don't mix well, but I am okay with that. He told me that I can't do Christianity by myself as that isn't what God would want. God knows I am wired, He knows where I am at.

I have asked the Lord to let me know what he wants me to be, I know He will tell me. I am hoping for God to give me a mentor, someone to correct me when I am wrong and instruct me. The only problem is this: is it like the people of Israel asking for a king? Because if it is, the last thing I want to do is reject God!!

17 September 2003

I have been having bad dreams similar to the one I had last year where I got shot and died. They have been very real dreams, I was petrified when I woke up.

9 October 2003

Just back from Cambodia. It wasn't as bad as some people make out. We look at it through Western eyes. Sure, there is plenty to be done, but you can see it is underway!

I went to prison to pray for the kids and spent a few hours studying the Bible with one of the group from Prison Fellowship.

Our business turned over more than $18k last month. I have two months left of this year of College and I think they will be the hardest yet. I must make sure I don't put my work ahead of my studies.

12 October 2003

We get the keys to our new house tomorrow, but because of everything going on, we won't be moving in for a couple of weeks. Everything is moving so fast! I need to slow down and put things in order of priority.

21 October 2003

We ended up moving in on the 17th, but we haven't had time to enjoy it. I haven't felt the Lord's presence as strongly as usual. Man, I need aim! I have asked God for some direction, like which church I should go to, but I will have to be patient.

31 October 2003

I am just asking myself why I bother to write in this book, I will probably never read it. I haven't been putting much effort in this term at College. I will probably only just pass second year.

Where do I go from here? Where do I fit?

Where do I belong?

7 November 2003

The other day I was reading *Jeremiah 39:18* which spoke to me, "I will save you; you will not fall by the sword, but will escape with your life because you trust in me," declared the Lord.

The main part that spoke to me was "... because you trust in me," how awesome is God to tell me to trust in Him!

Today, I am having a better day than I have had over the past couple of weeks.

15 November 2003

I was serving at Riverview tonight when Di started to prophesy over me, representing the Lord when she told me that I did not have to tell the person I had wronged, that it was in the past, and that I would start to see things happen as of tomorrow.

What I say is "Let it be."

16 November 2003

Today we had Outreach at Banksia Hill with over 60 people in attendance to see Lord's miracles, with the usual turnout only being 30 people. They were all ears. I must be mature and thank God.

What happens from here?

30 November 2003

My second-year exams are next week. I wasn't planning on doing my third year, but until He shows me another way, I will continue. I have a deep desire to serve Him, but where? What? And how?

I love you, Lord Jesus, please lead me in your Ways!

2 December 2003

I believe God is in control of the world with some of His people going in and out of it at will. A lot of strange things happened to me along my way to God, some very weird things and some strange people.

I am certain that the following people were important in my journey: the doctor at Midland, the old fella at Gingin, the people in Army greens, and the security guard at Joondalup.

Some have entertained angels and never knew it.

What if?

28 December 2003

We just returned from a week in Busselton/Dunsborough where the family spent Christmas, a well-earned break.

I know inside that I am growing, my first thought each day is *Jesus, I love you!*

I have organised with Tim to go to Banksia Hill for one day each week next year as part of the Alpha group. I have an overwhelming desire to help others but how, I don't know. It's good to be blessed by God, but I want to see other people's lives change like mine has. I often reflect on all He has done for me.

29 December 2003

I went to visit my mates Macka and Glen at Canningvale Prison today. Man, I feel sorry for Macka, he just got another two years on top of his sentence. He has spent eight of the past twelve years in jail, and when I speak to him, I see the chip on his shoulder. I think Macka won't change, but with God, anything is possible!

I have been reading a book called *Great Christians*, what a book! I am thinking of becoming a full-time evangelist, maybe through a scholarship, after I complete my third year. I am going to pray about it, I know God has my path planned. This thought is always going through my head ... what if I let Him down?

3 January 2004

My first entry for the New Year. Cathy and Duane came up to me at church and told me about a person they had tea with a few nights before with Duane's mum. He studies in England and his ministerial area is spiritual warfare. They suggested that I meet him. God's hands are on this, I feel. He knows best.

5 January 2004

I am going through a spiritual dry patch with my prayer, just not feeling it, only going through the routine. When will He show me the Way?

8 January 2004

On the way to the park tonight with my two boys, I saw flashes of light in the sky, things I hadn't seen for a long time. Sometimes, these flashes are only in the corners of my vision, and other times, they are right in front of me.

I feel sad about the world my kids will live in: the terrorism, other nations hating Western countries, Man's search for how the world was formed, the ozone depletion and Man's greed for money. God made the planet and everything in it. Man will find out one day.

Stephen Hawking — Big Bang — I know I will meet him.

I know.

9 January 2004

Today, I bought Amanda a Triton dual cab ute for $10k cash. How amazing is God? I love Him because He loves me. He loves me!!

19 January 2004

My spiritual dry patch continues. I went to the South Perth Church of Christ and was uplifted by their service. I plan to go there from now on. Two days ago, I felt a revelation about the cross and the sacrifice that Jesus made after I read Galatians.

Paul speaks of the justification of faith and I can say that I love Jesus more after the last couple of days. I think often of the dreams he has shown me, sometimes I worry that I am doing things that may cause me to miss their meanings. I need to forget about them for the minute and just trust in the Lord.

I love Him!!

23 January 2004

I need help!! I am having bad thoughts, I know they are not mine. One example is when I am speaking to a lady, my eyes go where they shouldn't, making me awkward and uncomfortable, if you know what I mean. I often feel voices in my head giving me the wrong thoughts — I have asked the Lord for help. He will help me control this part of me.

My wife and kids are getting annoyed with me stirring them up all the time. Sometimes, I act a bit childish and go too far, something I need help with. I haven't really been in the presence of the Lord for over a week and I feel empty!!

It makes me think of Joyce Meyer: I want — I think — I feel!

31 January 2004

I had my graduation the other night, but I don't feel like I fit in just yet. I am a normal guy now, running a business, not smoking or drinking or taking drugs. I now have a mortgage.

What can I say? Define normal.

I wasn't going to do my third year, but God will tell me if He wants me to concentrate my time on the business instead. We have the new ute plastered with the business logo and it looks great.

This is my final journal entry for this book (Journal 1) and I know there is a lot of dribble in it, but I am young.

If anyone reads what is contained in here, I am telling you straight: I see what I see, and have seen what I have seen, that is a fact.

DRIVEN BY PAIN
CHANGED BY GRACE

Part 2 Journal 2

MY STRUGGLE CONTINUES

7 February 2004

I am about to start my third year of Bible College. I am reflecting on how much has changed in the past two years.

I have:
- Stopped smoking and drinking
- Completed my parole and my 500 hours of community service
- Paid all outstanding fines as well as $15k in bills
- Completed two years of full-time study
- Started a business — $148k in turnover in the first year
- Travelled to Cambodia and Singapore
- Bought a house and paid cash for two cars
- Have my driver's licence and own a $5K motorbike

I thank my God for what He has done in and for me. I have a meeting at ten o'clock this morning with Balga TAFE's Department of Treasury and Finance about a tender for regular work. If we get it (worth $100k per year), our business will move into a whole new realm.

Where do I go from here?

I am supposed to start my third-year studies in two weeks, but I am uncertain about which direction to take. I do know for certain that my life is in the hands of my Lord and I trust Him.

I love Him so much!!

10 February 2004

We completed the tender today which came to over $135k, with over $96k of that being labour.

I spoke briefly to Duane about my uncertainties, and he told me to choose Bible College over my work commitments. In my heart, I will follow my God and I will have to be patient about knowing where He will lead me. There were ten other contractors offering their tenders to Balga TAFE. We have to wait and see!

Over the past couple of days, I have felt the spirit of God lead me, warning me to keep my mouth shut just when I am about to shoot off at the mouth. Most of the time, I do it without thinking. I feel myself growing spiritually. I know it will take time, I can't give up.

16 February 2004

I went to my orientation night for my third year of the Advanced Diploma of Theology. Wow, who would have thought I would make it this far? I thank the Lord that I could pay my $3k fees upfront.

Over the past six months, it has been money, money and more money. I am sick of it, life is not just meant to be spent on making money, but without it, well, you know what...

Tonight, I went to a cell group held for the first time at Braydon's house, an all-male meeting. I am committed to attending every two weeks for the next six months. I was hesitant to share my way-out testimony, and I am not sure God wanted me to share this and He will be unhappy with me. I saw what I saw, I know I did. It is as clear as day in my mind.

I know that this third year of study will be the hardest yet.

I WILL cross the finish line!

17 February 2004

I was reminiscing yesterday about being in jail for all of Rhyan's first year of life. After that, I was spending my time doing drugs. Two days ago, for the first time ever, Rhyan lay down with me without me asking him to. I know that there would be some hurt that he would feel because of how I was before. He is slowly coming to love me more.

20 February 2004

It has been a good couple of days. I am really trying to learn and respond to certain situations differently, with the help of the Holy Spirit, of course.

When I go to respond to a situation or a person in a negative way, I start to feel a tingling on my head that tells me to stop and think about what I am about to say before I say it.

The best example of this is the way I respond to Rhyan now. I used to respond to him in a negative way which isn't teaching him properly about right and wrong. The Holy Spirit is teaching me to stop and think, be calm and explain what he is doing wrong. It is having a positive effect on our relationship.

A friend from church, Arleen, rang me as she is having doubts about being able to do full-time Bible Study as well as being Mum to four kids. I continue to pray for her.

22 February 2004

The parable of the sower is so true! People are the seed. I ask myself what part I can play to have the seed grow in good soil in people's lives. It's all about foundation and Jesus being the cornerstone of that foundation. Bible College has helped me build my foundations firmly. I know that Jesus has helped me and He will help some of the people I have met lately who have fallen away from the Lord.

Mark 4:3-20.

29 February 2004

Today was a good day, we spent the day at Cable Water Ski in Fremantle with all my brothers and sisters. This is the first time that everyone showed up: Judy, me, Gavin, Graham, Cheree and all our kids. I spent the rest of the week flat on my back — I tend to put my back out every six months or so. It was so bad I couldn't even attend Bible College. Looking forward to a good week.

2 March 2004

Lately, I have felt empowered to relate to people better and it feels great. I was at Discovery tonight and the group that I had was really hard. What do you say when someone says they have brain damage and they hear voices.

Man, it was hard! I just love my God.

Today was the first day back at Riverview and I know it's going to be a full-on year.

4 March 2004

I just went to Royal Perth Hospital about my Hepatitis C treatment: injections once every week as well as a lot of other medication. I am so stressed out as my Type 1 strain is the worst you can get. There are many side effects such as depression, mood swings, loss of hair, aching joints and a general loss of energy to deal with.

I have Stage 1-2 liver damage meaning I have mild to moderate scarring. I could go on living for more than 20 years as it isn't until you get to Stage 4 which is cirrhosis of the liver. I have to have a biopsy every 4-5 years to see how far the damage is progressing. I am going to take part in a clinical trial where I will have double doses of medication in the hope to stop the advance of the disease. Unfortunately, at the moment, the success rate with Hepatitis C Type 1 is only 50%.

I worry about how I will be able to keep studying while undergoing such treatment. I plan to go to a support group for now, putting off treatment until the end of the Bible College year. With God's help, I will get through it.

At Bible College yesterday, we talked about the effects of generational sin. How I speak to my wife in front of the kids will be how they talk to their spouses in the future. I love my wife more today than the day we met, she is a beautiful lady. I thank the Lord for the rapid change in me in such a short time.

11 March 2004

I am very busy with lots of large assignments and with work. Amanda has started to attend a cell group with Maggie, somewhere she gets to wind down and feel the spiritual fellowship.

God has brought healing into our home, the kids and I are getting along well and I am getting better at reacting positively to them.

Work is exploding to the point we are knocking back work. I am not going to stress out about who I am not, but thank God for who I am!

14 March 2004

Last night at church, I was talking to a confused young man. I went to tell him about my own experiences when I heard a voice inside my head instructing me not to do that.

I must make it a point to follow that voice.

It is very sad to see people going through hard times, like my friend, Arleen. Her husband moved out, her phone was cut off and her car isn't working properly. What can I do?

17 March 2004

Today, Linus Perry and John Jacks from the U.S. came to visit Riverview as they have done every couple of years. Listening to these prophets is like hearing from God direct. It's awesome to see people weep as God speaks into their lives as only He can. Sometimes, people ask me if I see stuff, and I say yes, but only to spiritual matters. I know that I am growing and will **NOT** give up, no matter what comes up against me.

23 March 2004

Today at Bible College, I had a complete blank. I felt a noticeable presence and I could not think at all. God is so beautiful and wonderful.

Last Monday morning, clear as day, I saw a star moving in the sky. Three days before, I saw the same thing, but I watched for a longer period. I had seen this before during my first year at Riverview.

Why? I am 98% sure it was a star, but people would never believe me. I also see a lot of flashes in the day and night skies.

I keep all this to myself in the hope that the Lord will show me more. He has done great work in me and my wife.

25 March 2004

Today, I bought another motorcycle, a Honda VT750 2003 model. I traded my other one in for $5k and only had to pay $4,500 on top of that. A good buy that has only done 5,000 kms. A few problems, though. I only have my extraordinary driver's licence, so I might get done if caught for driving out of my class or maybe worse. I hope the Lord is not peeved with me!

I am feeling a bit guilty as I always make sure when I pull up somewhere that I can be seen, being proud and boastful.

I also tell people including my brothers about my new bike whenever I can. I have searched through my motives and I consider that it is just for the pure joy of having such a great bike, not showing off.

Man, God has brought me such a long way in such a short time!

28 March 2004

I have had a great day today, just doing things around the house. I was in the shed listening to the radio and I thought to myself that God made this possible; if it were not for Him, I would be in jail!

I have a burning desire to do something, but I don't know what. I want to help people but I don't know how to. How can I make a difference, a real difference? I have to do a ten-minute sermon in class on Wednesday. I am not a book person. I feel all over the place.

I just read the previous entry and what a load of baloney, it is pride and I need to get rid of it.

Two weeks left of Term 1 of my third year.

Please Lord, be the potter in me!

1 April 2004

Another college student friend of mine has fallen away from God. He got out of jail in January after doing two years. He has found it hard to fit in like I did at church. He was given an ultimatum by the Bible College to tell his missus to move out until they are married, get on Austudy and show his commitment to study. I think it was too much for him. What can I do?

7 April 2004

It's the end of Term 1 of my third year, and man, I have so many assignments. The other student from my previous entry has fallen away on drugs over the past couple of days. I saw him to try and help him out, we sorted out parole and urine tests, not to mention the problems he had with Bible College.

Now he has turned his back on it all, he is facing court next month and I reckon he had a chance to get off **IF** he got his act together. I feel he has blown that chance now! Can you help someone who does not want to help themselves? I can see the answers, but he can't.

10 April 2004

Yesterday I saw the Mel Gibson movie, *The Passion* which was, in my opinion, very graphic and at one stage, I felt sick because of all the blood. There were many times when I broke down crying. I know deep within me that Jesus did that for me, but the full impact, I believe, we will never be able to comprehend.

Yesterday was also Good Friday, and Gran, Uncle Lloyd and my two sisters came to church for their third time. The service was a little in your face, not too heavy, but not too light.

Tonight, I went to church because I do voluntary ushering and Phillip came up to me to see how Gran enjoyed the service at the end.

I still see flashes in the sky as well as spiritual stuff. I often wonder why but my awesome God will tell me when He is ready.

My friends Mick and Kim seem to be getting on better and have come back to the Lord. They backslid for a while, but thanks be to God, they are on their way back.

14 April 2004

Today I was contacted by a person about a prisoner about to be released who wants to turn his life around. I thought again about starting something, probably a Not-For-Profit (NFP) organisation aimed at ex-prisoners and drug addicts to help them change their ways. I will pray and ask God for His advice.

I look at my boys and my heart leaps with joy. Without God, we wouldn't be together. I love them so much, it makes me want to cry. Peter and Rhyan, if you ever read this, I love you more than life itself.

What to do?

21 April 2004

Tonight, the boys sat down with me and we asked each other what we think love is. *1 Corinthians 13*

We took it in turns praying for each other, the kids laid their hands on me and vice versa.

I still struggle being a dad as I am short-tempered and low in tolerance. I don't want them to hate me when they get older.

Tosha came over today and told me she is thinking about leaving school. I pray she doesn't because it will limit her opportunities later.

It must have been hard for her growing up without a normal Mum and Dad who were living together. My prayer is for her to find Jesus. I love her sooooooooo much, it brings a tear to my eye.

I can't help but think about the Lord every minute of my day, I love Him so much.

If only people could know.

25 April 2004

I search inside myself, but the Lord is a long way away from me, leaving me feeling empty.

Maybe it's my motorcycle?

No matter what, I will not give up!! After Bible College, I am thinking of writing a book about my journey so far, my childhood and how God saved me.

He is my foundation and I will not be moved.

Little Pete plays his second game of soccer today, how blessed and lucky I am to be there and watch him — everything God has shown me has happened.

I praise Him, I will honour and exalt Him above all that is in my life.

28 April 2004

Again, I have been feeling spiritually dry. **SIN** has been blocking my access to God. Yes, it was my motorbike, all I could think about was the bike. Another student got up in class today and said he felt that there was someone crying out for signs and wonders, but **SIN** was stopping them and that God doesn't tolerate sin. This really spoke to me, as I mentioned to Amanda yesterday that I felt this was directed especially to me. As of today, I will no longer ride the bike, but instead, I am going to put it in the paper. God's presence today was awesome, He touched so many people in many ways.

2 May 2004

I was up at 5 am this morning, praying for an hour, then reading His Word for another half an hour. Yesterday, I went to the farm for Amanda's mum's surprise 60th birthday. I have not ridden my bike since the other day, I have put it up for sale, probably going to lose at least $2k. After deciding to sell my bike, I feel that the Lord is also not pleased with other areas of my life. The first is when I drive out of the specified hours of my extraordinary licence. Amanda now often drives to the farm and back.

The second is about accepting cash for jobs without declaring it to the taxman. The third one is that I must stop giving place to the enemy, the wrong thoughts come into my head, like my observations about people, picking out their negatives rather than their positives. I also feel temptation when my eyes wander where they shouldn't, but I try to stop myself doing that.

Over the past few days, I have learned that the Bible says, "Blessed are the uncompromisingly righteous."

This means we cannot obey only part of God's Law if we want to obey Him. I have made up my mind to obey God in ALL things. I look at my family and know that God has given us a life that we never would have had without Him.

7 May 2004

At court today, the judge decided that I can drive from 6 am until 10 pm, every day of the week. In November, I will get my normal licence finally. During proceedings, just as I was about to tell the judge that I DID have my motorbike licence, the prosecutor jumped in and answered for me, stopping me from uttering a lie. I also now have an unrestricted bike licence, R-class as it is called. The bike has been in the paper for two weeks now and I could have sold it today. All I can do is thank God.

What is strange is if I had answered the judge yesterday with a lie, I would not have been able to ride the bike due to my guilt and conviction anyway.

14 May 2004

I just returned from a two-day Bible College camp. I often felt like leaving because I was uncomfortable, but it ended up being the best two days of the year so far.

Grown men were weeping, ladies were being slain in the spirit, lives were being healed in Jesus's name.

Pastor Ed prophesised over us. Some were spot on, some were placed on the shelf. Mine was that I would be released into ministry after two more spiritual tests. Seeing tears flow was a reward in itself.

I feel like the Lord wants me to get up at 4 am every day, so I will try it for the next week. I will ask God for a greater revelation of Jesus Christ and the work of the Cross. What direction does He want me to take, what does He want me to do?

22 May 2004

I have been getting up really early each day, watching Joyce Meyer and reading God's Word. The change in my life blows me away.

Little Pete has a big heart, it's good to see him reading his Bible and picking out scriptures on his own.

Young Rhyan, man, I love him so much. He is going to be very active when he grows up. You can see it in the way he runs everywhere.

I thank God for my children soooo much.

28 May 2004

Still waking up early each day, spending some time with God. I can't understand why some days it feels like I'm walking with God, then on other days, it feels like He is gone. I don't feel His presence as much when I pray now. Maybe it's a growth thing? I am not too keen on it as His presence is the blessing of blessings.

In two weeks, I have to present a thirty-minute sermon in front of my class. I pray that God will help me in every way.

I prayed before to say that I didn't want God to open doors until he thinks I am ready. Maybe that is the case now.

7 June 2004

I still feel like God isn't listening to me when I pray. I did my sermon in front of the class and it went well. I am supposed to speak at a church in Mandurah this Sunday, no way!

I just spent three days sitting in front of my computer. I came up with nothing. I was going to do my testimony but it doesn't feel right. I don't know what to do.

Why is God not talking to me and where is His presence?

10 June 2004

Today, I told Duane I couldn't go and preach on Sunday. After that, I thought I would give it another try and still got nowhere. I rang the pastor to say I couldn't make it, except he told me how much they were looking forward to me coming to their church. He didn't give me a chance to decline. This kind of reassured me. So on Sunday, I want to make it all about Jesus and what God has done in my life. I will wait and see what the Holy Spirit has planned.

Another student told me that he thought I had the spirit of David, the gift of spiritual deliverance. It started me thinking about moving to England to train and commit to the Lord. If everything falls into place, then I know it is His Will.

13 June 2004
Today I went to Mandurah's Holy Ground Ministries Church to give my testimony to about 20 people. I felt a lot more comfortable than the first time. It felt so good talking being able to stand before a group of people and talk about God and what Jesus has done for us. I love Him so much.

I wind myself up and stress over nothing!

18 June 2004
I bought a Honda VTX1300 Cruiser last week, brand-new for $19k. I own it outright, a bit of a spin. I know in my heart that Jesus is with me and He will never leave me. But I miss His presence, how He would give me a big cuddle in the past two years. I miss Him.

The other day, Peter from Bible College rang and told me that he had some good and bad news. My grades were all A's or A+'s, that was the good news. The bad news was I had failed Church History because I had too many absent days. I am devastated. I have considered pulling out of Bible College altogether after this. I am on a big downer at the moment, can't get a handle of things. When I was at Mandurah last week, I didn't like it, I can't see myself doing it full-time.

- Was it a mistake me starting this business?
- If I hadn't started the business, I might have spent more time on my studies.
- Have I let God down by not putting in more of an effort?
- Should I be attending more Christian events?
- Has my fire for God been reduced to a pilot light only?

These are the questions going through my mind.

23 June 2004

During prayer time, I felt an urge to tell JJ, one of the other students, that God said he was in the right place which seemed to mean a lot to him. God blessed us both: me by getting a Word from God and JJ by God speaking to him. How good is God?

Amanda and I were planning to go to Cambodia but I am a bit nervous because of that vivid dream that I mentioned in my first journal about being shot as I climbed through a window. I remember waking up at the time, sitting straight up in bed. I don't know if God has told me this to warn me or not, but if I am travelling with Amanda, I need to be very cautious.

God is **NOT** a God of confusion and Jesus has won the fight ... Amen! I also need to pray for direction. Kids, if you ever read this, God is an awesome God!!

30 June 2004

I loved God last night at Discovery, I felt blessed that God had touched people and worked through me. Today is my preaching exam, hope everything goes well.

18 July 2004

Amanda and I returned yesterday from our Southeast Asian eleven-day trip. We did two days' work at Phnom Penh in Cambodia, building a path at the youth prison. We then visited Singapore before catching a bus to Kuala Lumpur in Malaysia before returning to Singapore again. What a great trip.

I was reading the paper today which mentioned Stephen Hawking and I know that I will meet him.

How? God told me. Why? I don't know.

I won't let Him down.

29 July 2004

It's the end of the first week of the last term of my third year. I never thought I would get this far. I am still waiting on my appraisal for Church History that I failed because I was absent too many times.

My relationship with my kids is incredible. I still yell and scream sometimes and I am working through it. But we are together and I love them very much.

I don't know what I am going to do at the end of the year, maybe start that book about my life, before and after becoming a Christian. Why not? I will pray about it and God will tell me. I have to organise two speaking engagements, one at Riverview and I thought I might speak again at the Banksia Hill Detention Centre.

2 August 2004

I have been thinking about selling the house and buying a block of land so if we go to England, we will have property here for when we return. I will ask for the Lord's direction.

13 August 2004

I posted off the forms to England the other day, now I have to wait and see what they say. If us moving to Pommieland is not God's Will, I am sure He will close the doors. I get frustrated when I study, trying to find the information. I don't know why, but if the course outline tells me do one thing, that's all I do. I am not a studious person and I sit here and ask myself how I made it this far. I appealed the decision about Church History and they decided that I would pass the unit if I completed one extra assignment, so another good result there.

21 August 2004

I have heard back from Ellel Ministries in England, and it looks like God decided it wasn't what He had planned for me. I received an email from them saying there was no family accommodation and that I could go there if I could pay to do the course.

That would have cost me too much.

I will keep looking at options that come up and go. The lesson learned here is to keep things to myself until they are confirmed.

I know I have a lot more growing to do, both mentally and spiritually. During the past two days in prayer, I have felt His wonderful presence and I told Him how much I loved Him. I broke out in song.

I love Him so much!

24 August 2004

I went to see Glen in Canningvale Prison the other day and he told me he had been under surveillance by Federal Police on the outside. Everything Glen told me was similar to what I went through. So many weird things happened to me back then and now the same things are happening to him. I know God did awesome work in my life and the change in me is because of Him. There was someone there and nothing will make me think otherwise!

29 August 2004

I visited Jan from Prison Fellowship to see if there was something I could do. Since England has fallen through, I want to start something, I just don't know what.

Every second Wednesday, I am starting a group to help each other grow in what God is doing in our lives. I pray that the blessings of God are upon us.

1 September 2004

Yesterday, I held my first Growth Group session, just four of us including me. We want to try to work with God as He changes us. I enjoyed seeing people touched and inspired. God's hand is upon us and He will lead us.

I look at my boys and I love them so much, I want them to love me always. I wish Tosha-Lena could be in my life a lot more, but maybe that will change over time.

9 September 2004

I am not feeling good at the moment, the last three months of my course have been the hardest so far. No doors are being opened by God. I feel that I am very childish in some respects. I am happy, but not happy. I am happy about what the Lord has done so far in my life, and unhappy because I am not sure where it is all heading. Many parts of my life — my thoughts, my speech and the way I carry myself around church members — I still feel different from them. What if I let God down?

I must be going through another growth stage. One day at a time.

23 September 2004

I nearly had a punch-up with Ruben in class today. He told me to be quiet in class and it went from there.

Lots of things are not going well for me at the moment.

Some examples of this are:
- Receiving an $8k tax bill
- Having to find a school for Rhyan, meaning Pete needs to change schools too
- Not knowing where God is leading me

4 October 2004

We have to pay extra tax ($2.5k) every three months for the next few years on top of the normal tax payment of $8k from last year having received that information from the ATO.

So far, the cell I have started has met three times. It is all going great, being able to see the changes in our lives, with God's presence being with us each time.

I found a church down at Bunbury to preach at, I just have to organise a day to go there, God will let me know.

Only two months left of my final year!! Wow, ehh!!

Never thought I would do the three years. I am not who I used to be without Him, I had no purpose. I often think of the dreams that He sent me, they seem so far away. You could even say they were unbelievable, but that is from my viewpoint. I love Him so much!!

12 October 2004

What is wrong with me? I miss God's presence, I am going through another spiritually dry spell. Little Pete is sick with a high temp and he doesn't look too good. I look at him and see his little personality developing, man I love him so much.

Being a Dad is such a challenge when mine let me down, I do miss that relationship with my parents.

Have I let God down? I still say silly things without thinking.

What about the dreams He has given me? He is not a man who should lie. God **DOES NOT** lie.

Why am I not normal? I struggle when I am around others. I am happy with just the company of my wife and kids, is there more I should be doing? I am all over the place, I wouldn't use me if I was God.

There is not a word that can express my love for Him. Love is too small a word.

What then?

17 October 2004

I am scaring my kids, I am being too strict. How do I be a good dad where my kids will just walk up to me and tell me they love me?

I know I should play games with them, but that's not me. I can't stop using my past as an excuse for my future. I keep saying to myself that because I didn't have a dad, I don't know how to be a dad.

From today onwards, I am going to ask God to help me to hold my tongue and to be a better father. It's the boys' birthdays this week and I should be making it a special time, not being an ogre.

3 November 2004

Pastor Ed came to Riverview today, giving a prophecy over me about God blessing me, guiding me to take the name of Jesus into the corporate world. He said that I would be running a big business and helping lots of people. Pastor Ed said that the number 4 was going to be significant in my life.

I prayed for confirmation when I got home, some of what he says confirms in my spirit. I have always had a deep-down feeling that one day I would have a lot of money and be helping people. If this ever comes about, it will **ONLY** happen if God does it.

Let it be — I just need confirmation.

15 November 2004

Yesterday, I gave my testimony at the Bunbury Christian Outreach Centre. What a flop. I got all emotional and forgot what I was supposed to say. I got better as I went on. I honestly felt that God was not with me and that He left me alone to do it. I didn't prepare properly and I feel like saying "Never again."

Why has He left me? Why does He not talk to me? I don't feel His presence like I normally do.

21 November 2004

Today was a special day, my little big man Pete got baptised!!! And to make it even more special was that I was the one who baptised him with Mary-Anne at Point Walter Reserve Jetty! I look at my boys and I love them so much. I wish Tosha lived with me because without her, I don't feel complete.

Only two weeks left of Bible College!! I feel that I have let God down a little by not studying more. Maybe I shouldn't have started the business.

On a positive note, without Bible College, I wouldn't have this change come over my life.

My God is an awesome God!! I don't know where my life is taking me, but God does.

When in a fix: *Philippians 4:5-6*

24 November 2004

I love my boys and my beautiful little girl, Tosha-Lena. One day, kids, if you ever read this, just know I love you. Tosha, I think of you every day, I love you so much.

Just know that Jesus Christ is real. To be loved by Him will give you purpose. Please get to know Him. Don't do your life without Him.

30 November 2004

Exams today. Hebrews this morning, and tomorrow I have World Religion and Leadership. The end of three years, wow! Never in my wildest dreams did I think I would get this far.

I have asked the Lord four questions this morning:
- What do I do now? Focus on my business?
- Have I let Him down in regard to study in this last year?
- What study does He want me to do regarding those dreams He gave me (public speaking, travel, more Bible College etc.)?
- Are my dreams still alive? God does not lie, if He said they will happen, they will happen.

I finally get my normal driver's licence today, I have never really had one. How amazing is that?

12 December 2004

What is my purpose now I have finished my three years of Bible College? I have asked God for direction, but I have not seen it. The anticipation within me is strong. Maybe He has shown me, but I didn't know what it was. My business is fully booked right up until Christmas and then past it. Things are going very well with that.

Discovery is being moved from next year to 9 am on Sundays, do I stay there? I honestly feel like I have let the Lord down, otherwise, He would have fitted me in somewhere.

Growth Group is going well, all the guys are getting a lot out of the fortnightly sessions.

Kids, if you ever read this, Jesus loves you, He is real. We will live forever. Please get to know Him so we can be together. If it wasn't for God, I would have spent the rest of my life in jail.

I am sorry if I haven't been the perfect Dad, but if you could feel my heart, how much I love you all: Tosha-Lena, Peter and Rhyan. He is the king of all kings.

I love you, Tosha — just because you did not grow up in my house, you always grew up in my heart. I love you very much.

Pete, my little teddy bear — you are a walking barrel of love, I look at you and tears of love fill my heart. I love you, son.

Rhyan, you're a champion — the world is your footstool, my little man with the beautiful personality, you will go far, my son. I love you.

I know that one day you will all read this, it is all true what I saw in the sky and on the ground.

God loves you — I will see you again in eternity — Love Dad.

21 December 2004

Nine more days to go in the year and I think of all the changes that have happened since 23 September 2001, a little over three years ago.

We are going away for four days, me, Amanda and the boys. Looking forward to some quality time, although I know I let me past hinder me from moving forward. I have prayed to God about this, about helping me be a good dad. It's sad that Tosh can't come!!!

27 December 2004

We just got back from our trip. We stayed at Club Capricorn in Two Rocks for two nights and Jurien Bay for one night. We are planning to spend the day at Adventure World.

I walk around during the day and I can't seem to meet the desire in my spirit to be with Jesus. I crave His presence, His touch, His love, His company, His everything. Just to sit in my room telling Him how much I love Him and to feel His presence.

My sister Cheree was on the phone yesterday, telling me how she believes in Jesus. I am hoping that Jesus reaches down and opens her heart as He has mine.

2 January 2005

What a start to the year! I visited Uncle Lloyd in hospital and I led him to the Lord. He prayed the sinner's prayer. I thank God for answering my prayers because I have been praying for Uncle Lloyd for the past three years.

13 January 2005

I don't get to spend as much time in the morning with God as I would like. I think about Him every day. Why am I still mowing lawns? So many questions and few answers. I emailed Tim from Banksia Hill a few weeks ago but no reply yet. God has it under control, I will wait on Him.

21 January 2005

I am so confused. The way I came to know Jesus was so powerful. I spoke to Kelly-Ann and she told me how she was placed in Graylands for looping out or did she see what I saw?

I know that the drugs I was on made me loop out, and I also know I did see what I saw. I don't think anyone would want my brain or to be in my head. I might start my Hep C treatment soon which will knock me around a bit, but better than feeling the way I do now.

28 January 2005

I have been stressing out deciding where to serve. I plan to continue with Discovery and to start making prison visits to Acacia Prison. I will try it out and see how it goes, I don't know if God wants me to do this or not.

7 February 2005

Kelly-Anne has pulled out of church for more than one reason, most of which don't make sense to me. I am enjoying my Discovery time. I had Growth Group on Thursday and Raul didn't show up; no call, nothing. It was the same with ushering, he didn't even bother to call. If people are not going to be committed, what can I do? Every day, I thank Jesus for what He has done in me. I miss the closeness that we had when I was in Bible College. I just need solid direction!!

12 February 2005

Last night, I spoke to about 20 people at Riverview. At first, I was nervous, but I got better as it went along. Toastmasters is on every Monday night and I plan to go from tomorrow night. I feel like I am out in the desert at the moment as far as God is concerned. Every morning when I pray, I miss His presence, yet I know He got me here and He will get me further. The cry in my heart is "Lord, have your way in me," and I am prepared to go through whatever I have to if I am to be the person He wants me to be.

25 February 2005

I can't seem to relax around my kids. I love them, but I scream all the time. I want to be normal except I let the small things get to me. With any luck, I will start to chill out, I don't want to hurt them. I love them so much. Work is very busy. I am not sure what we are working towards yet, but **God does!!** He has brought me so far, words cannot describe my love for Him.

8 March 2005

I am busy with work, I volunteer as an usher on Saturdays and lead on Sunday mornings. I was going to lead Prison Fellowship, but I passed it up. Feeling slightly lost. Everything seems so rushed like at Growth Group where I feel that I am not preparing very well for the sessions.

I seem to be all over the shop. I am not happy when I am yelling at my boys. God will let me know what He wants me to do from here.

25 March 2005
Work has exploded, with us picking up two day-care centres, building a second trailer to carry the ride-on. I feel sorry for the kids when we work on weekends. Peter and Rhyan have started rugby training on Thursday and they play on Sundays. I had to pull out of Discovery so I could be there for them. I wish I could do more, but it is hard to change who I am but I will continue to try! I miss not serving God and talking to people about Jesus. I know His plans for me are still alive. Maybe I am just writing the second half of the book, the good part. Today was Good Friday and man, I love Him, words cannot express how I feel ... He is!!

17 April 2005
My service to the church has dwindled to ushering on Saturday nights and that is all! I feel like I am serving only myself by building my business. I thought that maybe because I don't fit in well with people, I have separated myself from God's Will. I can honestly say I have no friends. I spend my time with Amanda, my closest and best friend, I love her so much. Mum rang me the other day and told me about her dad, Grandpop, having to have his toes cut off because gangrene has set in. He probably doesn't have long to live and she asked me to say something at his funeral when he does pass away. How do you honour a man who spent most of it at the bar?

This life is just a stepping stone to the next.

22 April 2005
Gran rang me this morning to say Grandpop (Billy Baker) might only have two weeks' to live so I went to see him. He had trouble speaking but I prayed with him, leading him in a prayer to ask Jesus to be his

Lord and he did. God raised Jesus from the dead. I know I will see Grandpop again in Heaven.

26 April 2005
Grandpop passed away yesterday at 5.30 pm. I went and prayed with Mum, Uncle Lloyd and Gran.

RIP Billy Baker — 5 March 1929 to 25 April 2005, 76 years old.

8 May 2005
I was talking to a mate at church about God's provision. He shared his testimony of how God had opened doors for him in his business life, exactly what has been happening to us. We just picked up another contract worth more than $20k a year. I know it was God who has provided. As long as I walk in his ways, He has and will go before me to lay down my path. Eight weeks until our trip to Hong Kong.

18 May 2005
We have so much work on, it's hard to balance it all out. I start my day with God, but I feel that it isn't enough. I miss that closeness we had when I was studying. I am taking Pete to Bali next week, he knows where we are going, but he doesn't know when.
I'm going to pretend I am taking him to school, but instead, we will go to the airport. That will spin him out.

29 May 2005
A bit of reflection on what is happening. Spiritually, everything is okay, but it could be better. We work hard, six days a week, and I have not had quality time with the Lord like I used to. My focus is just on my business while the other students who graduated are working and helping in places like churches and hostels.

I am facing difficulties in my relationships and friendships outside of my immediate family. I really have **NO** friends, feeling uncomfortable around anyone other than my wife and kids. I don't mind it at all, but I ask myself if I am normal. God is my closest friend. I will always start my day with Him, no matter what, until the day my spirit knocks on heaven's door.

I leave for Bali on Tuesday with Little Peter, planning to relax and make sure he has a holiday with me he will never forget.

I look at my kids and I want nothing more than to be a good dad.

26 June 2005

Amanda and I go to China for ten days soon. I can't wait. I have put another van on the road a couple of weeks ago. The turnover for our business has exceeded $200k for the year so far, more than $70k more than last financial year. We now have two fully operational vans.

I miss the times I spent in the Lord's presence, overwhelmed by Him. People cannot fathom the change He has brought to my life, as well as to my wife and kids. It is the life I always dreamed of.

30 June 2005

This morning, I woke up to find my little man next to me, cuddling me and not pulling away from me, just like in my dreams. The way I used to be, my kids would not come near me but now there is love in our house. Thanks be to Jesus Christ. Three days until China!

17 July 2005

Returned from a great trip to China. Flew from Perth to Hong Kong, stayed there for two days, completing a ten-kilometre walk of the Great Wall. Went to Shanghai for four days, returned to Hong Kong via train. We had a two-berth sleeper, the trip took 24 hours. Awesome.

I start every day in prayer and in God's Word. Lately, I have been going through the motions, forgetting what I have read before the end of the chapter. Despite this, I will never stop starting my day with Him. I will try to find another way to draw Him nearer.

27 July 2005

We have put our business in the paper for sale. With any luck, it will sell fast. I plan to fly to Karratha soon to check out the situation there as we want to work for someone else for a while. What better place than up north with all the expansion projects happening?

The Bible says that Man might plan his path, but that God directs his steps! I miss His overwhelming love/presence!

My relationship with my family is better than it has ever been. I feel so selfish, I look at all He has done for me and I feel I am living my life for me instead of for those around me.

1 August 2005

We have three people interested in buying the business. This is when my doubts kick in, but I believe the Lord will send me in the right direction.

8 August 2005

Karratha was a good trip, but it is expensive to live there, rent-wise. I have an offer of $60k for the business, but I have told the potential buyer I will take $70k and we keep the ute. Waiting on his response.

During my prayer time, my mind wanders, but I will press on as the Lord will never leave me. Maybe when the business sells, I will have more time for Him. I pray that the decisions I am making over the coming months will be the right ones.

I hope to get involved at Banksia Hill or in a jail, let God lead me. I have so much to be thankful for, just a cuddle from my kids is a gift from God. After all He has given me over the past four years, I have no reason to complain ... forgiveness being the best.

14 August 2005

We have accepted the offer of $70k on the business, despite it being a low price. I feel like I am entering a new chapter of my life. What that will be, I am not sure.

Should I:

- Move to Karratha to work, getting more qualifications before I go or:
- Start a landscaping company using the proceeds of the sale of my lawn-mowing business or:
- Find a place to serve where I can help others change their lives

I will pray on these three options and trust that the Lord will lead me in the direction He wants me to go.

17 August 2005

Life is like a rollercoaster. We thought we had the business sold yesterday, planning to meet the buyer to get a deposit, when they pulled out. I had even drawn up a contract for the sale.

I prayed to the Lord yesterday that if the sale of the business wasn't what He had planned for me, that He would make the buyer's finance fall through.

The buyer rang me just before 10 am, telling me that the funds would not be released by the bank. And that the sale would need to be called off until he can raise the money! Is that God or what??

So instead of selling, I am planning to take the business one step further by buying a 2002 Iveco Diesel van with only 165,000 kms on the clock. It's worth $48k, I got it for $21k. Now all I need is staff.

I plan to stand on *Proverbs 3:5-6* and trust in the Lord with every part of me. His plan for my life is coming together, I feel it.

24 August 2005

I just paid $25k to get the van, the signwriting and, of course, the mower. All on credit card, mind you, but I am sure with the Lord's help, we will have that paid off in two months. I have a feeling that the next step of the business is getting a commercial property close to Como in South Perth. Now we have three vans going, I need to find a place close by to save on time and travel costs.

God has answered another prayer and has given us Selwyn, a worker who I really trust! He starts from the beginning of September. God is leading us, I am sure of that.

Next:
1. A workshop with a yard and exposure — Welshpool?
2. Software system put in place
3. A fourth van for mowing

Thank you, Jesus Christ!

29 August 2005

I have been thinking about Mum and Dad lately. I have not spoken to Dad since his mum's funeral three years ago. I have questions to be answered. He mentioned his new job at the time, and yet he never asked me about Bible College! He just kept talking to me like nothing has happened. The same with Mum. I never ring her, and when I do have to talk to her on the phone, she always finishes with "I love you," expecting me to say it in return which makes me mad. Especially when I can tell she had had a few beers.

I think I will write to both of them, asking them to write down about how they met and their version of events up to now. That might give me closure. I do have to forgive them, but how? I don't want them going to their graves without a relationship with me or knowing Jesus. I will ask for God's Hand to be upon what I do.

15 September 2005

There are just not enough hours in the day, we are that busy. We have just picked up another hotel contract and a few blocks of flats. At this rate, we can increase our services with a new van every six months. I often think of the times I spent with God when I was studying. I really miss those early days of being a Christian and feeling His presence.

23 September 2005

Four years old today! Spiritually, that is. The day four years ago when I walked into the New Life Church in Morley when I gave my heart to Jesus is memorable. No going back. I wish I could fix a few things, like the way I speak to my kids, I **always** seem to be so grumpy and I can't stand it. I do it without thinking and I hope to be able to change my ways before they move out of home.

My prayer time at the moment seems routine, not devotion. My prayer is that He leads me back to that secret place of worship and devotion. I **WILL NOT** ever start my day without Him, **EVER**!!

18 October 2005

Lots of stuff happening lately. Peter had his tenth birthday last week, Rhyan's sixth birthday is today, and Tosha turns 17 next week. Time is moving forward and I'm starting to feel old. My prayer for all of them is to know Jesus Christ and dwell in the House of the Lord all the days of their lives, in this life and in the one to come.

The business now has three full-time staff members and we recently picked up some more large jobs. My personal time with the Lord is lacking. The important thing is that I am where He wants me to be.

12 November 2005

I have noticed a change in the way I speak to the boys, particular Peter who is getting closer to being a teenager. I need to speak to him with respect, both privately and in front of others. God is working on me. I don't deserve all these blessings: my wife, my kids, my house, the business and the equipment, etc. I am debt-free except for the house.

I have been praying for my grandmother and I feel that He is at work in her life right now.

What can I say except I love Him so much!

26 November 2005

Reflection time — November nearly over, December upon us. It seems like yesterday when I finished Bible College. How awesome is God!

Business continues to improve, with the last two months' turnover being the same as the entire previous year. We are thinking about buying that fourth van to put on the road, probably in February or March.

The boys are growing fast, Rhyan's personality is starting to develop, they are both becoming little men. I haven't heard from Tosh for a couple of weeks, she never answers the phone. I love her so very, very much.

Every day is a gift from God. No matter what, I walk with Jesus every day of my life.

8 January 2006

It feels like years since I wrote in this journal. Work is booked two months in advance at the moment. We are advertising for another staff member.

When I start my day with God, I feel that I walk with Him still, but I miss the times when I felt His presence fall from Heaven. I am still working on being a better Dad. My temper is still not good, I carry on a bit, but God will help me through it. The last thing I want is for my boys to hate me when I am old.

Every day is a gift from God which I don't deserve. He chose to reach down and pluck me out from the Gates of Hell. He has stood me on a mountain and poured so many blessings on my life, to sit with my wife and kids at the table, to go on holidays, to have a house and a business!

Thank you, Jesus!

25 January 2006

Where is it all going? Every day is the same, what is the purpose? I can't see a change in the near or distant future, all I have to hang onto are the dreams that God gave me. I love Him so much, I think about him all day, about my dreams for my future.

1. Meeting Stephen Hawking
2. In charge of an organisation
3. Travelling the world, telling people how Jesus changed my life
4. I climb through a window and get shot — my life ends, not good!

I look at God's perfection, His flawlessness, and then I look at myself. How unworthy I am of all He has done for me. Thank God for Jesus! My prayer is that the Lord would have His Way in me all the days of my life.

Amen.

1 April 2006

It's been a while since I wrote in this book. I just paid $54k cash for a new Toyota Hilux 4x4, and I can't imagine telling the old Me about that. He would have laughed. I do feel like a new chapter of my life is about to start!

We sold the gardening/lawnmowing side of the business for $160k — we plan to pay off the house, put some in the bank, then we will be debt-free.

What next, I wonder?

I registered the name, Platinum Landscaping, to begin trading as of the first of July. We also plan to buy a bit of land past Wanneroo to build on eventually. This month, the business turned over $70k, well on its way to $500k this financial year. We used to borrow a lawnmower when we started, now we have four full-time staff and we are flat out.

Wow, God!

I still get customers from the pamphlets that I sent out. Most of the work I have is from God, I can tell story after story about how He has given us large commercial customers in a way only He could. Most people don't believe my stories when I tell them, but I know that God brought it to us.

In one month's time, I will own my home and be debt-free. Thank you, thank you, God, in just three years. Amazing!

I miss my encounters with Him during my Bible College studies, I still start my day with His Word, but I want Him to permeate my being, to serve Him full-time. He is my dad, my mate, my closest friend, the lover of my soul, my inner being. He is my everything.

10 May 2006

Platinum Landscaping is close to being up and running, with two vehicles paid for in cash, what a spin out. All the pamphlets, business cards, presentation folders, signage and letterheads are being done ready for a July start when we return from India.

We made an offer on an office on a two-acre block in High Wycombe. We will end up with a $250k mortgage, but that's okay, a large shed can be built which we can live in until we can afford to build a house.

I am still yelling at the kids, I am so unworthy. Lord, help me to hold my tongue and to be good to others. Help me to be a light in a dark place. I want to bring glory to God, help me be all you want me to be. I love you.

Amen.

23 June 2006

When my kids read this, I want them to know how much I love all three of them and that thinking of them brings tears of joy to my eyes. If it wasn't for Jesus, we wouldn't be together, I would be in jail. The key to getting to know God is to walk in His Ways, let Him help you. The important thing is to be teachable and obedient to what He asks of you.

Peter and Rhyan, I am so very, very sorry I am always yelling at you. I know it's no excuse, but it just comes out no matter how I try to stop it. Please know I love you and I am sorry.

Tosha-Lena, life has many turns. It is sad you couldn't grow up under the same roof as me, but you know in your heart and have known your whole life that I love you. I am sorry I have left you with some bad memories. I have many from my childhood and that is the last thing I wanted for you. *Proverbs 3:5-6*

Love Dad.

We are off to India in two weeks, it should be good. I think often of the shotgun going off — I wonder if it is this trip? I pray Amanda will come home safe.

I love you, Amanda.

31 July 2006

We got back from India in one piece, despite being close to some bombs going off nearby to where we were staying. It was a little hairy, I felt like getting on the plane and coming home when that happened.

Tomorrow is the official start of the new business, with a big landscaping job beginning. Amanda and I went and paid off our home loan last Friday, it took us just two and a half years!

How can I thank God enough?

5 September 2006

I just returned from two weeks in Melbourne, having taken Uncle Lloyd there to see his kids who he hasn't seen for forty years. Uncle Lloyd was born in 1913, being 93 years of age. I also took Pete with me.

It was good to see the joy on Uncle Lloyd's face when he saw his kids one last time before he moves on.

I still feel plugged into God, but then again, He also feels distant. Where am I spiritually? I feel like a scrambled egg, all over the place. I will press on and not give up.

I enjoy the times when Amanda is getting the kids ready for school, when we are all together as a family. We are still waiting on the two-acre block, but if it doesn't happen before the contract deadline, then we will have to look at what direction we will go.

Proverbs 3:5-6

12 November 2006

I visited Acacia Prison for the first time last week as part of the Ministry Team. It was good, I got up and spoke for a couple of minutes about how God can change their lives. I see a need for someone to help these guys prior to their releases to set boundaries so they won't go back to jail. There are things like Spiritual Discipline, Prayer, God's Word and Church Communities. I would also try to identify weaknesses such as pubs, friends, drugs, etc.

I have prayed and asked God about it but no reply. He will answer me when He is ready. Over the past six months, I don't remember hearing from Him at all!

Platinum Landscaping is up and running, with work booked until January next year. I am still doing Discovery on Sundays at Riverview, but I am not too sure for how much longer. I would like to work in the prisons, but waiting on God is frustrating.

We are trying to get Peter into a private school, Swan Christian College. We just booked our tickets to go to Tokyo, Japan in July 2007.

Can't wait. I have started having a few beers after work, they go down well. Apart from the beers, I can't imagine what else in my life would cause Him to turn His back on me. Does He want me to serve in the prisons? Is there anything I am doing that I shouldn't be?

1 January 2007
Start of another year, who knows what it will hold? We spent a week down at Mandurah and I would have to say it was the best Christmas ever. As a family, we started the day in Scripture reading about Jesus's birth, held hands and thanked Him and took part in communion before the kids opened their presents. Then I went to my mum's place and it was the first time in 15 years that I spent Christmas with family, it was good.

At Acacia, I plan to teach a course to build on the fire for God that I see there. I think this is my calling, and it has partially been approved by the Prison Chaplain, Allan F, and I will also be involving Phillip B at Riverview about what I have in mind.

7 January 2007
Phillip rang me on Tuesday about preaching at all services this weekend on the topic of making decisions. On Saturday evening, I spoke to around 500 to 600 people for over seven minutes, what a seven minutes it was! God moved through that place. How great is my God! Looking forward to the other three services today!

1. Give Him glory in all circumstances.
2. Say what He wants said.
3. It is not about me and my life.
4. It is about Jesus and what He can do in our lives.
5. Even in my weak and broken state, He can work through us.
6. The Bible says let all that has breath praise Him.
7. God is true to His promise.

After the service last night, many people came up to me and thanked me for what God had done in their lives, how He renewed passion, hope and direction. My prayer this day forward is that with **ALL** my heart, mind, body, breath, spirit, soul and movement, I praise the name of Jesus in the hearts and minds of all who I come across.

I pray that the words you hear from me are the ones you want to hear, that you carry the words that come from my lips and make them your own. Place them **DEEP** in the hearts and minds of those who hear them. Lord, be magnified, move through Church today in power, make tears flow, hearts repent, cause decisions to be made to follow You wholeheartedly.

Jesus = the name above every name.

Last week, a good friend of mine, Darren H told me he has cancer in his lymph nodes, all through his body, so he is going to die. Chemo will do him no good and radiation might prolong his life. He has three girls, what can I say? What could you say, how do you help? Darren's wife is not handling it too well, he is only 39.

19 January 2007

My course in Acacia has been approved, I will be Associate Chaplain when my commitment to Discovery ends. Maybe one day a week from next Thursday. Is this me? Am I trying to move myself forward, is this where God is leading me? Do I belong in the prisons?

27 January 2007

I had a meeting with Allan Shepherd of *Broken Chain Ministries* and *Agape Ministries* and I told him of my plan to start an NFP organisation and he offered the current organisation or the name if I wanted it. It's already set up as a tax-deductible NFP entity, saving me the process of applying to get it approved.

He has not only offered me this but the free use of the church, an office and phone, etc. I have approached Duane about this offer to see what he thinks. God's Hand is upon this, I know. There are a few details to work out, I can now plan on starting at Acacia Prison in the second term of this year.

13 February 2007

Things are moving slowly, I haven't heard from Allan F, the Prison Chaplain since our meeting. I am planning to cancel my upcoming meeting with Duane on Saturday as we are moving and I feel uncomfortable going to his house to discuss business.

God is amazing — I make mistakes and sin on a daily basis, and yet He loves me. We are in the second week of Discovery and I love it, I love watching the people cry as they discover God.

We had a baptism the other day, and it was a pleasure and a privilege to be a part of another person's journey discovering Jesus. The Holy Spirit touched lives and I feel that my life must be used by God to achieve His plan. Let it be. If I must die, let it be about Jesus and what He wants in the world, not just about me and my family.

I don't ask for business, I don't ask for riches or blessings, I ask for the eyes of the blind to be opened, those who do not yet know Him, the people who are yet to experience His Love. *Psalm 111*

4 March 2007

We moved from High Wycombe to Applecross, a blessing. A two-storey joint right on Melville Beach Parade, right on the water. Yesterday was the last day of Discovery and in a way, I am sad, I don't know if I am meant to start up the prison sessions or not, as I have no contact with the Chaplain whatsoever. It was only two months ago that I got to stand before Riverview Church and give my testimony. God has got it covered, I must trust in Him and wait.

We're all off to Bali, all of us plus Tosha on March 17. My mate Darren looks like he is going to be okay, he lost all his hair including his beard, so we will just have to pray and see how he goes.

6 April 2007

We had an awesome time in Bali, a whole week together, something for us all to remember for the rest of our lives. I completed a two-day security course at Acacia, and I am doing sessions on two days a week for the next fortnight. I am also at Wooroloo Prison on Sunday as part of the Chaplaincy Team. I am looking forward to it with great expectation.

Some bad news, Darren probably won't make it after all. He is very scared and I can't imagine what he is going through. God wants Mankind to be well, but when it is not meant to be, we should not let doubt enter our mind. Stand up! Believe and you will be healed. Am I like one of Job's mates who gave Job the wrong advice?

My advice to Darren was to take stock of his situation, look at his life, putting into place steps that will enable him to leave something behind for his wife while he is still able.

They have tried everything, but even the radiation isn't working. So now he is having palliative care in his home.

I don't want to be Job's mates, I don't want to plant seeds of doubt in his mind — but what if — what if — what if he leaves it too late to leave behind something special for birthdays and special occasions?

Me, I would leave:

- A message video for Amanda, telling her to get another partner and not to live alone, that it would be okay
- Leave messages on tape for my kids for their weddings and other special occasions
- Something to let them know regularly throughout their lives that I loved them.

What can I say?

29 April 2007

I have been going to Acacia twice a week for the past month. I have written a course: *Keys to Change* that will start up in mid-May, running for ten weeks. I am also going ahead with the ministry called *Broken Chains,* and I am having a vision/prayer night at my house around the same time next month, sharing what we expect to undertake.

God is so great, He has brought key people across my path who are planning to come along with what I am about to do.

They are Belinda, Duane, Barbara and John from Riverview; Alan, Brett and Brian from Acacia; and Joy and Tony from Prison Fellowship.

There are many things that *Broken Chain Ministries* (BCM) will attempt to address, like the following:
- Biblical Foundation/ Fellowship/Church
- Pre-release Assessments
- Employment/Training
- Home/Accommodation

I feel strongly that this is what God had in store for me, who am I to hold Him back? The work of the Holy Spirit must be powerful in all our group sessions and in the lives of the BCM participants if the Ministry is to be life-changing.

29 July 2007

A lot has happened since I last wrote in my journal. I have been up at Acacia now for a couple of months and I have since found out I am not a teacher. Steve W has been doing the past three sessions and the boys enjoy his style.

My best mate Darren H passed away last week — 22 July 2007 — leaving behind his wife and three girls, aged 10, 7 and 5. The funeral is tomorrow. Amanda and I just returned from another overseas trip on the 21 July.

This time we did Singapore, Malaysia, Phuket, Bangkok, Kuala Lumpur and back to Singapore. The kids went to the farm for two weeks. Pete is becoming a teenager and Rhyan is a mature little man. I love them so much. It blows me away to cuddle them and to say, "I love you, son."

Thank God I am not where I was six years ago. I miss Tosha a lot, but she has her own life, starting work up in the mines as a Geo's Assistant, making real good money.

We had a vision night a couple of months ago, a really good turnout of around 26 people, choosing a working party of six to put together a board for BCM! I can't help asking: "Where is it all going?"

I am trying to build fellowships with those seeking God for a change in Acacia with my twice-weekly sessions. Every participant in the group responds differently in the group sessions. Do I want to be there? Yes! Why? I want them to know Jesus and know that another life is possible through Jesus.

God moves so slow, it's not happening fast enough for me. I wish He would do stuff in a mighty Way. Sometimes I feel like telling everyone to piss off! It's too hard. It's going too slow.

Working three days a week along with ministry is a slight pain because I like to give it all when I get into it. It's just too slow. Is it me? Have I done something wrong? I honestly feel like throwing it all in. All I have to do is switch it all off, not care what other people think. But I **CAN'T**. I can't. Because I am where God wants me.

2 September 2007

Today is Father's Day and I am blessed with my two boys who brought me breakfast in bed and cards they made me. Peter bought me a Hillsong CD, Rhyan gave me a $2 gift and an awesome card. My beautiful and amazing daughter, Tosha-Lena is coming over to see me tonight. Wow! Lord God — I want to thank you for letting me feel the cuddles of my children, to thank you just for hearing the words "I love you" from their lips. God, you have taken me from a place of sorrow to a place of joy and blessing.

How can I thank you? Tears fill my eyes as the pain in my heart for wanting to love you more comes to mind. I love you, Lord.

I cannot express my love, I can't put it into actions or words. I do not deserve what you have given me. Please let me have the chance to stand before thousands to tell of your great and awesome love.

Psalm 33

26 October 2007

I have just finished reading *Psalm 42* and in it, David praises God even though everything around him is going wrong — I will do the same. I miss the swirl of the Holy Spirit within me. I am still going to Acacia and I am about to start a course in J Block (Protection), running from 29 October until 11 December — called Discovery!

I have a few blokes I met up with on Saturday/Sunday nights, we are planning a Bible Study or something similar for Tuesday nights. I cannot see where this is going and I feel inadequate. I pray that this is what God wants.

28 November 2007

Where do I start? I went to a prison fellowship concert at Wooroloo for about 50 prisoners, enjoying the preachers and the band, when the preachers asked if we wanted to go pray.

Many of the prisoners wanted to go but didn't because the other prisoners would have made fun of them. One prisoner got up and boldly encouraged the others to stand up and go and pray. Only six or seven of them did.

Dreams:

The next morning, I awoke crying! Sobbing! I had experienced two dreams. In the first one, I was on a bed, with someone stroking my head and saying it was okay and not to worry. He was telling me God can see those who want to come to Him and not to worry. The second I woke up, I sobbed, I knew God was hurt when those prisoners didn't come to Him. It made Him sad, people around us have or can have a drawback influence on their lives. God wants all people to come forward. Last night, I saw 90% of people wanting to come to Jesus but they didn't because of what the others might say!

I rang the prison in the morning and asked to speak to the Assistant Superintendent and I shared my heart and vision with him. I mentioned wanting to come alongside Wooroloo's prisoners — both in and out of the prison — requesting complete access to the jail to walk and talk with the boys. He said yes.

God yesterday opened another door of a prison to me. Wow, with my background and a door has opened and I will start straight away! This morning I had two very vivid dreams. In the first one, I was travelling down a country road, with barely enough room for my truck. There was a person near the verge ahead of me pushing a wheelchair. As I drew nearer to the wheelchair, I slid off the road itself, taking the wheelchair onto the bull bar. I was only doing two or three kilometres an hour at the time, but the truck ran through a paddock, knocking down fences along the way. Incredibly, no-one was hurt. But when I went back to the person's home, their family tried to bribe me for the damages they had received, for them not to report the incident to the police. I paid them, but they then gave me some counterfeit money in return. When I woke up — God has told me **NOT** to lie and always tell the truth, lies will only reap negative consequences.

The second dream — I was preaching in an open space, a drive-in or something similar. Belinda from Riverview was there. I was telling the small crowd about my experiences, telling them about God's Word, His

Love, His Truth. It was not about Peter but about Jesus. More people came, crying as I spoke, and more and more people kept coming to listen.

When I woke up — God has told me that I must speak the truth and for it to be about Jesus, Jesus, Jesus, not about me. I have been called to proclaim His Word, to tell people the truth of the Gospel! I must always be humble and respectful of all God has laid before me, to walk in His ways without compromise.

6 January 2008

Already the sixth day of the new year! On 31 December, I told God, no more alcohol. So far so good.

I went to the prison to confront Alan, the Prison Chaplain after a two-week break. My first reaction is not to go back until he apologises, a big gamble as this would change the direction my life is going.

We went to Kalbarri for a week, good times spent with Amanda and the boys. All week, us fellas only wore shorts and Amanda took an interesting photo of the three of us from behind, pants dropped to the ground with our arms around each other. A boys' thing. Every day is a gift. Everything will work out as God has planned.

10 January 2008

Last Thursday, I went to the prison, wandering around the blocks telling people about the Bible Study sessions. Around eleven, I wandered into the Chaplaincy Office to get ready for lunch. Alan was there with Brett. To cut a long story short, I had to give up my security card which had the word 'Chaplain' on it. I told Alan I would not be back until a new card was issued.

Over the next few days, I thought about working there two days a week unpaid for the past eight months, but it's not about the money! It's the way the Prison Chaplain went about things, his demand that I give up the card. I emailed him, mentioning that I was not planning to return to Acacia.

Two days later, I received an email from him with an apology for the way he behaved. I feel this is not enough.

I am about to sell my business and intend to work full-time in the prisons voluntarily. My whole life is about to change. If the Prison Chaplain behaved like that once, he might treat me like that again! There's nothing to stop him.

The fire and desire to go to Acacia is gone, I honestly miss the prisoners and do not intend to go there until:
1. Alan apologises
2. I get a new security card
3. I get access to Acacia assured for 3-4 days per week
4. I get a set of keys

I expect a $10k deposit to arrive for the business sale tomorrow. No matter what happens at Acacia, I would like to try something new. I would like to give God this year.

We had our first get-together the other day for ex-prisoners which went well. I was planning to organise a sponsored walk to Albany for ex-prisoners and ex-drug users to raise awareness that there is more to life than drugs, crime, etc.

29 March 2008

A lot has happened since my last entry. I didn't end up selling my business after all. I am back at Acacia two days a week, working with Steve, John and Joy, we make a great team. Everything is okay with the Prison Chaplain, Alan. I get disheartened, as prisoners say one thing in jail, then when they get out, they do the opposite.

Last week, we bought a house in West Swan for $630k, nearly an acre. That should give me something to do with my spare time!

Today I am taking Little Pete, Gavin, Billy and Chook over to Rottnest Island for the night, should be good. Next month, Little Pete and me are going to Singapore, Malaysia, Phuket, Bangkok and Hong Kong. I am looking forward to spending time with him. I wish Rhyan would come, I think he will on the next trip. I love my boys so very much. I want to leave them with good memories. Please help me, God.

27 April 2008
Just got back, I enjoyed spending the two weeks with Pete and look forward to the day when Rhyan comes too. Before I left, we had put an offer in on that one-acre property with pool, stables, shed, etc. in West Swan. The offer has been accepted and we move in on 4 June. We borrowed $350k. The fire I had for the prison doesn't seem to be there anymore. I feel like I have let God down. I have been drinking over the past two weeks.

What do I do when I catch up with the boys on a night out? I am also disappointed with the lack of commitment shown to the organisation of the sponsored walk by some of the boys. They make me feel like I am tracking them down about the walk when I see them.

There are some Christian leaders within the prisoner group who do not see their potential to rise up and lead God's children. I think from next week, I will cut down my hours at the prison. I don't want to let God down, but I feel I am the wrong person for the job. I plan to continue to do my 'little bit' each week and pray that God will have mercy on me. I AM SO VERY, VERY SORRY!!

3 May 2008
I am still having 3-4 beers every night, I feel far from God, but I know He will never leave me.

- Has God called me to build my business? Are things falling into place? — Yes.
- Has God called me to minister at the prisons? Due to the access I have — Yes.

Therefore, I will continue to go up there one day a week and ask for God's grace and strength to sustain me. I have just read what I have written, stop feeling sorry for yourself.

Look what you **DO** have:
1. Jesus Christ!
2. An awesome wife and kids
3. A new house, cars, bike and boat
4. Money in the bank and being 100% debt-free
5. Lots of travel
6. Equipment for the business

I want for nothing and I still struggle. Sometimes I have a beer, I want to make a difference in people's lives, but some of the words that come out of my mouth are not right.

My prayer — Lord Jesus, please forgive me, Lord, help me live for you, to helps others to know you, to walk in your Ways always, to let me shine! *Matthew 5:14*

Now I have to think about whether I am selfish. There are so many people out there with major problems who don't know Jesus.

Lord, help us!!

2 August 2008

I am reminded of an old dream I once had in Karnet Prison Farm, a dream where I was taken by angels up in the sky over the jail.

I looked down and yelled to the boys below, "God is real, Jesus loves you. Hey, look up!"

During my daily morning prayer, I felt affirmed that my place is within the prisons. My one concern is my need to have a beer or two at the end of the day. He wants me to stop, but I find it hard.

Amanda and I were ordained as pastors last week on 27 July by the ICAG (International Christian Ambassadors of God), giving legitimacy to small ministries such as ours. Much has happened, with Amanda and me recently returning from Vietnam, having had three overseas trips in the past few months.

18 January 2009
NOT GOING GOOD.

Over the past few months, I have been trying to get my drinking under control. I emptied a whole carton down the sink and told myself no more. Then the next 40-degree day came along and after a hard day at work, I had a beer. Then I started the cycle again, 3-4 beers each night after work, even after church on a Saturday, usually grabbing a few beers from the bottle shop on my way home. I can't stop at one or two, God Almighty knows it.

That's why He told me: Stop drinking, obey me, and feed my sheep!

The past 6-12 months have been the hardest to keep my spiritual discipline. All my excuses — I deserve it, I work hard, I only have it at home, I am not hurting anyone — don't cut it with God.

Please, please help me to stop, help me to obey you!

So many things on my mind, like how the attendances have dropped off for Bible Study sessions. I must be obedient.

I didn't go to church last night but stayed home (to have a beer). Both Amanda and I agree that having a beer at six or seven pm is not on! Around 7 pm, I started thinking I had let God down. I drank five beers, got a bit depressed and you guessed it, I thought about having a whack! Meth. I rang a few people and got some from a mate.

I have no grounds to justify my actions other than the beer. I must stop!

To live life in the presence of the Holy Spirit is so awesome. I had that for years, and now I want it back!! I have no real friends, only Amanda, my truly supportive wife. God will welcome her to Heaven one day as his good and faithful servant. I love her so much, I don't deserve her. I will remove all drugs and alcohol from the house and ask God for His help. Three times, God told me to give up pot, and I did. Three times, He told me to give up drinking, and I have tried, but haven't obeyed Him as yet.

NO GOOD.

I don't want to go back to my old life.

Help me so I can help others.

Serving God for the past 7 years, I have noticed a few things:
- The more you obey Him, the more you feel His hand on your everyday life.
- He acts in small ways, and yet you know it is Him.
- You must be patient, He works to His timetable, not yours.
- The choices I make have a flow-on effect, both positive and negative consequences.
- When you speak to those who want to listen, your words might sound silly to you, but not to them. God makes it so for those God wants to minister to.
- Life must be Christ-focused and centred.
- Jesus must come first.
- With obedience comes blessing.

I feel lost. I feel like He has left me to do my own thing because I didn't obey Him, I want Him back in my life: the joy, the passion, the fire, the anointing you feel when walking in His Will which is so incredible.

Will He give me another chance? Will He restore the Joy of His Salvation to me? I know I don't deserve it, but please. Amen.

It's been hard ministering to others when I am feeling so low myself.

2009 is a new year, it is after three-thirty am on 19 January.

I don't want to go back to my old life!

I need to remind my kids, I don't always mean to be angry and grumpy and short-tempered. I love you all so very much. My head is a battleground between the way I was brought up by Mum and Dad, the streets, the institutions, the drugs. My boys are lucky they have an awesome mum, same goes for Tosh Nosh — your mum turned out A1+. She chose to focus her life on giving you a good life and that was the main reason she left me. "Good job," I reckon. Praise God every day, talk to Him, read your Bible, thank Him. He always listens.

I think I mentioned that we bought a house in West Swan. In six months, I have taken out all the palms, put in an extra-high fence all the way around and erected a shed with a 32,000-litre water tank.

Also picked up a Bobcat for $22k, worth $50k. Plus a Scania tipper, too big for what I want to use it for, going to sign up for an Isuzu 2009 model, to use it to cart bobcats. We still have Ryan working for us, we do not deserve him. I plan to give him a company car with all the gear next week, he is moving house, and I think I will up his hourly rate.

In closing — I will obey God. I will keep trying, I will not give up, I will find somebody to speak to, I will trust God on His Word.

"HE WILL NEVER LEAVE ME NOR FORSAKE ME!"

8 February 2009
I think I broke down or had a mental breakdown, trying to do too much. Business, ministry, doing up the house, working seven days a week for the last couple of years.

I organised a mate, Dion, to come and paint a room, except when I got home, he had stripped the hallway, bathroom, laundry and toilet as well as one bedroom. He had also made a start on a second bedroom.

This sent me downwards into a mental spiral. I could not think, could not make decisions, could not even go to the toilet, my brain was in lockdown. I remember three times where I curled up into a ball and cried. Despite how I felt, I know God was with me.

Thanks be to Lord Jesus.

We have now made some serious choices about the direction of my life. We have laid off half of the staff, deciding to focus on landscaping and the prisons only. I feel God is pleased with these choices of mine. No more beers or drugs.

Last week, my brother-in-law, Callum, lost his daughter to a drug overdose. Gemma, Tosha's cousin, only 17 years old. So young, the funeral is this Wednesday.

Tosh — after the last few weeks, I feel we have been getting closer. I love you, please know it.

Pete — you are turning into a fine man, very responsible, never be afraid to show your love to either man or woman as love is life. Express it, that is the challenge.

Rhyan — God has a plan for you, you are a deep thinker, always try to keep Jesus as your resting place.

Amanda — next to Jesus, you are my rock. How on earth you put up with me, I will never know. I know I will die before you, waiting at the Gates of Heaven so we can enter together, if God is cool with that.

I love you all soooooooooooooo much!!

12 March 2009

The last two weeks have been life-changing for me. I have obeyed God by cutting down my business by half, only doing landscaping. I have been struggling with beer — no more. What I have gone through the past week, I never want to go through again.

Graham got married, and I had a few beers, went to the casino and did some drugs. God took His presence from me. The following day was Hell.

I curled up into a ball, crying out to God for forgiveness for what I did on the weekend. It seemed as if I were to die, life would go on for my wife and kids, it was like I didn't exist. The pain of being separated from God was more than I could handle. Why, oh why, do we not listen to God? I felt like I went through what Adam and Eve did in *Genesis 3*, being separated from their God.

Like David in *Psalm 6*, "I cried out to the Lord and He heard my cry for mercy." I have made an oath to God — I will obey Him.

25 April 2009

I have so much to write and know that I won't be able to get it all down on paper. Much like my previous entry, the last month has been mind-blowing and it has changed my life. I attended a four-day course with Brett, the chaplain from Acacia. I looked up to him like a father, but now I consider him to be a life-long friend and mate, a person who I will and can trust with all things.

The course was called Kairos, held at Mobilong Prison in Murray Bridge, S.A. From the day I arrived in South Australia, I was in God's presence. I arrived in Adelaide before Brett and stayed at a motel for one night alone before Brett and I drove to Murray Bridge.

Once we got there, all we received was love! I was blown away! We met the volunteers who worked with the prisoners, what a privilege to serve the Lord. I met the 24 participants taking part, I will be calling them 'Brothers in green' from this day forward. I felt at home with them.

At the end of the course, the 24 lives had all been impacted in some way through forgiveness. Forgiveness: for their closest loved ones, for the prison officers and for parents and mates who had let them down.

At the end of the four days, they were all in tears and forgave, despite what they had been through, no matter how tough their exteriors were, Jesus Christ worked through them.

A few prisoners who stuck in my mind were:
- Henry — doing life with still 12 years to go before he gets to the minimum, he works in the visitor centre.
- Peter — Like myself, he was raised in institutions and what he has been through in prison isn't good.
- Chris — Another lifer, and only 25 years old.
- Ang — What a bloke, I will never forget him. In and out of jails all his life, cut off the offender's penis after he raped his daughter
- Will —Grew up normal but then drugs stuffed up his life, this is who I was teamed up with.
- Ricky — Friend of Will, tried to act the class clown, but God was on the case. He went away changed.
- Reg — With a soft heart, but has done so much jail time, trapped in the system, cried throughout the course.
- Darren — A young Aboriginal fella, blew a promising football career by making bad choices.
- Kain — A muscled-up guy on the outside, a big soft vessel of love on the inside. Supposed to go to court on the last day, but the Lord worked a miracle.
- Carlo — An Italian fella who had his faith restored.

These are just a few inmates who stood out. I have come away from the past five days with a deeper appreciation and love for my family, not to mention my extended family.

I know my home is with my brothers in green. I have to be among them to tell them about Jesus! I have greater respect for the Christian community who serve within Kairos, seeing the impact first-hand.

I have a stronger desire for Jesus. To my family, you are a gift.

My prayer — 18 April 2009

Lord God,

I want you to have your Way in me! Please, whatever I have to go through to be all that you want me to be, put me through it!

Be the potter in my life, make me, shape me, mould me into a vessel that you can use to touch the multitudes, millions upon millions of people, Lord God. Make my heart and mind be clean and may my motives always be pure in your eyes.

I also ask that you put deep within me a burning desire to live for you every minute of every day, let not one day be wasted. Place within me your love for the salvation of all humanity and your desire for them to truly know you! Show me how to show them.

I ask for wisdom far beyond my years, to minister your Word faithfully, respectfully and honestly. Help me to forgive those who may offend me, and to ask forgiveness from those who I have offended.

Lord God Almighty, I ask that the Holy Spirit work in and through me in a powerful way. I ask for a triple portion of your spirit, your anointing Lord, that you may be magnified in my life in all that I do. Always keep me humble, may I never be proud, help me to serve and may I never live for my flesh.

I ask all this in Jesus's Name. Amen.

25 April 2009 (second journal entry)
I forgot to mention the same dream I had on three separate occasions while I was away. The first two times, I was too tired to write the dream down, but after the third time, because God was telling me to do so, I got out of bed and wrote it down.

God is going to ask me to lead a group of people.

He has told me that I am going to be disabled, that the only way I can communicate to others is similar to how Stephen Hawking does, through some sort of device in my mouth. Apparently, I am disabled by the shotgun blast from my very vivid dream from ages ago.

God has told me that it is very important that I tell Amanda this as people must know!!

EVEN THOUGH I AM THE WAY I AM, I CAN STILL COMMUNICATE!

God Almighty is going to speak through me to give important instructions. I saw myself in a wheelchair, unable to move, with many people around me, waiting to hear God's Word.

The dream matches up with parts of two previous ones I had when I first became a Christian: the shotgun blast and the use of a device similar to what Stephen Hawking uses. May God be glorified in and through me until my last breath. I love you, Lord. Jesus Lives, He lives!!

1 June 2009
When I reread my last entry, I realise how frightening that is. It makes me think of Amanda, how I want her to not stop living her life, making time for herself, despite what might be happening with me when this occurs. I love you so much, what a wife you are! I have never met such a noble, selfless woman as you, Amanda. I pray we enter God's Kingdom together. Me, I'll be happy being a doorkeeper. I love you, Amanda! Pete, Rhyan and Tosha, please know I love you.

11 July 2009
Well, it's nearly midnight and I just got out of bed. Amanda and I went to Thailand, but I cut our stay short by a week. I just couldn't help myself: I was drinking. God was not happy with me, and my guilt is great. Unfortunately, Amanda could have done with the extra week's break which makes me sad.

18 August 2009
I have one week left of the Clinical Pastoral Orientation (CPO) course that I have been doing at Joondalup Health Campus as part of Chaplaincy training. Still doing my two days a week at Acacia. I am into my second week of teaching a course called *Drawing Near* which is going good. I want to serve Jesus full-time, my desire to do so is strong. Again, I am trying to sell my business.

27 September 2009
In the past three or four months, I have sort of been running a men's group, both in the prison and outside of it. God has been working in ways I have never experienced until now. The Holy Spirit has been healing people, baptising them with spiritual gifts and when praying for people, He touches them in a big way.

I feel I have five options in front of me at the moment:
1. Work full-time
2. Pull out of the CCWA (Council of Churches WA) and continue at the jail just doing the courses
3. Work and stay with the CCWA
4. Jail, work and *Men of Might*
5. Sell my business and do full-time study and the jail sessions

I am tending to get ahead of myself, I need to let God give me direction to all of it or only some of it. I need to slow down and learn more.

There are no doors open externally at the moment. I must remind myself daily, who I am in Christ. My love for my family is getting stronger each day. Thank you, Lord Jesus.

20 October 2009
Had a real bad night, it was like there was a battle going on for my spirit. I had a dream where I was in a house with Steve W from Acacia. He was playing with his son when people came over, trying to score drugs from me. I refused, they wouldn't go away. Then there was a divine battle between me and something or someone in the air. It was trying to take me, but I said: "… greater is he who is in me (Jesus) than the one who is in the world" from *1 John 4:4*.

It felt evil. This presence/thing tempted me by saying that I had to go with it or else I would be left behind. I refused to go. I am left scared and shaken by this dream. I do not understand it fully.[4]

23 October 2009
The Lord has been waking me at 2 am every night for the past four or five nights. The Holy Spirit is raining down in drops, soon we are going to have an outpouring of His Spirit. We must obey, we must obey.

Dreams: past and recent — I have experienced what I believe is Hell, another place, so lonely with no comfort, and the Gates of Heaven being closed to me, being left behind.

To my family, I love you, you are special to me. May my life be an offering to God. Have your way with me, Lord Jesus. We must obey!
    He loves us!

---

[4] 19 February 2010 — this dream is God telling us that we must obey Him. He has given us the power to do so those who refuse will be shut out.

24 January 2010

I think I have been going through a growth trial which I failed.

Where to now?

Psalm 46:10 NSAB talks about being still before God. Stop striving, that is big for me, stop striving.

Two days ago, I met John Bevere at his conference, it was awesome! He made a DVD for the boys at the prison to encourage them in what they are doing. I am waiting on God.

Yesterday, I had some great one-on-one time with my boys, spending time with Rhyan, driving around having a chat. I wish Tosh had grown up under my roof. I long for her to be more in my life but I suppose at 21, you have a lot to experience.

8 February 2010

Off to the jail today (Monday) to teach the second *Drawing Near* course by John Bevere, with another course on Thursday.

The last few weeks, God has been teaching me to rest in Him, to walk in obedience to Him. When I go to the jail, I see Him ministering, not me. It's His grace, His power. God is in control of my business. After a dry two months, the phone calls and emails have started again.

Trust in Him — Obey Him — Cease striving — Know that He is God.

NOTHING is impossible for Him.

16 February 2010

Grace, God's Power.

Faith without Works is dead.

Faith with Works is life.

Faith with Works produces results.

Results should be a change in nature.

Galatians 5:16-26 Live by the spirit

2 Peter 1:3-11 Growing in faith

19 February 2010 2.15 am

Yesterday I had a meeting at Wooroloo, funny, it was at 2.15 pm!

I spent the afternoon walking around the jail, seeing the need for God to be up there. It's a dry place waiting for God to move. As God has opened the door, I must enter. I plan to spend one day a week up there. I am just a vessel.

I must trust Him, I must walk in obedience to what He asks.

One day at a time.

24 March 2010

God gave me this scripture at two-thirty this morning.

Revelations 2:10 — Don't be afraid of what you are about to suffer. The devil will throw some of you into prison to test you. You will suffer for ten days. But if you remain faithful even when facing death, I will give you the crown of life.

I know this scripture is for me as it is the second time it has been given to me.

Lord, give me the strength to endure death or suffering so that I will remain faithful to you.

4 April 2010

Amanda is at Phuket with her sister, Ursula, for nine days of 'well-deserved rest'. Especially for putting up with me.

Pete has gone away as a leader for a three-day youth camp. I am so proud of him, he is growing up to be a fine young man. My main man Rhyan has gone away to the farm by himself and is having a ball. I sometimes walk past his room in the mornings and see him reading his Bible. ☺ Yeah, man! Thank you, Lord.

That leads to me being at home alone with 2 dogs, 2 cats and Amanda's plants!

Amanda flies back on Wednesday and I am off to South Africa next week for Angus Buchan's Mighty Men's Conference. Four hundred thousand men. Going to be sick. Hey, sick, a new word I must have picked up from the kids.

I'm having trouble focusing on business and the jail at the moment. I want for nothing, God supplies all my needs and yet I still whinge! I want so much to serve Him full-time so much it is affecting me, I have lost all interest in the business to the point I want to shut it down, but is that His Will? If I sold all my assets today, I would last a year — but in my heart, I don't have peace about it.

I've been getting a lot of revelation regarding sanctification. Some of the scriptures God shows me are full-on. I feel that in the days, weeks, months and years to come, I will suffer and it's not going to be good.

Prayer — Lord God Almighty, give me the grace to endure, don't give up on me, I know I am unworthy. Whatever I have to go through to be all you want from me, I will be. Strengthen me to obey you!

To my three kids, I am sorry for the mistakes I have made when bringing you up. Things like sports, smacking you, telling you off when you cry, not doing the normal stuff dads are supposed to do. Learn from my mistakes, don't do these things to your kids when the time comes. You are my all!

Don't ever give up on Jesus. He is the Way, run to Jesus.

Run fast — don't look back.

16 May 2010

Since returning from South Africa, I feel like I am being pushed in a new direction. I am shutting the business down, selling all the gear. God is moving me into full-time ministry. I seem to have no desire for money or work or for anything this world has to offer. I just want Jesus in my life. I turn 40 in three days, feeling old on the outside, but so very new on the inside.

2 July 2010

I have spent the past few months shutting the business down, getting Ryan set up as well as my own affairs.

The sellers of the two-acre property in High Wycombe we put an offer on pulled out of the deal with no reason, so we have recently started the process of taking them to court.

We had mediation today about the property, explaining to the judge that we believed that the sellers pulled out because the zoning was going to be changed from Special Rural to Light Industrial, hence they broke the contract. The Judge and the sellers saw our side of the story and we ended up walking away with over $500k compensation, we would have settled for less than a third of that. It was never about the money, it was the principle of the matter. How great is God! God has a plan for us, we are 100% debt-free again.

Where to from here? I feel I need a father's heart for my children. Peter is growing more into a man each day, I am scared because I don't know how to teach him how to live. I don't want to force him to do anything.

I am not sure what to do now, I have no plans, no idea what I can do up at the jail, I will wait for God's guidance. Paul from Riverview finished up the day before yesterday. We had our first meeting with the MMC (Mighty Men's Conference) Perth Coordinator.

Amanda now has a van set up and plans to do full-time garden maintenance.

To my family, Jesus Christ is our Lord. Love Him — Seek Him — Serve Him. He loves you.

Matthew 6:33 Seek Him with all your heart.

Have mercy on me — a sinner!

In the journal at this point is a letter from Peter Junior to his father.

6 September 2010

Who are you to judge us?

We don't know what you know, we don't understand what you understand, and we don't think like you think!

What you think is rude, we don't understand, you can't expect us to know everything you do. You think we are self-focused but you don't know what we really think. We think it's rude that you judge us when you don't truly know us. I love serving in kids' church and coaching sports. I love helping people and kids, it's one of the passions of my life.

For you to come to me and say I am self-focused breaks my heart and brings me down when you say these things. I am here in bed, wondering why I do these things if they portray me as selfish so I will ignore you when you say things like that to me.

Jesus understands me. It gets harder to do these things as I grow older. Just remember that some of the stuff you do to us is bad!! I hate it when you just walk in saying: "... because I'm the Dad!"

My main points:
- We don't know what you know.
- We don't understand what you understand.
- We don't think like you think.
- What you think is rude, we don't know.
- You can't expect us to know everything you do.
- I try so hard to help others, but then you call me selfish and that makes me cry in my bed at night.
- Some of the stuff you do is unacceptable to us. Treat others like you want to be treated.
- I hate it (yes, hate is a strong word) how I can't stand up for myself.
- We could have yelled at you that after being a parent for 21 years, you might have the swing of things.

Peter Senior responded:

Peter! I love you, son.
You are becoming a great man, I am proud of you.

There is break in the journal here, with several pages ripped out.

25 October 2011

The last year of my life has been the worst. That's why those pages have been ripped out. Anyone reading these journals of mine will say that I am extremely pathetic and stupid and I am now paying the price.

I got pretty low in October last year, taking meth. We went to Phuket and I was taking Valium because my mind would not stop thinking. Back in Perth, I was struggling with my decision about shutting the business and the prison is shut to me after my criminal record became known to the DCS.

In October, I had meth and my life has not been the same since. On 5 November 2010, I was driving to Armadale to pick up a part for Amanda when it was like all Hell came in me.[5] It was the same feeling I got when God tried to warn me many times before.

I spent three days curled in a ball, I didn't eat or drink. The last year I have been under massive spiritual oppression like the Lord has lifted His hand off my life. I start most days in tears. I find it hard to pray or read His Word. It's like I've been cut off.

I have a **tangible** spirit latched onto my head that torments me all the time. My mind, body and spirit are very tired and worn out from the constant fighting. It's been ten days short of a year and I am exhausted from fighting.

I have been very stupid and I can't believe I have done what I have done. I am scared, I don't want to be away from my wife and kids.

---

[5] These events are also mentioned in Section 3.

I am in Dunsborough trying to fast to seek God for direction, I can't even do that properly. I believe all doors for ministry have closed to me. When the opportunity shows itself, I try to serve. I don't know what to do, every day is a fight. When I look back at the past ten years of my life, I am extremely saddened by my stupidity and my actions. I cannot fix what I have done but wish I could.

What I am going through is like a sci-fi movie, nobody understands. I feel like I have let Jesus down, but also all those He was going to reach through me! I am so very, very sorry.

My half-hearted attempt at a fast will continue for the next few days (drinking tea only) then back to Perth to continue the fight.

I will **NOT** take my own life and scar my wife and kids, I will continue to fight and trust God. God is a good God, I honestly love Him with all my heart.

It's been a year since I felt His presence — I miss Him so much!!

DRIVEN BY PAIN
CHANGED BY GRACE

Part 3

THE DARK NIGHT OF THE SOUL

In 2010 after coming back to Perth, I had no clear direction and still had this tangible yet invisible presence on my head that continued to fill me with doubt, fear, abandonment, rejection, hopelessness and a whole heap more. It was the darkest few years of my whole life, a period that happened for well over seven years. No-one understood — I had to keep it to myself as everyone I tried to talk to about it thought I was nuts. I actually read up on what I was going through and found on Google a spiritual experience where they called it 'The Dark Night of the Soul,' everything it said about it was exactly what I was going through and a whole lot more.

It was the most horrifying, indescribable, petrifying, life-destroying yet life-changing experience I have ever been through in my life.

It did not last for one year, but rather seven years at all depths and levels of torment, fear, anxiety, abandonment and much more over that time.

It all started when I finished at Acacia Prison. I didn't know what I was going to do with my life. I did know I was not supposed to go back to work landscaping, the jail door shut on me, I was very lost and double-minded. You would think after all that God had done in my life and all the full-on spiritual encounters I had with Him that I would trust Him and wait on Him, but sadly it was like a washing machine inside my head.

I remember after a couple of days of being like this that I heard a voice in my head.

"Stuff it, you might as well get off your face."

All I remember is grabbing my keys off my desk and jumping in my car without telling Amanda where I was going. I rang an old contact and had organised to get an eight ball of meth from her. I went to her house to pick the gear up. She had fresh needles so I quickly had a shot. The second I did, I had sex with her. I binged on the gear until I used it all up and went home a couple of days later only to tell Amanda what I had done. I could not believe that after all that I had been through that I could fall so far down to the point that I did. I used drugs for two days, slept with prostitutes, smoked cones and after waking up at home a couple of days later, I sat there and watched the tears fall from my wife's face as I told her what I had done.

Man, I was so blooming sorry. I felt dirty, sick, angry and confused.

How could I do that to God, my wife and my children?

I took all my clothes that I was wearing because I felt so dirty, inside and out and put them in the bin as well as my wallet. I even got a hammer and smashed my watch and wedding ring to pieces, everything that I had on me when I did what I did, I destroyed. Little did I know that this was to be the beginning of seven years of hell.

I was lost and broken, not sure what God wanted me to do with my life, I was a mess. A couple of days later when Amanda was working in South Perth, she asked me if I could pick up a water feature pump for her in Kelmscott.

I headed in that direction, driving along the train line when I heard a voice whisper into my ear: "You have committed one too many sins for God."

"Yes, that's right."

The second I agreed to the voice, it was like every demon in Hell entered into me and I was more than overwhelmed with a total absence of God, and when I say total, I mean total. It was like the opposite to when God entered in me and I was completely and utterly overcome. I had to get home, but I did not know how to.

I just remembered yelling that I was sorry while crying profusely all the way home. I went straight to bed; I was a mess. I couldn't move from the bed, crying, cuddling my pillow, saying I was sorry over and over again. At the same time, I felt my spirit was cast into hell. Inside me, I felt fear, anxiety, torment, pain, rejection and abandonment like I had never experienced in my life and that I did not believe possible for a person to feel. What I went through was not of this world, it was like I was in Hell. I don't want any person EVER to experience a complete and total cut-off from God, I have no word to even describe what happened.

I lay on my bed for three days rocking and crying. I did not get out of bed, eat food or drink water or even go to the toilet for three whole days. I was very seriously thinking of taking my own life, I could not handle what was happening to me. I needed professional help, except I knew my troubles were not physical, but spiritual. Amanda took me to the doctor on day five and all I did was cry. I was an absolute mess, I really needed help. The doctor gave me with a whole heap of tablets to settle me down, but I was a little scared to take them because I had just pissed God off and I couldn't handle this getting worse. I seriously can't describe to you what I went through back then; however, I know I was in a place that was 100% without the presence of God.

It's like I felt the wrath of God, like being put in a fire where I was being tormented by everything that was the opposite of God.

Every day, Amanda would go off to work and I would just seek God, crying in spiritual torment, begging Him for mercy, repeatedly telling Him that I was sorry. I remember laying on my bed with a whole heap of Xanax, Serepax, Seroquel, Valium and a whole heap more Benzos and other pills.

I wanted to kill myself.

All these thoughts were flowing through my mind, I didn't want to go to Hell forever, I didn't want to lose my wife and children. I couldn't believe how stupid I was to get to this point. It took months to teach myself how to hold back the overwhelming presence of evil that was tormenting me. Every day, I could feel the very clear sensation of a hand on the left side of my head. No matter what I did, I could not remove it unless I lay down on a bed. As soon as I got up, the feeling returned. If I put my hand on my head, the feeling would transfer to my hand.

I was scared.

My brother Gavin came over from Tasmania and used to drive around with me. He saw what I was going through. When I would drive with him in the car, he would sit next to me with his hand just above my head to give me a break. It was not only exhausting but surreal and terrifying. Imagine having a hand on your head wherever you went, you could feel it, but you could not get rid of it.

From 2010 to July 2012, I worked as a volunteer at many rehabilitation centres trying to help people. I no longer worked for money; I just want to help change lives. I battled through that spiritual oppression for close on seven years and at various times, I felt it slowly decrease its intensity on and in me. I had to fight mentally and physically and have hundreds of prayer sessions.

Through that experience, I lost all love for the material things of the world: my car, house, gold chain, money.

Nothing had a value, only people.

It would be fair to say that I was smashed, humbled and broken except I loved people and families more. I look back to all those fellas who went in and out of jail when I was a chaplain and every time they went in and out, I used to say to them, "How dare you leave God at the gate, you're a Christian, you get straight out of jail and look at what you do."

Man, was I humbled.

Though this spiritual fire was the most terrifying experience I have ever been through, I would not change it because it actually changed me for the better as a person. How I think, how I speak, how I treat my wife, my children and others has all changed. Everything about me has changed.

From 2010 until today, I've often felt like I was in a science-fiction movie. What I went through was real, my Dark Night of the Soul.

Again, what happened to me was bad, but at the same time good. I had a spiritual experience that was absolutely petrifying to myself, it was like I was placed in a massive big fire and my whole spirit on the inside was burning. I honestly believe I went or experienced what Hell was like. For those three days, I could not stand, I lay curled up on my bed in tears, I felt like every demon in Hell was in me, and this experience went on for nearly seven years.

Going through this humbled me, it brought me to my knees in deep submission to God. I know He is real, we are not just a fart in the wind, He is real and when we croak, then it's either Heaven or Hell, but again, how do you communicate what you know to be true without pushing religion down someone's throat like I did for nearly ten years? The best way to communicate what you know to be true is by shutting your mouth and living what you know to be true, that our actions would speak louder than our words.

**DRIVEN BY PAIN
CHANGED BY GRACE**

Part 4

SHALOM HOUSE: THE STRICTEST REHABILITATION CENTRE IN AUSTRALIA

In 2010, I went down to Dunsborough with a mate, Damien to fast for three days to see if I could hear from God about what the heck this thing in my head was and how the hell I could get rid of it.

I was not in a good place. I started to panic to the point I was mentally about to pop.

I heard this voice in my head yell 'TRUST ME,' then my mind calmed down. I knew it was God telling me to trust Him. Little did I know it then that the words I heard, 'TRUST ME' were to strengthen me for the next ten years. We returned to Perth and I still had no clear direction except that I know I was supposed to give the business away or I should separate myself from it and that I was no longer to be up at the prison, I became a full-time volunteer and I still am to this day, nine years later.

I stopped writing in the journal in 2010 after I got back from Dunsborough and it's now March 2020 and I'm sitting here about to tell you what has unfolded over the last ten years.

Today, I run Australia's largest and strictest residential rehabilitation centre with over 140 men, 15 families (husbands, wives and children), we have 70 to 100 staff and volunteers and we are and always have been 100 per cent self-funded, it's called Shalom House.

The reason why I called it Shalom House was that one day in 2009, I was speeding (drugged out) off my dial and had not slept for a few days due to the gear, but I was walking up the beach in Cervantes, hanging for a drink of water. I came to a caravan park and when I walked into the grounds of the caravan park, this old fella was laying back on his chair. Behind him, he had a wooden sign saying 'Shalom'.

I said to the dude, "What does that mean?" and he told me it meant *Go In Peace*, so I figured, that's pretty cool, it was a word that stuck in my brain.

A few years later when I started Shalom in July 2012, I was thinking to myself what to call this place and I kept getting the name *Shalom* in my head, so I googled "What does Shalom mean?" and up came this information. It is a Hebrew word meaning peace, harmony, wholeness, completeness, prosperity, welfare and tranquillity, not to mention love in its purest form, truth, faithfulness, compassion, mercy, grace integrity, honesty and it can also be used idiomatically to mean both hello and goodbye.

Pretty cool, hey, so I thought to myself, *I'll call it Shalom Discipleship House.*

Between 2010 and 2012, I volunteered at some rehabilitation centres, helping where I could. I also spent time on the streets helping a few homeless people. I kept running into many people I had previously met when I was working at Acacia Prison as a chaplain, mainly at a detox facility in the city.

They asked me, "Pete, help me change my life like you changed yours." I'm not joking, I used to get heaps of them. I had a very close mate named Geoff Walker who ran a men's rehabilitation centre in Mandurah, so I used to take these fellas down there as I knew his centre worked well for those that stuck around. Once I took eleven fellas down there, but only four decided to stick it out and stay.

If you had asked me if I ever wanted to start a rehabilitation centre, I would have said that you were out of your mind. NO not me, that's the last thing I ever wanted to do as I have always been reliant on ME, the last thing I ever thought I'd be doing is running a rehab. One day, I was told about this fella who felt he was called to start a rehabilitation centre and that he wanted to meet me to gain some ideas.

I was introduced to this fella named Jason Bresanello. We met and Jason told me that he felt God tell him to start a rehab and he wanted to know the best way to go about it. I told him that the first thing he should do is get a bunch of strong Christian men and meet once a week for three months and pray into what he felt God had laid on his heart. So I helped him gather a few men and we met in my shed for over three months at 6 am every Wednesday morning for an hour of prayer.

Around the end of the third month, I thought that I might take Jason down to Mandurah to meet Geoff to see if he would give Jason some time at his rehab as a volunteer. On the drive down, we were having a conversation about starting a rehab and how it should be done, it was a drive that I will remember forever.

Jason said he would do one thing and I was saying the opposite, then it came to the point where he turned to me and said, "Maybe you should be the one to start one."

The first time he said that, I rebuked it, saying there was no way, it wasn't happening, there was no way I was going to open a rehab.

Jason felt God was telling him that I should run the rehab — nope, not happening, not interested.

As I mentioned before, the last ten years have been the hardest years of my life as a Christian man, very hard, so much has happened in such a small time. There is no way that I can communicate it all to you without rambling on for hours. I've been full-time volunteering now since 2010 and at Acacia Prison as a chaplain three days a week from 2005 to 2010. Amanda supported me financially while I devoted my life to helping people. Amanda pays the bills and gives me my spending money. I just want families to experience what I wanted: a family, Mum, Dad, family holidays, one school, playing sports and all that stuff, to experience everything that I never had but always wanted, I just wanted to be normal.

Anyway, one day I was driving past the Bandyup Women's Prison and I saw this house right next door with a *For Sale* sign on it so I went and had a look as it was open for inspection. When I walked through, you could see that the property had everything needed to make a good rehab. I mean it had 4 bedrooms, 2 bathrooms, a big shed on a very quiet street, it looked good.

At that time, we owned our own home and I felt God tell me, "Peter buy the house."

I looked over the property seriously and then rang Amanda and told her that I felt God told me to buy the house and to use it to start to disciple men.

So it all started from there. I thought if God wanted me to buy it, I'll make a stupid offer and if the fella rejects my offer, then I don't have to and if he accepts the dumb offer, I wouldn't have to. I NEVER wanted to start a rehab, I just wanted to help people. He had it up for sale for $650k, I put an offer in at $450k and told him that's all I was prepared to pay, that I couldn't move from that, as I had no income and had to mortgage my home if I was successful.

As it turned out, he was in a hurry and wanted out due to his health, so he took up my offer and in July 2012, the house was mine and away it went. Within three weeks, I had six men in the house with a few volunteers to help me.

I thought it would be as easy as opening a house and sticking a few fellas in it and it would just work and go from there. How wrong I was.

These last seven and a half years have been full-on, my gosh, have I learned about people.

I often tell people that I spent twenty-six years in and out of prisons from the age of nine, even when I was not in prison, I was in prison. You see, you can take the prisoner out of prison but then you have to take the prison out of the prisoner. Even when I was not in prison, I was still in prison, everyone that I felt comfortable around was doing what I did not want to do. My whole life I just wanted to be a geek, a normal person, a productive member of society, but I did not know how to do any of it.

I know I tried to hang around the geeks, but I felt really uncomfortable like I did not fit in, that they were better than me. By the way, a geek to me is a normal person, one who is free from the influences of drugs and substances. They go on family holidays, go to one school and get to run up the corridor in the morning and jump into bed with Mum and Dad for a cuddle. You see, I have never done that sort of stuff. My whole life consisted of being put into foster families, children's homes, prisons and living on the streets when I escaped. I would have given anything to be normal.

Today, I'm a geek, a normal person, a productive member of society, free from the influences of drugs and substances. Little did I know that what I was about to embark on, starting and then running Shalom House would give me the tools to radically help men, women and families change their lives.

The last seven years have taught me everything I need to know about why I was where I was, what caused me to go down that path as well as how to get the prison out of the prisoner.

Well, when I started Shalom in July of 2012, I started with one fella for three weeks while I spent my time painting and getting the house up to scratch. I got a mortgage on my home and had to buy all types of sheets, blankets and other types of stuff for the house. When we first started Shalom, everything came out of my family's funds.

Over the years of me being locked up or out in the community, I have had to undertake many courses that the government or social welfare people forced me to attend and for me personally, they were wastes of time, I never wanted to do them but had to because I was ordered to.

If you put twenty people into a course and if two people want to do the course and eighteen don't, then those eighteen unmotivated people spoil the experience for the two people, but they all are made to complete the course. If they don't, they might be sent to jail or be given a worse penalty.

I wanted Shalom to be different than anything that is around, I am really selective about who I let into Shalom and take probably only one out of every twenty people who call me for help. They must be 200 per cent determined about doing whatever it takes to want to change their life. If they are not serious, I won't put a 70 percenter with ALL my men who are 200 percenters. They, like me, want to be geeks but they just don't know how to become one.

Shalom House's program is based on what a normal person in society would do. Out of bed at 6.30 am, free time from then until 8 am during which each resident is expected to shower, eat breakfast and do their daily devotions. What I mean by daily devotions is that we are a faith-based rehabilitation centre based on Christ. Devotions start from 8 am where we will get together as a group, do our devotions where each person shares what they got from it and close in prayer, ending about 9 am. Work starts every day from 9.30 am until 5 pm, Monday to Thursday and then Fridays, the fellas finish at 3 pm. On Saturdays, we do an activity and on Sundays, we go to church.

What I learned in the first year of running Shalom was that items such as television, mobile phones and newspapers were distractions for the fellas' mental growth and that also it's not one program that fits all. If I had seven fellas in the program that means we had seven programs. You see, the second we are born, we are being programmed by the way Dad is Dad and Mum is Mum, how Dad treats Mum in the home as well as in the community, how they model fatherhood/motherhood and how they carry himself or herself in the community. They need to model what they want their child to be, not just in the words they speak, but in how they live their lives.

We are also being programmed by the schools we go to, the kids we hang around as well as the way teachers teach. Lastly, we are also being programmed as we live life. We will all face the circumstances we do and do not create, and as we face those situations, we are the ones that make the choice how to handle each circumstance that determines the direction of our lives, no-one can make the choices we must make except for us, you cannot violate a person's free will.

My program is different than the next program, it took me a while to work out, for example, if I have seven fellas, well then, how can I communicate to them? All the fellas through Shalom come from different backgrounds than I did, they spoke differently, were struggling with different stuff than I had. They had experienced stuff that I had and had not.

Most fellas who enter Shalom do not come from a faith-based background. Many fellas had experience with organised religion but wanted nothing to do with God because of what they had been through growing up, where they had religion pushed down their throats or were forced to go to church and I don't blame them. You should be able to tell from how I'm writing in Part 4 compared to my journal entries in Part 2 that I have personally changed dramatically. At the beginning of this book, I wrote when I was detoxing off drugs when I was last raided by the coppers in 2001, that's when I was selling two and a half kilos of meth a day, heaps of guns, etc.

The encounter I had with Him in Part 3 was off the charts, unexplainable on many fronts. I moved out to a caravan park in Gingin to break off all ties with the people I knew and slept a lot. I felt at that time to sit down and write out my whole life as I remember it. I would wake up, sit on the computer for a few hours then go to bed. When I woke up, I went straight back to the computer and typed some more.

This happened for about three months, right up to the point where I was raided by the TRG and got done for a pound of pot, two handguns, intent to sell and supply and a whole heap more.

When I got up to that point, I felt God tell me, "Peter, now we have written the first part, let's write the second".

So I stopped writing in 2001, it was last year in 2018 that I actually found the first part and now He has told me to write the second.

You should have seen how I communicated in 2001, mate, lots and lots of swearing. I had to get my editor to clean up all the swearing, it was shocking, even I could not read it, let alone put it in this book. From 2002 to 2010, I kept a couple of journals in which I kept a record of all the things that were happening to me as well as what I was experiencing, a lot of it was way out but real, very very real.

I understood that I had become a full-on God botherer, I honestly thought that I was doing the right thing. I only realise now that I had done the wrong thing. I used to send out scriptures to people even if they didn't want them. I would also guilt-trip my whole family into coming to church. Again, I honestly thought I was going good, but He showed me that I was getting ahead of Him and that I was too full-on.

This section that you are reading now is nine years after my journals and eighteen years after I wrote my life story, so it's taken close to twenty years to put all this together, forty-nine years to live it and twenty years to write it.

Everything about me has changed: my wife, my children, my grandchildren, the last forty years of my life prepared me for the last nine years of my life and now I'm about to turn fifty, I am prepared to equip and empower people not to do what they want to, but what they need to.

So back to Shalom. Seven fellas mean seven programs, and by law, I can have seven unrelated people in a house without the Shire's permission. Shalom was growing and I was also leading large men's group meetings and felt that I had to create a board to keep me accountable and make sure what we were doing was legit so I approached a few fellas to be on the Steering Committee to get it all going: myself as CEO, Amanda was the Secretary, Mark Turner the Chairman, Steve Wilkinson did the accounts as well as Phillip Hirschberg, Murray Preston, Frank Tyson, and Craig Dorrington were all directors. It was a great mix of fellas plus Amanda. Mark Turner was incredible, he literally completed the application process alone to register Shalom House as the West Australian Shalom Group Incorporated operating as Shalom House. He registered the entity as a Not-For-Profit (NFP) charity with deductible gift recipient (DGR) status as well as a charitable collections licence.

When the numbers of the house started to get up to about seven or eight fellas, we put in an application to the City of Swan to rezone the property from a residential property to a community purpose use which would allow us to run Shalom lawfully. The ad went in the paper telling the community of our intentions as well as a sign placed on the front fence, standard practice. I also had to lodge documents into the Shire telling them about Shalom, its program and its stages.

I didn't expect the backlash from the community, it was off the charts. We started to get letters from locals that they did not want a rehab in the Swan Valley and that I would increase the crime rate and devalue their properties, etc. Even when we attended the City of Swan meetings, I could feel the hatred aimed towards me. Strewth, all I was trying to do was help people. I called it Shalom Discipleship House, not Shalom Rehabilitation Centre.

People kept saying it was a rehab and I would argue and say, "No, it's a discipleship house."

This happened almost daily to the point, I waved my white flag and agreed that we could call it a blooming rehabilitation centre. I was sick and tired of explaining the difference, but hey, just for the record, it is a Discipleship House.

The house kept getting bigger so that I had to rent another house and that's when we moved a few fellas to Stage Two of the program. What I'll do now is explain the five stages so that when you read about Shalom from here, you will have a bit of an idea what is expected from the fellas and what happens before they can advance to the next stage.

THE SHALOM HOUSE PROGRAM

STAGE ONE

The first stage in the Shalom House program goes for approximately three months, depending on the resident. If they give it 200 per cent, then they can move forward faster, but if they drag their feet and are unteachable, then it could be a year or more. I have had one fella who stayed at Stage One for a year, he kept restarting over and over and has only just gone up to Stage Two.

Stage One is about us getting to know the client and the client getting to know us; it's also about detoxing them from any substances or medications that they might have been on. It's also about getting them used to the unique Shalom environment, the routine and the people, the way the program functions and how we do things.

Many people entering a structured program like Shalom House often come from a background of addiction to drugs and alcohol or from a lifestyle of isolation from others. The length of time it takes for them to settle in will depend on the individual, the culture and the background they come from. At Shalom House, we do not have one program, we have 140 programs because we have 140 men. If we had eight men, we would have eight programs.

RELATIONSHIPS

What we do at the Stage One program is to work out what we are dealing with. We gather information on the resident's family, relationships e.g. Mum and Dad (are they together, if not, when did they split?), brothers and sisters, ex-partners, children, uncles and other relatives or close friends to whom the resident may have unintentionally hurt with their actions.

FINANCES

We also get a copy of their Baycorp Credit File because we want to work out what department they may owe, not just on the credit file, but also to banks (including loans), energy providers, water corporations, communications providers such as Telstra and other organisations. Everyone who completes our program and again, I say COMPLETES our program leaves Shalom 100 per cent debt-free and with money in the bank. This is true for every resident regardless of what they originally owed: $5,000, $50,000 or $1m, they ALL leave Shalom House debt-free. Pretty cool, hey? Most people ask how, well, you're going to have to come out and have a look, hey.

GENERAL MATTERS

The gathering of information at the start of the program is really important as we want every one of my fellas to leave here with their whole lives on track: North, South, East and West, it's all this stuff that used to hold me back in my old life. The generators could be an unpaid drug debt, outstanding debt, a house that needed to be cleaned up and the keys handed back. We let their close family know where the resident is and our process with regards to visitors. You would be surprised at some of the stuff we must deal with early in the program as we want the fellas to focus on themselves as they focus on doing what they must do, we focus on them.

DIRECTION FOR LIFE

At around the 8-week stage in the program, the fellas, no matter what their age, sit with our Employment/Directions Officers who will ask them what they want to do with their life. It could be working as a boilermaker, tiler, plant operator or even a kitchenhand. Whatever it is, the Employment Officer will find a work placement for them for when they start Stage Two. We also sit the fellas through work preparation courses such as gaining their white cards.

DEPARTMENTS

As you can see by all the information we have gathered, we have a great deal of work to do with most residents depending on their history.

Resident Care — Looks after all current residents' daily needs as well as for intakes.

Finances — looks after the details of getting fellas to leave Shalom House 100% debt-free.

ID Services — Gets all the fellas 100 points of identification.

Medical — Looks after the fellas' medical issues across the board.

Movements — Looks after any transportation needs of the men to their necessary appointments.

myGov — We create a myGov number for each resident so we can streamline the resident's taxation, superannuation, Centrelink as well as anything else such as Medicare. This makes it easier for the resident to look after all their own affairs when they leave us.

Program Manager — Makes sure that certain tasks are initiated at the best possible times in the fellas' programs.

Office Manager — Runs all the above departments.

We also have many other departments related to the working day. When coming into the program, all residents are clearly made aware that Shalom House is a working rehabilitation centre: if you can't work, you're not coming in here. Normal people work, well, so can they. The whole program has been put together in a way that it simulates what modern society does, so do we. It re-establishes the body clock, gets us back into a working routine, teaches you how to cook, clean and all that important stuff.

STAGE TWO

When a resident has been with us for about eight weeks, we sit with him to map out a plan for their future. No matter what the resident would like to do with their life, we believe that it's possible (within reason) and we do our best to come alongside them to make it happen. Whether it's starting a business, going to TAFE, taking up an apprenticeship or completing a trade that was never finished, we believe it can be possible.

Beginning paid work depends on what a resident decides he wants to do in the future. We endeavour to have our residents starting work in their chosen field. If their behaviour is all good and at the three months' stage of the program, (heading towards Stage 2) we will try to find our fellas two days a week of paid work, but they must remember that paid work is not an expectation, it is a privilege, that goes for their entire stay at Shalom.

We find employers who are on the same page, meaning going out of their way as an employer to provide a safe working environment for our resident, making sure that they don't team him up with a person who is struggling with addiction or with issues that might rub off, but rather someone who will be a positive influence in his life. All the income the resident receives while working is used to help him move forward financially in his life. We begin to facilitate paying out their unpaid fines and debts that they may have accumulated. We also help them get their driver's licence, buy a car, etc.

We find we have most fellas are off Centrelink benefits by the four-month stage of the program. We believe that Centrelink was set up by our government for people in short-term needs of crisis, not for people to live off. Centrelink is abused by thousands of Australians and it's not okay. We want our men to take responsibility for their choices, I don't believe the government of our day should pay for another person's bad choices. It is sad because those who are genuinely doing the right thing are being punished because of those who do the wrong thing.

We find this gradual progression back into the workforce helps us monitor whether they are putting into practice what we are teaching them at Shalom. If there is a reason for concern, we can taper it back to where we feel they need to be. This balance provides us with an opportunity to see if they are maintaining their progress by making the right decisions and the way they behave.

If it looks like the fella is putting into practice what we have taught them in the workplace, we increase the paid days of work from two to three and then again, from three to four days a week. All the funds the fellas earn on the delegated days of work we use to facilitate the resident becoming debt-free, how awesome is that?

STAGE THREE
Stage Three not only sees the resident increase the amount of paid work they receive externally and continues to plug in with the men in the earlier stages. We allow the resident to purchase a mobile phone as well as a car and the freedom to come and go from the Shalom properties with an 8:30 pm curfew.

The whole idea of the program is that when residents come into Shalom they lose 100 per cent control over their life and let us make the decisions for them. We look at all the problems they have and gather the information and based on that, we put together an individualised program. Over time as we fix their problems, we slowly hand control and the decision making back to the individual with the long-term goal of completely stepping aside in all areas. By Stage Three, most of the bills are either sorted out or they are on a payment plan, financial and general issues sorted out. Many family relationships should be restored. The resident should be in some sort of routine with regards to work and can relax on weekends (something they have not experienced before) without all the bills and worldly problems that life throws at you, it's a good feeling.

This gives the resident a sense of freedom and responsibility whilst keeping them accountable to the leadership at Shalom. They grow in their independence whilst having people to fall back on and continue to receive guidance for the issues that arise. If they do stuff up, we teach our men to tell the truth and depending on what it is and how long it took them, we just give them a warning; however, we expect the Stage Three fellas to lead by example and put back into the fellas who are coming behind them.

STAGE FOUR

In Stage Four, the resident can choose to be moved out of the main house and into shared accommodation with other senior residents. By this stage, the resident has a lot of independence to make choices in their own lives. We want to see the resident working hard and building relationships with their families, friends and the community.

We consider mentoring to be a vital part of our program. We want to see all senior residents giving back to the program by encouraging the newer residents and helping to maintain the Shalom culture.

Through Stage Four, we start handing control of everything over to the resident. When I say everything, I mean everything. They make all their own medical appointments, organise paperwork, paying their own bills, looking after their myGov account, they pay rent as well as everything else as part of society. They must be in control of all this to be eligible to qualify for Stage Five.

By now, they are a good example for the rest of my men, are 100 per cent debt-free, all the family relationships are restored (for those who will work with us, that is), they own their cars and are volunteering one day every fortnight at Shalom helping the fellas.

STAGE FIVE

Stage Five is a period during which the residents have full control of their life and are making choices on how to live and what type of life they want to pursue. During this period, we will continue to monitor the resident's progress and we carry out random drug testing on them just to make sure they are doing well.

The residents are to demonstrate all the moral and lifestyle choices they have learned in the program to show they are ready to graduate. How well they can cope with the temptations of everyday life and how they deal with their loved ones will determine if they are ready for the next step. By this stage, they have moved out of Shalom and are living in their own home and working five days a week. With all our Stage Five fellas, we fully deck a whole house out for them with near-new furniture, cutlery, pots and pans, a fridge, a washing machine and a TV, whatever they need, we give it to them for free.

GRADUATION

When the resident has demonstrated that he is capable of living free from the program and feels ready to graduate from Shalom, they make an application telling us why they feel ready. We then assess each application and speak with the resident to make sure that a support network is present and that they are set up to fully succeed. We take many things into consideration when approving an application to leave our program. What we want to see is that they are putting into practice everything they were taught at Shalom and being a productive member of the society that they have now entered back into. When we graduate a person, we are saying that not only do we support and honour them in what they have achieved, but also that we are confident that they will not go back to their old ways.

The resident's graduation is done in the presence of his peers and family and is a major event in the Shalom family. After graduation, the resident is so well connected in his community and has a network of friends, mentors, counsellors and family that life simply carries on with a sense of achievement and purpose and it's also how I get paid. I've been a full-time volunteer now for over 10 years and how I get paid is by seeing families being restored, lives changed, the broken being made whole. Husbands and wives restored, parents and children, brothers and sisters, one of the greatest gifts we can have is family.

EXPANSION

Anyway, back to the house. It kept getting bigger to the point where I had to rent another house up the road. Not only that, three of the fellas were ready for the next stage of the program and that's when we moved a few fellas to Stage Two. As you can see by the stages detailed previously, you will know what happens and what I'm talking about. When I rented the next house and moved the three fellas over, more men came to me wanting help to change their lives. I never advertised what I was doing, but for some reason, I was getting all these people asking me to help them change their lives like I had changed mine.

Both houses started to get full very fast to the point that I had to look for a third house. Up until this point, everything was coming out of our savings. Sure, I was charging $300 per week (each resident's Centrelink payment) but when you are feeding and transporting men and the numbers get up there, the money doesn't last too long or go too far. I remember when we went out places, we all had to go to activities or church, there would be 10 men, me and my wife squeezed into our Troupie.

One night I was driving to church and when I looked in my rear-vision mirror, it was full of blokes. I just started to cry, the reality of the job I had on my plate came upon me, it felt like I was giving everything I had and I was exhausted. I couldn't fit any more men in my car, I had no money left, trying to work out how the heck I could work all this out was taking its emotional toll on me. Don't get me wrong, Shalom was working, but it was hard work.

I remember crying, saying that I needed a bus. When I went home that night, I prayed and asked God for a bus. I looked at a few car yards and at ex-rental companies, the one that I wanted was $32k so I planned to sell my Troupie to buy a Toyota Hiace 14-seater bus.

It just so happened that weekend I had organised about 70 men to head down to Albany for a four-day camp. I'd hired a couple of buses, and I called the camp, *'Get a Life Weekend: Real Blokes, Real Stories'*.

First up, I got a few fellas to tell us what they had been through, then we broke into groups of six to unpack what we had each taken away from our discussion. We shared personal things we have struggled with or had done in the past that we had never told anyone else. The camp helped fellas open up about hurts of the past: pornography, unforgiveness, sexual abuse, a range of addictions, marital unfaithfulness, all those issues and more.

Anyway, when the fellas were going out to a day activity, I went into town to buy some groceries. I had just pulled into the shopping centre carpark in Albany when my mobile rang. I answered it and some fella asked me if my name was Peter and of course I said it was.

"Peter, I don't know what it is, but you have been in my heart for the last few days and I felt that I had to call you. Is there anything you need for Shalom?"

I responded that I needed a bus because the fellas couldn't fit into my car anymore, that it was like sardines. He then said that he felt God had told him to ring me and give me $20k.

Mate, I just burst into tears in the middle of the carpark.

"Peter, are you there?"

Me, I honestly could not answer, I was sobbing. He kept asking if I was still there, but I couldn't talk.

"Listen, call me on Monday and I will transfer the funds."

After I cleaned the snot out of my beard and trying to compose myself, I rang my wife in tears.

"Hey, woman, this fella has just rung me up and told me he was going to give me $20k for a bus. God's bigger than that, I reckon He can give us the whole $32k as I had found the perfect bus at Thrifty's second-hand car yard. So together we prayed and asked God for the whole $32k, not just the $20k and we asked Him for it before Monday. When I got back to camp, I told the other fellas who were helping me run Shalom and so Damien, James and me also prayed, thanking Him for the $20k, but saying we believed that He was bigger and that if He wanted to, He could give us the $32k.

When we got back to Perth, we cleaned out all the buses before dropping them back to the hire joint. I was walking from Shalom House to my home about 400 metres away when I listened to my voice messages. There was a message from the guy who said he was going to give me the $20k, but as soon as I heard his voice, my first thought was there goes the $20k, but the opposite happened.

"Peter, I don't know what it is, but ever since I rang you on Friday, I have been getting an overwhelming prompting that I am supposed to give you more, so I am going to give you $30k. Give me a call when you get this message."

I was in shock. Again, I was crying big time, realising that after counting the funds leftover from camp, I had $2,000, which meant that I had the $32k cash for the bus.

God had answered my prayer.

For some people, that may not mean much, but for my family, that gave Amanda and me the confidence to continue to do what we were doing as God was there with us, giving us what we needed. Not just the bus, but the fact that He was supporting us and hearing our prayers meant so much to us. I got some licence plates for the bus: 'Just Pray', so now we call it the Just Pray bus.

I had been looking for a third house for a long time and I ended up coming across a property in Park Street in the Swan Valley, not your normal house. This thing was huge, actually three houses in one.

On the day I looked at Park Street, the real estate agent showed me house number two and she told me house number one was also available for rent in two weeks' time.

I was excited.

I thought that I may as well sell the one we had bought as it was a big overhead for us and we did not really want to have a mortgage and the other rental lease was up for renewal. Amanda was the only one working in our family; I was a full-time volunteer. So I signed the lease on the two properties. They would hold more men than the other houses and they were side by side which was a bonus.

It wasn't until we had moved in a few weeks' later that we found out that the people in the third house were a bunch of FIFO workers using drugs, getting drunk and a whole heap of other stuff. I rang the real estate agent and told her that this wouldn't work. Either they had to go or we would. I told her that we were a rehabilitation centre, that I couldn't have my men around that.

"Well, if you want them out, you will have to rent it."

I agreed. Their lease was up in six weeks anyway, so we made do until then.

Meanwhile, I cancelled my Shire application to have the zoning on the old place changed as I stuck the property up for sale. Funny, as the property sold within a few weeks.

Shalom kept growing, employers were coming on board and people started to volunteer to give me a hand. For example, Damien did not get a wage for two years as I never had enough money to pay him.

Me, I never have and will never take a wage from Shalom.

After a while, funds started to trickle into the account to the point over time, I could put Damien on five days a week. The number of men increased to seventeen.

The board decided that we should obtain the owner's approval to put a Change Of Use application to the Shire to see if we could get the zoning changed from rural to community purpose. I thought that it would be no problem at all, the only problem that we had with the first one was the community making a huge noise. It was pretty bad actually, with everyone saying: "Not in my backyard, you don't."

it was really sad. I lodged the Change Of Use form into the Shire for 157 Park Street, Henley Brook and within 7 days, I had the City of Swan come and put the public notice up, and according to the requirements, another notice went in the paper.

No sooner had the notice gone up when it was taken down again and after another 24 hours, I received a directions notice from the City of Swan, saying "A decision has been made under delegated authority that the application was cancelled and that Shalom House was to cease operations within 30 days or appeal to the State Administrative Tribunal (SAT)."

I went into panic mode as I had not been in this position before and I felt very intimidated by the letter as I was not expecting it. I put up a post on Facebook with a big HELP sign explaining what had just happened.

We had to appeal to the SAT. As part of that process, I had to write a detailed description of Shalom, what we are about, explaining every stage of the program. I must admit that when I sat down and started to write, I was blown away when I realised I had a rehabilitation program with proven results over the past two years plus. Not just in restoring the lives of men, but also supporting women and families in our community with a fully 100% self-funded rehabilitation centre.

When I put my notice up on Facebook for the call for help many people put their hand up, I also rang a lawyer mate, Leigh Warnick and told him my problem. He put me on to his nephew who was a barrister, Peter Lochore. He started the ball rolling by lodging our SAT application, but in response to my cry for help on social media, lawyers Simon & John Steenhof, my brother-in-law, Simon O'Sullivan and a few other people offered assistance. It was humbling as I never openly asked anything from anyone. I remember at the first house we opened, I felt so alone and as if I was doing it all on my own. One day, I had a plumbing problem and I called who I thought was the Singing Plumber, but it turned out to be his son Craig from Dorrington Plumbing & Gas. Over the phone, Craig told me that there was no problem, that he would help me free of charge.

I broke down crying.

I've always just relied on myself, I never asked anyone for anything, but all this was too big for me.

Never in my wildest dreams would I have thought about running a rehabilitation centre, especially one that would turn out to be Australia's largest and strictest. Well, while we waited for the court date to be set, Shalom kept growing, men were coming from everywhere, my phones wouldn't stop ringing. It was like I was the Pied Piper but I did not have a pipe. I tried many times to speak to a local Councillor or member of the state government to no avail.

I did manage to get four City of Swan councillors to come and look over Shalom, but not one of them would speak openly on my behalf. It did not make sense. I had people at the end of hope, people taking their lives, people who sincerely wanted to stop taking drugs and needed a hand to do so, yet it was like I was a hot potato.

I met up with many of the councillors privately at a coffee shop to ask them why they were not speaking up for me publicly. I needed help, I was already housing 27 men, all my houses were full and I did not know what to do or who to turn to for help. Each councillor said that they could not speak up for me publicly because if it came to a vote, they would be asked to leave the room and that their vote would not count as they had to remain impartial. I accepted the answer, but it still did not make sense to me.

Over time, I managed to get a few politicians to visit: Andrea Mitchell, Helen Morton, Ken Wyatt, Michael Keenan, Joe Francis (Former WA Corrective Services Minister), even the Governor of Western Australia, Kerry Sanderson and retired Chief Justice Wayne Martin.

All of them said that there was nothing they could do as I was caught up in a legal court case and while the case was before the courts, they could not intervene.

I did not understand too much about the process of the SAT, but I was under the assumption that when I got to the court, I would get an answer that same day.

How wrong I was.

Little did I know that this was the beginning of five years of court battles, costing my legal teams over a million dollars. By the way, they did the work for us on a pro bono basis from beginning to end. It took me nearly six months to get the first hearing date set in four months' time. We were growing and I mean growing, I ended up with 36 men in Park Street.

We were chockers; just in case you don't know, that means full.

Our court date finally came. It started with the City of Swan and their lawyers as well as the planning team and my lawyers doing a walk around the Park Street property with me explaining how it all worked. I explained the routine of the men, what they did from day to day and how much rent they paid. I also shared in detail how each Stage worked. From there, we went into Perth City where I was questioned by all parties on Shalom, its operations, how we were funded, as well as how we came to be.

I left the court that day feeling a little deflated. All I was trying to do was to help people change their lives and I had all these people who hated me for starting a rehabilitation centre in the Swan Valley. I didn't mean for it to get so big. On the hearing day, I heard so many false testimonies from a few locals who did not want us in the area, the grape growers especially. Rehabilitation and the Swan Valley don't mix.

I then found out that I would have to wait for up to another four months to get the verdict from the courts. I kept trying to reach out to the Shire because I needed help, but they kept saying that it wasn't up to them, to wait for the outcome of the court case.

In the meantime, Shalom kept getting larger: around forty-two men across three houses. Finally one day, the verdict was handed down by the SAT that we had won the case, meaning that the City of Swan or the powers that be would begin to work with me, or so I thought. Apparently, the City of Swan had 28 days to appeal.

I sat back waiting over the next month for a letter from the City of Swan, hoping for some sort of meeting, but nothing happened until on the twenty-eighth day, I got a letter saying that the City of Swan was appealing to the Supreme Court of WA. My lawyers were very surprised, they reckoned that it wasn't standard procedure, so this meant I was in for a long wait to receive a court date for the Supreme Court.

I couldn't wait any longer because of the growth of Shalom so I had to look for another house. I found one not far from Park Street and put in the application to the City to start up another Shalom House venue. I signed the lease, put out the call for unwanted furniture and king-size single beds and I split the men into the houses, half in Park Street and half in the new one at Forrest.

Our offices were also bursting at the seams, with staff working on top of each other so I went hunting around and found a building that was previously used as an art gallery on West Swan. I looked over the place, it seemed reasonable to me, $770 per week so I filled out the paperwork for the Shire, lodged it, signed the lease on the offices and started to move in. It was good, lots of room.

By then, I had about 40 staff and volunteers and growing, this meant that I now had three applications going through the SAT. Over the next few years, we were to go through many court cases, the first one where we won and the City appealed to the Supreme Court. When it got to the Supreme Court, they spent nearly a week arguing over whether it was a community purpose building in the context thereof or if it was a residential building in the context thereof. My lawyers were arguing it was community purpose and the City was arguing that it was, in fact, a residential building.

The judge asked both parties: "What happens if I find it is both residential and community purpose?"

The lawyers said, "Well, it would have to go back to the SAT, Your Honour."

So back to the SAT it went, with another four months to get a date and then another three months to reach the date, and all the time, Shalom House was growing.

What do you do when all your houses are full and every rehabilitation centre in Perth has a three to six-month waiting list, someone comes knocking on your door and they say to you that they will do whatever it takes to change their life, do you turn them away or take them in? Me, I took them in, Park Street ended up with 36 plus fellas in it, Forrest Street ended up with 42 fellas, I had beds in the lounge rooms, in the hallways and even in the garage. We turned the four-car garage into a large bedroom, we even had beds in the corridors with partitioning to give the fellas a little privacy.

Now put yourself in my shoes. For the life of me, I could not understand why not one local councillor of the City of Swan, nor politician would advocate publicly on our behalf. I started to call out the local Council on social media for their lack of willingness to try to engage with me as I was very frustrated. I didn't understand why no attempt was made by them to assist me in helping their constituents, fellow human beings. They are elevating policies and procedures above human lives and I don't believe that is okay. The stories that were and still are coming out of Shalom House were about men's lives being changed, families being restored and yet it was like they did not care.

A local election was coming up and I thought to myself about running, all the pieces were there. Milena, one of my main staff members, came from a background in politics and she had run many campaigns. I had a printer help me with discounts on printing. I thought to myself that there was no reason why I couldn't, so I put my hat in the ring. We put together 200 corflute posters, heaps of pamphlets and

200 t-shirts with my head on it. I ran for the local council as I wanted to find out what the heck happens behind those closed doors that would cause a person to elevate policies, procedures, rules, acts and guidelines above human lives. I soon found out how it all worked.

I mean struth, we have Australia's largest and strictest rehabilitation centre that is working at changing not just the lives of the men in the program, but all the families in turn.

I won with a landslide vote and knocked the Mayor off his position and was elected as a Councillor for the City of Swan. I was on Council for close on two years. As Councillor, I saw what happens behind closed doors and what I saw repulsed me and still does. I decided to upskill myself by studying two-thirds of the course, the West Australian Local Government Association Diploma (WALGA) as well as the Australian Institute of Company Directors course (AICD) and graduated so I now have initials after my name, Peter Lyndon-James (GAICD), qualifying me to run companies as a CEO or to sit on a Board of Directors.

Around that time, I caught up with a highly regarded gentleman who held a high position in the state government.

He often challenges me in the decisions I make which I appreciate.

One day, he asked me, "Pete, what are you achieving on council?"

"Nothing, they have a muzzle on me due to what I swore to uphold when elected. Also, many of the Councillors have been here for anywhere between 18 to 30 years and they are a closed shop to me. Trying to work with them is like eating concrete, every time I walk into the room, there's silence."

So he said to me, "What are you doing there then? Take the muzzle off your mouth, you have learned what you needed to learn."

I took his advice. My gosh, best thing I have ever done. But I must say, I learned a great deal.

So today is the start of 2020. I plan to put into practice everything I have learned, not just over the last seven years running Shalom House, but the last forty-two years of my life. From 01/01/2020, I am devoting my life not just to help other self-funded rehabilitation centres start, but also putting into practice what I have learned to see if I can make a difference at a much higher level, a level that will make positive changes to our state.

I might think about trying my hand at West Australian politics, I reckon I would be good as a politician, the only thing I can't do that some politicians are really good at is telling lies as well as telling you what you want to hear in order to get your vote.

That's not me.

We need change. I've spent my whole life trapped in a world that I never wanted to be in. I broke free from that life and then I got put in a position where I had to deal with local government councillors, politicians and other rulers of our day. Personally, in my view, most are no better than the blokes I grew up with in jail except the system protects them.

As a politician, or should I say Councillor, I am elected to serve my community above self, I had been elected by the residents and ratepayers of my local council to be their voice, but due to the code of conduct I swore to uphold when getting onto council, a muzzle was placed on me, this should not be.

I have devoted my life to making a difference and I will make that difference, I am determined to do so. We must change the policies, procedures, rules, regulations, acts and guidelines that govern not just our state, but our nation, we are over-regulated and common sense has gone out the window, many blooming politicians are corrupt and in it for the wrong reasons.

We must have change.

www.toughlovebook.com.au/

www.peterlyndonjames.com.au

My Business Award Winner (Not-For-Profit), 2019
WA Representative for Australian of the Year, Local Hero, 2018
Telstra Business of the Year WA Finalist, Social Change Maker, 2018
WA Finalist for Australian of the Year, Local Hero, 2017
Western Australian of the Year Winner, Community Award, 2017
Telstra Business of the Year National Finalist, Charity Award, 2017

ART BY CHERIE MONGONY

This piece of artwork took over 1500 hours to complete. The right-hand side is an oil painting and the left-hand side was created with a soldering iron.

TESTIMONIALS

Gavin Lyndon-James's testimony

Peter's Past

What a wasted life ... what crime, filth, violence, depravity and wrongdoing, what a cesspit of garbage called life did he crawl from ... anybody that truly knew my brother 20 years ago could easily ask themselves these questions about Peter.

We grew up in an extremely dysfunctional family, our mother and father separating when we were very young. They didn't really know how to be parents, both being young and not equipped to deal with life. I place no blame on our parents, they made some poor life choices as do many of us. I love them, I honour them and I forgive them. We all make mistakes, and none of us is perfect.

Having said that, our father left us for his own reasons with our mother left with 5 kids under the age of nine. It was too much for her to cope with and she struggled, so all of us kids ended up being placed in the care of the State.

Peter and I share a birthday, being born exactly one year apart. For seven years in a row on our birthday, Peter was incarcerated, birthdays for us have never been a good thing. It dredges up bad memories, we have not had a birthday together since I was 6 years old.

We have lived shared experiences and walked different paths. We were put into our first children's home together at the ages of six and seven. We have both been fostered, lived in hostels and we have both lived on the streets; however, Peter so, so much more than I ... I know the feeling of sleeping in a clothing or paper bin, of having to steal food to fill an empty stomach and of being young, alone and afraid. It does not define us, it simply teaches us life lessons. For me, it was not a path

I wanted to walk; for Peter, it's a life he immersed himself in. He faced the same choices I did.

I have been mistaken for him many, many times in my life. I have been bashed, assaulted and had people try and kill me because they thought I was Peter. Life wasn't pleasant for me as a child and then as a young man when you followed in Peter's wake ... so if these things were a regular occurrence for me, then how bad were they for Peter!

Peter made conscious choices to do the wrong thing. Did he know better? No, he made the choices — right, wrong or indifferent — Peter could not be told or controlled. His path was one of self-destruction with a strong rebellious streak.

At one stage, Peter was recognised as Western Australia's worst juvenile offender. No matter how bad he was — we were brothers, and I loved him. All I ever wanted was to spend time with him — even if things went bad which they normally did.

There came a time in my life where I had to cut him off. I joined the army at the age of 17 to get away from that life. Four years after I served my time, I ended up back with him. Life was not good, it was always about crime and drugs. I am not a criminal and will never be one. I have tried to live my life 100% within the law, but many times I failed at this. I made stupid choices as a kid because I wanted to be with Peter — my brother who seemed to thrive on living against the law.

There is way too much history in Peter's background to write down all of the stories. It would simply take forever. So I will only offer a few.

An example of Peter and his disregard for the law was on one occasion when I returned to Perth from the army on leave. We had ended up out on the town when things went bad, getting involved in an altercation at a hotel. Peter caused a fight, but we were vastly outnumbered by a group larger in number than ourselves. We were both covered in blood and bruises. It was unnecessary, uncalled for and purely Peter's fault. He caused a violent and wild confrontation, people got hurt ... how we walked out is beyond me.

Peter was smiling, a sinister grin that I hated seeing. He was proud of what had happened, it was his usual living in the moment thing ... he looked at me then shook my hand and told me he was proud of me for standing tall — it meant something! We were then arrested and spent the rest of the night in the lockup.

When attending court the next day, the judge read out about 30 charges in my name! I was flabbergasted. Peter had been using my details whilst I was in the army! He admitted to that in court and I said goodbye to him yet again as he was led away to the cells. If he had not have owned up to those charges, I would have been jailed for who knows how long. I was not a dog and would have taken the rap for him.

I am or was my brother's keeper...

I considered him my protector (not that I had a right), he was my older brother who left me in his wake and many times with the consequences of his actions (unbeknown to him). When we were together and he was doing crime, there were times I wouldn't participate and he would either try to shield me or belittle me. Peter had a habit of tormenting me. I never saw myself as a criminal, it was not my lifestyle, it was his.

I was introduced to hard drugs, sex and the criminal lifestyle Peter lived from a very young age, something I am not nor will ever be proud of ... I could not embrace or immerse myself in that lifestyle like he did. Peter was yet again incarcerated, so we had Amanda and the boys staying with us. I visited Peter in WA's maximum-security prison, Casuarina. Peter told me that I would make a good screw! (Prison Officer) I told him in no uncertain terms where to go!

"I'm serious, Gav, you would make a good screw, there is an advertisement in today's paper for prison officers, you should apply..."

So I thought I would have a look at it when I got home ... as I went to leave the visitors' area, the prison officers told me to return to my table — they thought I was Peter!

I had met the love of my life by this time and we had three children. I wanted stability and security so I applied for the job. How I got it, I will never know, I declared my past. I was applicant number 1079 and I got the job ... wow.

I ended up being an Operations Manager and then Industries Manager at the largest prison in Western Australia.

When I worked at the prison, my old life was gone and my new life was going well. I was promoted quickly, happily married and all shades of my previous life were gone. I had cut my brother off, I wanted nothing to do with his lifestyle. I was on the straight and narrow! Of course, I still loved my brother and kept tabs on him. When I was at the prison, I was firm but fair, I truly enjoyed the job. I was not a hypocrite, my only vice was drinking and I hated drugs and what they did to people!

When I turned the prison locks on cells, I was always conscious that it could have been my brother I was turning the locks on...

Peter continued on his path of extremes, guns drugs and everything that went with them, a world I would no longer welcome in my life.

What I heard on the grapevine about Peter was all bad...

We had drug dealers operating out of a house opposite where we lived when one day I observed a car pull up out front and Peter step out. Across the road I went.

"Hi, Pete!"

He was taken by surprise.

"You can visit druggies, but you can't visit your own brother across the road?"

"Hang on, Gav, I've got something for you!"

He went to the boot of the car, pulling out 2 x .44 Magnum pistols, one in each hand.

"Here, I've got a gift for you!"

This was in the open in the middle of the street, I stepped back and told Peter I would see him later, walking back home across the road ...

I didn't see him for some time after this.

I then found out a few years later that he had found religion ... what I called a Godbotherer ... he had apparently given up his old ways. When I heard this, I was sceptical. I wondered what angle he was working, then I found out he was for real, he HAD turned his life around. We did not speak much at this time as I was absorbed in my work and couldn't associate with him anyway because of his criminal record. I wasn't prepared to risk my job.

One day, I was surprised to find that Peter was approved and on the official visitors' list for chaplaincy within my prison. This went on for some time ... church attendances within the prison also appeared to be growing.

I witnessed changes in my brother that were hard to fathom, he had grown a heart for others. I thought this may have been just a 'thing' that would pass, but it did not. His faith grew and grew. At first, he was trying to push his religion down everyone's neck, he even studied theology! And he graduated! He asked us many times to come to church, but I found him to be too full on. After some interesting years, Peter became much better at showing, sharing and living his faith, rather than forcing it upon you.

After many years of working at the prison, I was still carrying some heavy life issues that eventually caught up with me. Our family has an addictive nature and I had turned to alcohol to deal with some of my past ... it didn't work ... I eventually came crashing down. My brother was there to pick me up, he shared his faith and prayed over me and for me ... things then started to change in my life.

He invited me to a BBQ for blokes and by the end of the night, I was left wondering what they had that I didn't! There was something different about the fellas there, they all seemed to have this unexplained peace about them. I remember saying to Peter that whatever they were on, I wanted it!

My brother led me to the Lord, I had a number of overwhelming experiences, and now I have that same peace upon my heart ... I am eternally thankful for my salvation. I am also eternally thankful to my brother Peter because his sins do not define him, he was bad! In fact, he was one of the worst, but Peter now is a far cry from the previous Peter! God's grace as I have found is immeasurable!

Having made so, so many mistakes, having committed so, so many crimes, having banked so, so much sin! Nothing can separate you from the love of Jesus Christ! The old is washed away and the new takes hold. Does this make us perfect? Absolutely not, we still have our struggles, we still have baggage, we still have our faults and flaws ... we just learn to commit them to God, and the void in your heart becomes filled.

What fruit is now being produced by Peter?

Peter always had the ability to do well in business, he had tried on many occasions to get his life right ... unfortunately, he would get back into the drugs and the businesses would take a back seat ... this went on for years until he became a Christian.

Peter gave everything up, anything that was related to his past life, he gave away. He actually told me about the time he was sitting in Hungry Jacks in East Perth, he had already given everything away or binned it. He thought he had nothing else to give (the only thing left was the pushbike he was riding), and apparently, some young fella walked in and asked him about the bike. He told Peter it was his! Peter then told him to please take it.

Stripped bare, stripped down to the change in his pocket with his wife and children to support, with nothing in the world to do so.
Amanda and Peter started a lawn-mowing round which did amazingly well and in no time, they had some big contracts and a number of employees. They bought a house, did it up sold it, bought land and sold it, they made a big profit and bought another house with pool, built a massive shed, developed the property and sold it.

God blessed the work of their hands ...

Peter committed himself totally to running Shalom House and it was growing exponentially! Amanda continued to operate their business, going from strength to strength ... they even sold it a couple of times, but it kept coming back to them. I have never met nor will I likely ever meet such a hardworking and loyal woman such as Peter's wife, Amanda.

She would be up early getting her kids ready for school, prepping the work vehicles and the tasks for the day. Upon finishing a full workday, she would then plan out the next day, looking after her boys, preparing the meals and keep an amazingly well-functioning house.

As well as being there for Peter whenever he needed her ... I have worked alongside Amanda and she has a more devoted work ethic than ANY man or woman I have met! Amanda has been Peter's one constant, she has been his rock and their love has only ever gotten stronger!

Peter was having men's gatherings, consistent numbers in the hundreds ... out of this, he realised that many of these men needed to escape the chains of addiction from life-controlling issues, exactly as he had! Peter and Amanda bought a house to place some of these men with the intent to get alongside them and mentor or disciple them. Peter had unintentionally started what is now known as Shalom House, otherwise known as a drug and alcohol rehabilitation centre, a label he does not like!

Shalom House now has approximately 160 men, several properties, a fleet of vehicles, a number of businesses and approximately 80 staff members.

They are in the business of changing and transforming lives. Countless lives saved, countless families reunited and restored, pulling people out of the depths of despair the drug cycle hooked them into.

They learn how to return to society as a contributing member, they learn selflessness, compassion and even learn how to love again. They learn respect, honour, integrity and how to give back. They learn to build their life on solid foundations.

Parents getting sons back, husbands repairing the damage done to the family unit. They learn routine, how to return to the workforce, how to be responsible within a normal social environment and how to function as normal, everyday human beings. Priceless!

I worked as a custodial officer for 10 years and have seen the prison revolving-door syndrome firsthand ... one person's drug habit costs is generally a heck of a lot more than the average person's wage! Do the maths, they have to spend far more on addiction than any income they could possibly earn. Addiction then demands to be fed which then obviously equates to increased crime.

People argue that because they are druggies that they deserve to be in prison, but I have met many people who would simply have been better suited to a place like Shalom House.

I have encountered many Shalom residents over the years who had been incarcerated where I worked. The change in these men at Shalom has been phenomenal ... it's like meeting two entirely different people. I have been blown away on many occasions having witnessed these men from both sides of the fence ... the changes in these guys at Shalom is nothing less than amazing. They have people who truly care about their welfare looking after them! Which, in turn, they then do for others ...

I have some major differences of opinion with Peter, we butt heads and unfortunately, getting a point across to him can, at times, be extremely hard work ... yet if you show him something that works, he most certainly is open to change and he is always trying and willing to do things better, as long as the changes are proven and positive. It takes hard work matched with complete and total dedication to do what he is doing ... something myself and those I know would not be able to do as he does ...

I know the heart behind Shalom, Peter is my brother and yes, he gets some things wrong, he is certainly not perfect — None of us is perfect. I don't agree with everything he does nor the way he is with people at times. I believe I know Peter better than anyone other than Amanda.

Peter is a product of his own terrible past, he has learned by that, he changed from being the worst of the worst to someone who can show others how he changed his life. The Peter I see now versus 20 years ago is as different as dark is to light! I see the personal toll it takes on them and it is not a burden many of us could carry, I know I certainly couldn't. He and Amanda live it 24-7.

Amanda is and will always be Peter's constant, she has the innate ability to balance him out. She understands Peter at a level most of us would never imagine, comforting him when he has lost another fella, whether it be by drugs, death or departing Shalom! I have nothing but respect and admiration for them as a team.

If only you took the time to realise they only mean the best for these men and families. How fully vested they are in helping others ...

Peter is different, he is not everyone's cup of tea, he is the way he is through living a remarkable life. When he was bad, he was truly bad, but that bad no longer exists — he is good and to God gets all the Glory! I am sure God will say Thank You to his good and faithful servant when Peter's time is done!

Written with Love and Respect,

Your Brother and Brother in Christ, Gavin

Christian Gee's Testimony

My name is Christian Gee. I am forty years old. I was born in the south-east of England, one of six children: four sisters and one brother. I am the youngest of the six and have a wonderful, loving mum and dad who are still to this day very much in love. They are a shining example to many what a happily married couple looks like. Upon reflecting over my childhood, the first time I felt a bad seed planted in my heart was when I was about three years old.

I overheard some friends speaking distastefully about my family. One nasty comment seemed to fuel another, and so it continued, never seeming like it would stop. I felt an overwhelming compulsion to intervene and tell them to stop because in my heart, I knew it wasn't right. I was scared they wouldn't listen to me and then I would just be told to be quiet. After all, who was I to tell them what they could and couldn't say? I was only three years old.

That day, I felt a feeling of resignation come over me which disempowered my soul. This seed was planted in my heart, telling me I would get told off if I spoke up and that my opinions would not be deemed credible. I went to a local primary school where I did not feel comfortable or welcome. I was picked on by the older children for having darker skin than the rest of the children due to my Burmese ancestry. No-one else at school was as dark as me. Racist comments were thrown at me daily. This, combined with not speaking up for myself, led me to be very unhappy at school and a second bad seed was planted in my heart which said I was not good enough and I was not worthy enough to be liked.

This unhappiness manifested itself into nervous compulsive habits such as nodding my head and clicking noises I would make with my tongue. By the age of seven, I still couldn't read and my parents, witnessing what was going on, were very concerned. They decided to take action and removed me from the school. They then put me in a private school.

After the first day at my new school, I came out and ran over to Mum and Dad, telling them I loved it. I was so happy to finally feel like I fitted in. I had a sense of belonging. There were children from all over the world at this new school: Chinese, African, Spanish etc. Racism was not tolerated and everyone was treated equally. Within three weeks, I was reading and writing fluently. By the end of the school term, I was awarded prizes for my academic progress. It felt so good to be achieving and to be liked by my peers at school which was all I ever wanted. By now, I had lots of friends and I loved where I was.

Sport was a big part of our school curriculum, and by nature, I was very competitive. Unfortunately, my skill level didn't cut the grade and I was never really good at any particular sport. This used to frustrate me because from a very young age, I always dreamed about being great and being a champion of some kind in sporting events. I didn't enjoy team sports because if the team lost, I would take responsibility for the loss due to my poor skill level. Despite this, it didn't deter me from someday wanting to be a champion in the sporting realm.

At the age of eleven, I was introduced to the sport of rowing. Part of our training was making ourselves stronger so we could row faster and have better endurance. We were taken down to the school gym one day to train with weights. There wasn't much tuition so we were left to our own devices, training with the equipment. I found myself developing a fascination with getting stronger and wanting to develop my muscles.

I had always admired physical strength. Soon, my hunger for weight-training became an obsession. It overrode my desire for rowing and even overtook my priorities in regards to my studies. I found that through my determination and willpower, I was able to get stronger and stronger. This gave me a great sense of accomplishment and made up for the shortfall of how I felt about myself and my performances in other sports. The seeds that planted themselves into my heart years ago were still looming and controlling my thoughts which, in turn, led to actions as we are all a reflection of what we think about ourselves. These thoughts of not being good enough, not being heard and not being liked. I then used this mantra as a motivational tool in my training to prove them wrong. My love for weight-training led me to the often controversial sport of bodybuilding.

By the age of sixteen, I entered my first competition as a junior competitor and won! This win fulfilled all my aspirations of the feelings that come along with success. I felt worthy, I felt like I mattered, the feelings of victory were sweet and oh so addictive! I continued to train hard with a burning desire to battle and conquer against myself in the gym. I made a declaration to myself, that one day I would become a heavyweight national champion in my sport of bodybuilding.

The romance of pumping iron had begun!

I moved to Australia in the year 2000 at the age of twenty-four, still pursuing my bodybuilding dreams. I was working three jobs: personal training full-time during the weekdays, sports massage on the weekends along with security work at nightclubs. I loved the party scene which involved money, drugs and women. I didn't sacrifice my bodybuilding and stuck to its regime religiously. Still pursuing the glory of one day winning that prestigious Mr Australia Heavyweight Title. Never once giving up on that dream I had when I was a child. I wanted it all and I was prepared to work for it! I would do whatever it took to achieve it.

In 2001, I competed in my first Australian competition, winning the overall title. One week later, I came second in the WA state titles then flew to Sydney to compete at the nationals where I didn't place. The competition was stiff, so I came home and went back to the drawing board.

I burned the candle at both ends, filling my life with bodybuilding and partying, working around the clock to fund my habits: anabolic steroids, ecstasy, methamphetamine, dexamphetamine and all types of sleeping tablets. Women came in and out of my life, but I never managed to hold on to one. They couldn't keep up with my manic lifestyle. Though at the time it may have been exciting, it was exhausting.

In 2007, one week before the nationals in Sydney, I was due to compete at the WA state titles. The night before, a friend came over with some meth. The next day, I competed and won the state titles and carried on partying, taking drugs for another two days.

By the time it had ended, I had been up for four days taking meth with the competition thrown into the mix. The next week leading up to the nationals was the hardest week of my life. My body was exhausted and coming down from drugs. I pressed on, nonetheless, not losing sight of the national title on the weekend to come. The inside of my mouth was lacerated from the side effects of grinding my teeth. My bones felt dry and painful as a result of the weekend's antics, combined with the heavy lifting in the gym. Every rep was torturous, as all my body wanted to do was rest.

I went to Sydney that weekend and came a close second. I wondered had I not partied the weekend prior whether I might have won that year. Who knows!

All I know now is that my drug use was getting out of control and it was starting to infect my life and dreams, like a slow-working poison. I got back to my hotel room after that competition day and cried, finally I could rest and I didn't have to be strong anymore. Over that weekend in Sydney, I was presented with three fantastic opportunities: a sponsorship deal with a leading sports nutrition company; a photoshoot with a leading world-class sports photographer so that my pictures would be published in fitness magazines in Australia and the US; and lastly, Luke Wood, Australia's number one pro bodybuilder offered to train me for my next show, having seen my potential and wanting to take me into the pro ranks!

Things were happening for me in a big way and fame and glory were starting to become a reality and I loved it! In 2009, I was planning my assault on taking out the nationals title in Sydney, vowing to myself that I would never stop until I won. I had the confidence, work ethic and hunger in my heart as always. That title was going to be mine, no matter what. Then came the biggest setback of my life when I tore my pec major tendon clean off the bone in an arm wrestle. I was intoxicated on amphetamines at the time and obviously was not in the right state of mind.

I had an inner voice telling me so loudly: DON'T DO IT!

Three times it told me.

I know now that it was the Holy Spirit telling me, trying to protect me from danger, but I ignored it and I paid for it dearly.

Such are the consequences for not listening to God …. within three weeks, I was in surgery to have the tendon reattached. It took me a whole year to rehab it back to full strength. Still having my sights set on that national title, it was on for 2010 instead. I had a six months injury-free clean run at the title. My training was manic and all I had in my head was that the only thing that could stop me was if I died.

I would train for up to four hours a day with the intensity of a man possessed. God willing, my endeavours paid off and I took out the title that year of 2010, winning the National Heavyweight Mr Australia. Being the best in the country that year, I had achieved my lifelong ambition and my childhood dream was now a reality. I felt on top of the world, oh what a feeling! As far as I was concerned I had it all, all the things I thought I needed to be content, happy and secure.

I had a wonderful partner, the bodybuilding title, a luxury apartment in Northbridge, a brand new four-wheel drive and a flourishing personal training business located just a short walk from where I lived. I told myself I would rest for a couple of years and enjoy the fruits of my labour. So I did just that.

Looming in the background though was my drug habit and an insatiable urge to seek out the highs in life. After having so many of them attached to the past few years in my training, I now searched for them by getting high from smoking methamphetamine. I never did mainstream day-to-day living too well. I found myself using meth more and more frequently and it was starting to affect my work life and every other area of my life.

Coming into work high was not a good look. Along with my drug habit came a corrosion to my soul, my morals, ethics, with my respect for myself and others being destroyed. The more I used, the more desensitised I became to the sins I was committing in my life. I didn't care about who I hurt in the process. I was too high or coming down too hard to be present to emotions of remorse, but really, I was just kidding myself. Guilt and shame were very apparent in me. Over a period of five to six years, I continued on this path of self-sabotage and destruction, resulting in the loss of everything I had ever worked hard for: my partner, my sister, my brother, my friends, my apartment, my car, my business and I was in a whole world of financial debt.

Worst of all, I lost myself and, in turn, my soul.

I had lost all respect and honour for myself and I had disrespected and dishonoured God. I had become complacent, fearful and wasn't even a shadow of the man I once was. I was numb to all emotion; I had even lost my ability to feel happy or sad. I was so empty and as far as I was concerned, I was in a state of oblivion. I was fearful of everything, even answering the phone in case it was from a debt-collecting agency or an angry associate due to my lack of integrity.

Drugs stripped me naked of everything.

I had suicidal thoughts but I didn't even have the motivation to follow through with it due to lacking in the energy to make it happen. It was a pathetic state of affairs. It was only at this point did I admit to myself that I needed help and for the first time in my life, I knew this was one battle I could not win through my own strength. I was defeated and I chose to surrender my problems and turn to God for help. I rang up my only friend who also happened to be my ex-partner and I told her I wanted to go to church to ask God for help.

The urge within me to seek the Lord seemed to be inherent, like it was part of my DNA. I now know that in the scriptures it says we are all made in God's image and we all have Christ in us. She gladly obliged and I started going to church (this was a few weeks before entering Shalom House). Every time I went, I was in tears for reasons I cannot explain. I know now it was the conviction from the Holy Spirit, convicting me of my sins.

It was at this stage I asked God back into my life as I always had knowledge of God, I just hadn't practised being a Christian for many years. I realised that God really loved me throughout my entire life and had given me everything my heart desired without compromise. The only thing I hadn't done was to thank him for everything he had done for me because I thought it was due to my own strength that I had achieved everything in my life. I hadn't put Him first, therefore, God was disciplining me by taking it all away so that I would finally humble myself and realise that I couldn't do without him in my life.

In my brokenness, I found God and I am so grateful. My friend told me about Peter and his rehab at Shalom House. I was willing to do whatever it took to have a life again because what I had wasn't even worthy of calling an existence.

After a meeting with Peter, he accepted me into the program. I have been here now for six months. I have a smile on my face and laughter in my soul. Love and joy are back in my heart, all thanks to Peter and the forgiveness and grace of our God. I have my soul back again and along with it my self-respect, all of which have been restored.

I won't trade them in ever again.

I no longer believe the lies I told myself all those years ago as a child. I am worthy and I am loved.

For it says in the scriptures: *For I know the plans I have for you, declares the Lord. Plans to prosper you and not to harm you. Plans to give you hope and a future. Thank you, Lord, all praise, glory and honour go to you.*

NB: You can have everything, but have nothing. You can have nothing, but have everything. Lose your self-respect, honour and integrity and you can have all the world has to offer, but inside, you will have nothing but emptiness and you might as well be dead.

One's identity is found in Christ, not the things that we can attach ourselves to in the world. Everything of real value is found in Christ and through him, we will have eternal life...

From Peter to Amanda

It talks about my wife in the Bible, she rises at 4 am every morning, gets herself ready, spends time with God, gets the kids' stuff ready, feeds the cat, feeds the dog and then about 6 am, she comes back to bed to wake me up with a tickle. ☺

While I shower, she gets breakfast ready and by the time I get back to my bed and get on my knees to start the day in prayer and in the Word of God, my crumpets and tea are laid by my side, we suck face three times and she goes to get ready for the day.

Amanda works flat out all day putting everyone ahead of herself. By the time she gets home, it's straight into cooking tea, by the time bedtime arrives, it's normally 11.30, then she sets the alarm only to do it all again the next day, 29 years on, still the same.

My wife is a gift from God not just to me but to this world, she is like a pearl of great price who has captivated me since the day we met. Who on earth could walk through what I put her through, her strength and beauty inside and out shines, and I am a lucky man, after all, I have put her through and done to her, I am allowed the honour and privilege to still gaze upon her glory, I still get the fluffies on the inside of my heart, looking forward to the next 25 years.

HAPPY 25th Amanda Lyndon-James

❤❤*I LOVE YOU BIG TIME*❤❤

Proverbs 31:10-29

A wife of noble character who can find?
She is worth far more than rubies.
Her husband has full confidence in her
and lacks nothing of value.
She brings him good, not harm,
all the days of her life.
She selects wool and flax
and works with eager hands.
She is like the merchant ships,
bringing her food from afar.
She gets up while it is still dark;
she provides food for her family
and portions for her servant girls.
She considers a field and buys it;
out of her earnings she plants a vineyard.
She sets about her work vigorously;
her arms are strong for her tasks.
She sees that her trading is profitable,
and her lamp does not go out at night.
In her hand, she holds the distaff
and grasps the spindle with her fingers.
She opens her arms to the poor
and extends her hands to the needy.

When it snows, she has no fear for her household;
for all of them are clothed in scarlet.
She makes coverings for her bed;
she is clothed in fine linen and purple.
Her husband is respected at the city gate,
where he takes his seat among the elders of the land.
She makes linen garments and sells them,
and supplies the merchants with sashes.
She is clothed with strength and dignity;
she can laugh at the days to come.
She speaks with wisdom,
and faithful instruction is on her tongue.
She watches over the affairs of her household
and does not eat the bread of idleness.
Her children arise and call her blessed;
her husband also, and he praises her:
"Many women do noble things,
but you surpass them all." [6]

---

[6] Courtesy of Peter's Facebook Page

Here are four generations of Peters:

My grandson, my son, my dad and me.

Photo taken at my Dad's 70th Birthday celebration, 8th February 2020

www.ingramcontent.com/pod-product-compliance
Lightning Source LLC
Chambersburg PA
CBHW070249010526
44107CB00056B/2397